A Primer on

U.S. Housing Markets and Housing Policy

THE URBAN INSTITUTE PRESS
Washington, D.C.

THE URBAN INSTITUTE PRESS
2100 M Street, N.W.
Washington, DC 20037

Library of Congress Cataloging in Publication Data

Green, Richard K.
A Primer on U.S. housing markets and housing policy / Richard Green and Stephen Malpezzi
p. cm.
Includes bibliographical references and index.
ISBN 0-87766-702-0 (paper : alk. paper)
1. Housing policy—United States. 2. Housing—Prices—United States.
I. Malpezzi, Stephen. II. Title.
HD7293.G687 2003
363.5′8′0973—dc22

2003017863

Printed in the United States of America

A Primer on

U.S. Housing Markets and Housing Policy

Richard K. Green
and Stephen Malpezzi

THE URBAN INSTITUTE is a nonprofit policy research and educational organization established in Washington, D.C., in 1968. Its staff investigates the social, economic, and governance problems confronting the nation and evaluates the public and private means to alleviate them. The Institute disseminates its research findings through publications, its web site, the media, seminars, and forums.

Through work that ranges from broad conceptual studies to administrative and technical assistance, Institute researchers contribute to the stock of knowledge available to guide decisionmaking in the public interest.

Conclusions or opinions expressed in Institute publications are those of the authors and do not necessarily reflect the views of officers or trustees of the Institute, advisory groups, or any organizations that provide financial support to the Institute.

Preface

This volume is aimed at students of housing policy and others requiring an overview of U.S. housing markets.

Some parts of this volume were previously published in other form. Sections of it draw upon the following sources:

- Richard Green. 1996. "Should the Stagnant Homeownership Rate Be a Source of Concern?" *Regional Science and Urban Economics* 26 (3/4): 337–68.
- Richard Green and Patric Hendershott. 1996. "Age, Housing Demand and Real House Prices." *Regional Science and Urban Economics* 26 (5): 465–80.
- Stephen Malpezzi. 1996. "Housing Prices, Externalities, and Regulation in U.S. Metropolitan Areas." *Journal of Housing Research* 7 (2): 209–41.
- Stephen Malpezzi and Richard Green. 1996. "What's Happened to the Bottom of the Housing Market?" *Urban Studies* 33 (10): 1807–20.
- Stephen Malpezzi. 1998. "Rental Housing Markets in the U.S." *Netherlands Journal of Housing and the Built Environment* 28 (6): 773–96.

Specific references to these and other sources are given in the text. A companion volume, *Practical Housing Market Analysis,* is under way, and will focus in greater detail on techniques of analysis for those undertaking hands-on research.

Stephen Malpezzi and Richard Green are professors and Wangard Faculty Scholars of the Department of Real Estate and Urban Land Economics at the University of Wisconsin, Madison. The authors are indebted to John Clapp, George Galster, Patric Hendershott, Steven Hornburg, Isaac Megbolugbe, Henry Pollakowski, and Susan Wachter, among many others, for comments on previous versions of this material. We are especially indebted to Anthony Yezer for detailed comments and encouragement. Support for some of the research presented here was provided by the University of Wisconsin's Graduate School, and the Center for Urban Land Economics Research. Views expressed in this volume are those of the authors alone.

Contents

1 Introduction

Many housing advocates, housing policymakers (*wonks*), and housing economists think that among themselves they know the answers to certain questions about housing in the United States. Examples of such questions include the following:

- Do regulations drive up the cost of housing?
- What will happen to house prices in the future?
- Is homeownership becoming unattainable?
- What's happening to the bottom of the rental market?
- Does the housing market "work" for minorities?
- Is homelessness a housing problem?

Unfortunately, the questions that advocates, wonks, and economists care about do not entirely overlap. When the questions *do* overlap, advocates give different answers from wonks, who give different answers from economists. The reasons often have do to with perspective: advocates are fighting what they (often correctly) perceive to be crises on the ground level, wonks are trying to intervene (or not intervene) in the market in the best manner possible, and economists are just trying to understand the market.

Our purpose in this volume is therefore to review housing policy from a particular perspective—that of economists—but in doing so relate economic concepts in such a manner that they are useful to noneconomists, and to provide answers to questions such as those listed above.[1] That is, we are attempting to give advocates and wonks a sense of how economists look at housing markets, and why that perspective is valuable. We also hope to help economists who are not housing specialists to understand housing a little better. Housing is not a homogenous good like wheat or oil, so that simple textbook models of demand and supply are only a starting point for analysis. We will do our best to give economists a sense of the institutional and social phenomena that often strongly influence housing markets. While we are economists, we appreciate that social and political phenomenon can lead to policy outcomes that do not efficiently allocate the supply of housing.

This volume is an overview, and makes extensive use of both housing market and policy literatures. Still, this is not just a literature review, because it presents some specific empirical work to shed further light on several housing policy issues, including those listed above.

Chapter 2 presents a broad review of the market for housing services in the United States. It includes an analysis of the following:

- A conceptual framework;
- Demand and supply (overview);
- Measuring prices and quantities; and
- Basic data sources.

The third chapter contains a brief review of housing programs and policies, with an emphasis on a unified treatment of different interventions. The fourth chapter focuses on the current policy questions listed above, and the final chapter concludes with a brief review of current housing policies and programs evaluated in light of the facts we presented in the earlier chapters.

This volume has already been used in urban and housing economics classes at the University of Wisconsin, the University of California, Berkeley, the University of Pennsylvania, the University of Florida, the University of Connecticut, and the George Washington University. These classes have comprised both undergraduate and master's level students in business, planning, and public policy. We hope that policymakers and advocates, as well as students and economists new to the study of housing, will find this book useful.

NOTE

1. This is exactly what chapter 4 , "Six Questions for the Next Decade," attempts to do. Also note that more technical reviews of housing literature include Arnott (1987); Maclennan (1982); Muth and Goodman (1988); Olsen (1987); Rothenberg et al. (1991); and Smith, Rosen, and Fallis (1988). Less technical material can be found in, for example, DiPasquale and Keyes (1990), van Vliet (1998), Whitehead (1999), and several recent thematic issues of *Housing Policy Debate*.

2

The Market for Housing Services

Introduction

After food and medical care, housing is the largest consumer expenditure in the United States. In 1994, personal consumption expenditures on housing were about $2,600 per capita, or 14.9 percent of household budgets.[1] Further, the bulk of expenditures in one of the next highest categories, household operations (i.e., furniture and utilities), are linked to housing. From the investment side, housing is the largest single form of fixed capital investment in the United States, comprising more than $9 trillion, or roughly half of this nation's gross fixed private capital. Other than human capital, housing and land are more widely held than any other form of capital.

But concern about housing stems from more than just concern for economic efficiency and growth. Shelter is one of those areas, like education, that cuts across concerns for both efficiency *and* equity. Housing is the largest asset of most American households, so the housing market profoundly affects the distribution of wealth; housing's location and tenure could well affect the behavior of its occupants; and housing issues are bound up with several important racial issues. It is fair to say that the sociological implications of housing market outcomes are as profound as the economic implications.

This chapter is organized to characterize the market for housing services. First, we give an overview of how housing markets work in the

United States. We then present a series of facts about the various components of the housing market in the United States: demand, tenure choice, supply (including filtering and new construction), and prices. Next, we develop some concepts that are especially important in studying U.S. housing markets: property rights, externalities, market definition, and capitalization. Finally, we discuss some methods for measuring the price and quantity of housing, including hedonic methods, repeat sales methods, hybrid methods, and user cost.

How Housing Markets Work

We begin with a schematic diagram (figure 2.1) of how the housing market works. *Inputs,* such as land, labor, finance, materials, and infrastructure, are combined by *supply-side agents,* such as landlords and developers, to produce housing services. Homeowners, and to a lesser extent, renters, are also producers, because they maintain and upgrade their houses. *Relative prices* provide producers of housing services with information that helps to determine whether to provide more or less housing, and whether input suppliers should provide more or fewer inputs.

In the United States, as in most countries, the market for housing services per se can be approximated as a competitive market.[2] Housing production activities (the middle box in figure 2.1) have few barriers to entry or large economies of scale. Few landlords or developers are large enough to exert significant market power.

Whether the market for *inputs* is as competitive is more debatable. It can be argued that the ownership of some inputs, for example, land, is more concentrated. Large economies of scale may make the production of some inputs a natural monopoly, as with some types of infrastructure. Government regulations could conceivably restrict the competitive allocation of inputs, especially developable land.

Figure 2.1. *How Housing Markets Work*

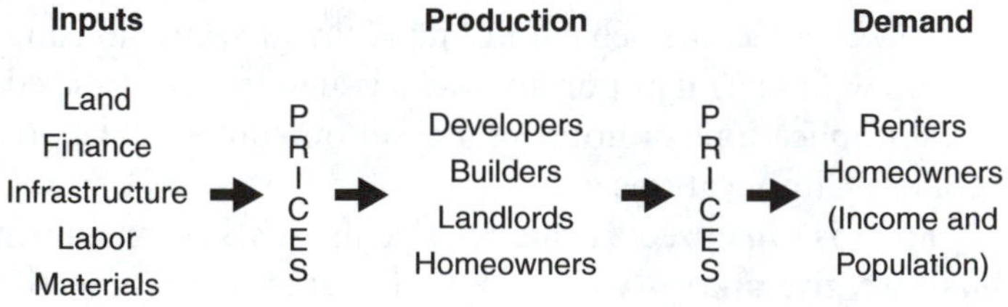

Many housing problems can be traced to low incomes, and they need to be addressed by raising those incomes. Other problems in housing markets can be caused by problems in the input markets, especially land, and in the regulatory and property rights framework of the market. In chapters 3 and 4, we will discuss the effectiveness of government intervention in the housing market, including what we feel works (actions that directly attack problems) and what does not (actions that distort market signals).[3]

Some Facts about U.S. Housing Markets

Housing Demand

In the broadest sense, demographics and incomes drive demand for housing.[4] Many studies implicitly or explicitly assume that demographics primarily determine the number of households, and thus demand when measured as number of units; and incomes primarily determine the size and quality of those units.[5] But a number of studies demonstrate that incomes and housing prices affect household formation in turn; and demographics affect household size and hence demand for space. Other studies focus on how age of household head, household composition, and so on, affect the type of unit and its location.[6]

Figures 2.2 and 2.3 present some key demographic data. One of the demographic trends that will affect housing is a presumed stable popu-

Figure 2.2. *U.S. Population by Age*

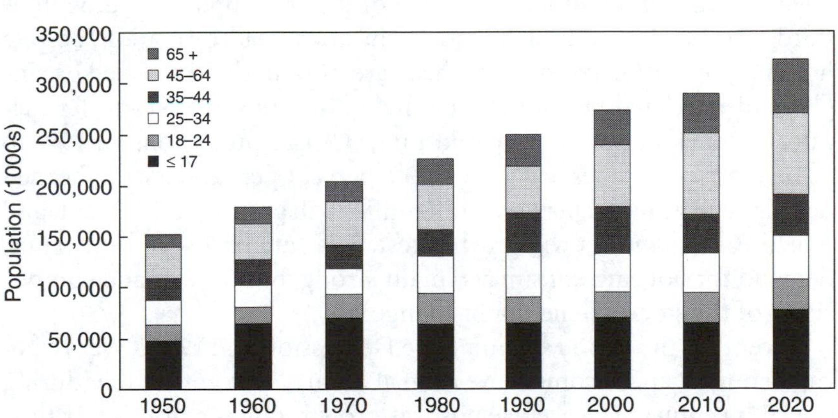

Source: U.S. Census Bureau.

Figure 2.3. *U.S. Households by Type*

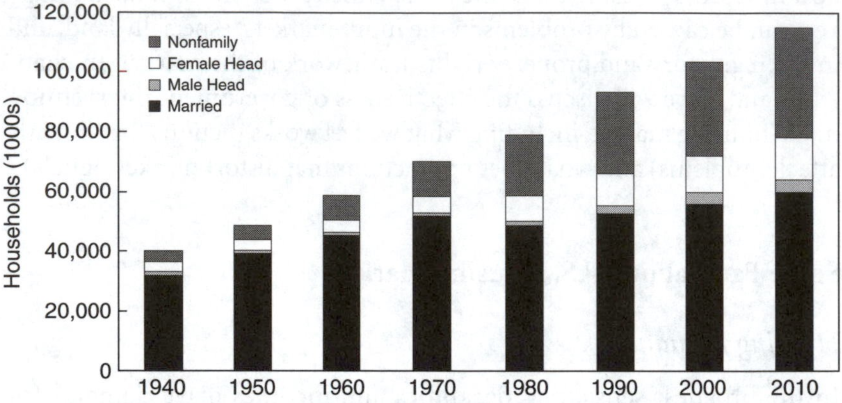

Source: U.S. Census Bureau.

lation growth rate, estimated to be about 1 percent per year over the next few decades, much of which will be driven by immigration.[7] The U.S. Census Bureau's mid-range projection of population growth is 0.9 percent per year from 1990 to 2020; deviations from this projection will likely be due to changes in the rate of immigration, which is difficult to forecast.

Another trend is the aging of the post–World War II baby boom population, which means the elderly will comprise a larger share of the population, reaching about 40 percent of the population in 2040. The growth rate of the population over 65 is projected at 1.8 percent from 1990 to 2020, or about twice the rate of general population growth. A third trend is the continued increase in household formation, despite holding population constant, as the share of households headed by singles and unrelated persons sharing living quarters grows, and fertility rates remain low. According to mid-range Census projections for 1990 to 2010, married families will grow by 0.7 percent per year, female-headed families will grow 1.2 percent, nonfamilies will grow by 1.5 percent, and male-headed families will grow fastest, at a rate of 2.4 percent. Thus, demand for housing *units* may remain strong, but the size and composition of the stock will no doubt change.[8]

Except for the period spanning the Depression and World War II, per capita output and incomes have risen at about 2 percent *per year* during the 20th century. The average postwar growth rate is a little lower than the prewar rate (1.7 percent versus 2.1); what is really remarkable is the decline in the *variance* in the postwar period. Omitting the Depression/War years, the standard deviation of annual real changes in GNP per capita before WWII was more than 6 percent, but in the postwar period it has been about 2.6 percent, a remarkable shift to say the least.[9] Purchasing power of households can be measured by after-tax disposable personal income, which closely tracks GDP per capita.

The relation between income and housing demand in the United States can be roughly but fairly represented as follows: *within* particular markets, households spend more on housing as their incomes increase, but the increase is less rapid than the increase in incomes. Economists define such a relationship with a unitless measure called *elasticity.* For example, the income elasticity of demand for housing is the ratio between the percentage change in housing demanded and the percentage change in income:

$$\varepsilon_Y^D = \frac{\Delta Q/Q}{\Delta Y/Y}$$

where ε represents elasticity, Q the quantity of housing services, and Y income.[10]

Literally hundreds of studies have been carried out examining the demand for housing.[11] Early studies, such as those by Reid (1962) and Muth (1960), examined housing demand using aggregate data on how housing expenditures and incomes changed over time. These studies generally found income elasticities around 1.0. If the income elasticity is 1, then the fraction of income devoted to housing stays constant as income rises and falls.

In the 1970s a large number of papers appeared based on household survey data, such as that from the Experimental Housing Allowance Program, and later the American Housing Survey.[12] Generally these studies found lower income elasticities, and (to the extent that comparisons are possible) lower price elasticities, than the aggregate studies. Of course, these studies are not without their own problems. From Muth onward, analysts have wrestled with the proper specification of income. Friedman's (1957) permanent income hypothesis posits that current income can be decomposed into so-called permanent and transitory components. Further, households "smooth" their consumption by making consumption decisions mainly on the permanent (or long-run) component. Positive transitory income is saved, and if current income is below permanent income, households borrow against or use savings.

Since permanent income is never directly observed, different papers adopted different proxies for it. Some studies rely on an instrumental variables approach; that is, using a regression model to predict or estimate permanent income based on age, job status, and other life cycle variables. Other studies use total consumption for a proxy. Polinsky (1977) pointed out that the omission of a price term in many studies not only ignores an important parameter, but also may bias the estimated income elasticities. Papers such as Goodman (1995), Hanushek and Quigley (1978), Ihlanfeldt (1981), Lee and Trost (1978), and Weinberg, Friedman, and Mayo (1981) and grapple with such issues that a given cross-section sample may contain many households that are temporarily out of equilibrium—that is, consuming more or less housing than their true underlying demand, because of the high costs of moving or other changes in housing consumption. Papers by Ihlanfeldt and by Goodman and Kawai (1985) analyze demand based on those who have recently moved, who would be presumed to be closer to equilibrium, with corrections for selectivity bias borrowed from the labor economics literature.[13] Lee and Trost (1978) and Hanushek and Quigley (1978) are among papers that examine housing consumption as a decision combined with tenure choice and/or moving.

Elasticities from cross-sectional studies are generally less than 1.0. Many of the more recent studies, particularly those that examine recent movers, have found higher elasticities than earlier studies. Which elasticity is relevant depends upon the purpose. For example, demand estimates based on proxies for permanent income, and limited to recent movers closest by their true demand curve, may best reveal the true underlying elasticity. Often estimates from such models suggest unitary or greater elasticity. But such estimates may be of little direct use in explaining observed patterns of housing expenditure within the market, which clearly exhibit inelastic behavior. The latter estimates may be more relevant when, for example, predicting housing budget shares for programs where eligibility is, indeed, based on current (not permanent) income. And only a few papers, such as Follain (1979b) and Rothenberg et al. (1991) examine the proposition that "the" elasticity actually varies systematically in different segments of the market.

Figure 2.4 uses American Housing Survey data to illustrate the inelastic demand within the United States (i.e., rents paid rise less rapidly than household incomes). The household sample of about 60,000 households was sorted into household income deciles, and the median gross-rent-to-

Figure 2.4. *Housing Expenditure: Rent-to-Income Ratios, by Income Decile (Renters)*

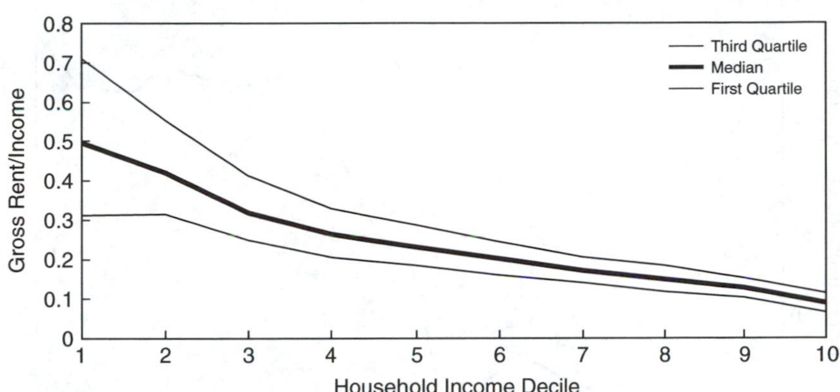

Source: 1993 American Housing Survey.

income ratio calculated *within* each decile. First and third quartiles were also calculated to examine variance within deciles.

The pattern is strong and obvious. Budget shares fall as incomes rise, consistent with inelastic demand. Further, the variance within deciles falls dramatically as income rises. This general pattern holds up even if we control for other household characteristics. Homeowner demand, not shown, is similarly inelastic. However, there is some evidence that housing expenditures *across* markets increase at least as fast as income.[14]

These patterns of owner and renter housing consumption are surprisingly similar across countries. For example, in the Malpezzi and Mayo (1987) study of 14 cities in developing countries, for both tenure groups the cross-section elasticity is less than 1, and the long-run time series elasticity is about 1, but the *level* of owner consumption is higher.

Housing Tenure: The Rise of Homeownership since World War II

Figure 2.5 shows the dramatic increase in homeownership in the United States, especially since World War II. The percentage of homeowners has increased steadily but leveled off and even slightly declined from 1980 to 1990. The U.S. Department of Housing and Urban Development (HUD) estimates show that the rate rose a bit from 63.9 percent in 1990 to 65.4 percent in 1996, virtually indistinguishable from the 1980 high of

Figure 2.5. *U.S. Homeownership, 1890–2000*

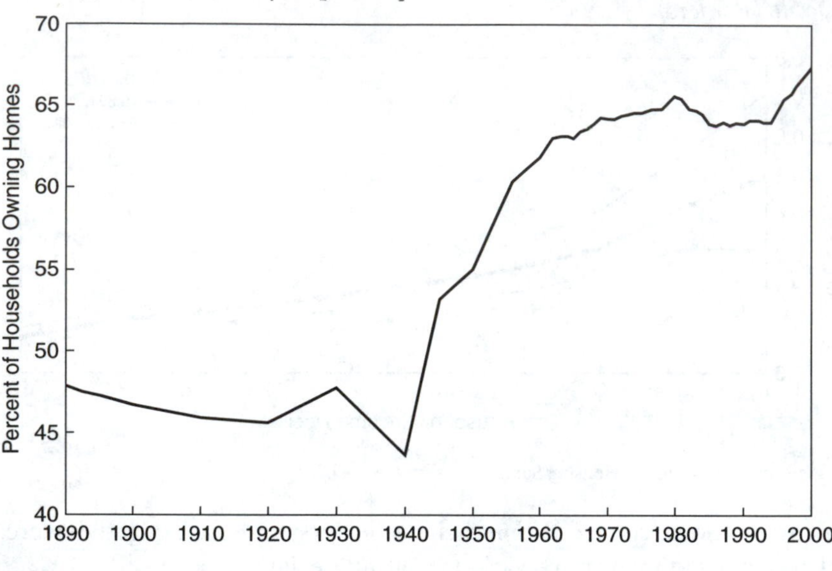

Source: U.S. Census Bureau.

65.6 percent. Most recently, the rate has increased to 67.5 percent, but this growth rate remains slow relative to the rate that existed between 1950 and 1980. As homeownership has for some time been part of American politics and culture,[15] the slight decline through part of the 1980s caused concern in some circles. It will be argued below that this drop-off was probably due to a combination of demographic shifts and an increase in the user cost of owner-occupied housing relative to rental. Nevertheless, a number of additional subsidies for owner-occupied housing, especially for first-time homebuyers, have been enacted or are under consideration.

Figure 2.5 implies a large decline in the *share* of renters in the postwar period, which masks the fact that as the number of households in the country grew, the *number* of both owner and renter households grew. During the past twenty years, the number of owner households grew just under 2 percent per year, and the growth rate of renter households was almost as large. Population growth, on the other hand, was about 1 percent per year. Many new single-person households and households comprising unrelated individuals formed, so the average household size dropped from 3.2 persons in 1970 to 2.6 persons 20 years later.

Recent figures for the number and percent of households in each tenure category can be found in table 2.1. This table shows that most housing in the United States is private and not *directly* subsidized,[16] and the majority of private households are homeowners. This housing is governed by private contracts, regulated mainly by state and local governments. Governments also regulate rents for part or all of the market in about 200 cities in the United States, mostly in New York, New Jersey, and California. These cities contain about 10 percent of the U.S. renter population, and roughly 4 percent of the total rental stock is controlled. These regulations are almost all local.[17] Virtually all urban jurisdictions have local land use and zoning regulations, which greatly affect the housing market, as will be discussed below. Table 2.1 also highlights that although roughly 6 percent of U.S. households lived in subsidized rental units in 1997, this was a substantial increase from as recently as 1970.

Determinants of Tenure Choice

Tenure choice is usually examined as a dichotomous choice, where households either rent or own.[18] Many early studies used simple models where the probability of homeownership was found to vary with income, household composition, and so on. Other papers focused particularly on the role finance and tax preferences play in tenure.[19]

Table 2.1. *U.S. Households, by Housing Tenure*

	1950	*1960*	*1970*	*1980*	*1989*	*1997*
Homeowners						
N (in thousands)	23,560	32,796	39,885	52,516	59,916	68,838
Percent	55%	62%	63%	66%	64%	66%
Renters						
N	19,266	20,288	23,565	27,566	33,767	34,896
Percent	45%	38%	37%	34%	36%	34%
Public Rental						
N	Nil	478	894	1,196	2,466	1,860
Percent		0.9%	1.4%	1.5%	2.6%	1.8%
Other Rent Subsidized						
N	Nil	Nil	102	1,813	2,594	4,375
Percent			0.2%	2.3%	2.8%	4.2%

Sources: Census and AHS, various years.

Given the wide variation in method and data, some remarkably robust findings emerge. First, and probably least surprisingly, higher income households have higher probabilities of homeownership, in both the simple models and in more complex variants. The literature suggests this is partly because of greater tax advantages (hence lower user costs of homeownership), and partly because of fewer liquidity constraints. Older households are more likely to own, all other things being equal, as are more educated households. However, the relationship between these variables and the probability of homeownership is nonlinear.[20] Blacks are generally found to have lower probabilities of homeownership, even after controlling for differences in income and other measures of socioeconomic status.

Findings on the effects of inflation and taxes are less settled. In particular, given federal tax policy in the United States since 1986, when inflation increases, user cost for owner-occupied housing generally falls relative to rental—if financial markets are "perfect" and contain no institutional constraints. But as Kearl (1979) first pointed out, inflation also shifts the real burden of payments forward in the fixed rate mortgage, resulting in the so-called "tilt" problem. And if financial institutions use fixed underwriting ratios, high nominal interest rates reduce the size of a loan for which a particular household qualifies.

Housing Supply

When most people think of the term "housing supply," they think of housing starts. Figure 2.6 presents this bellwether data. Increases in real income, in household formation, the attainment of some economies of scale in both house production and housing finance, led to a large structural shift in housing starts after World War II; but housing remains, as it always has been, cyclical. In fact, volatility in starts has *increased* since the 1970s.[21]

But starts—new construction—are not the only source of supply, or even the largest. In any given year, most housing is supplied by the existing stock. Starts have not exceeded 1.8 million units since 1978, while according to the 1997 American Housing Survey the size of the entire housing stock is about 110 million units. Nationally, less than 10 percent of the population lives in a unit that is less than five years old.[22]

Figure 2.6. *U.S. Housing Starts, 1890–2000*

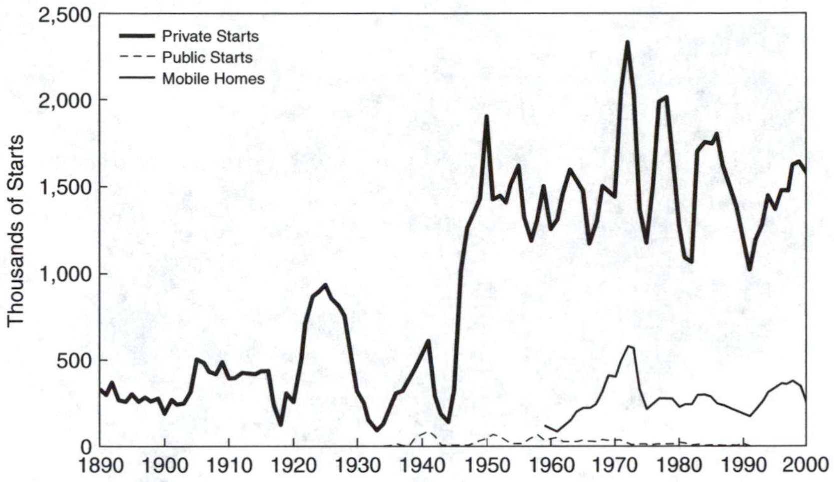

Source: U.S. Census Bureau.

Figure 2.6 also illustrates the growing importance of mobile homes and manufactured housing. As many as half a million units have been placed in a single year. In recent years, manufactured housing has comprised as much as 20 percent of new units.

Even when attention is limited to *changes* in the stock, there are other significant sources of supply. In addition to housing constructed in place, and manufactured housing put in place, changes in vacancies, demolitions, and conversions are important sources of supply. Comprehensive data on these sources are unfortunately lacking, but Hendershott and Smith (1988) have prepared estimates of the sum of demolitions and conversions for some recent years. According to national accounts data, expenditures on improvements to and maintenance and repairs of housing units are roughly comparable to the value of residential construction contracts.[23]

Aggregate numbers mask a very wide variation in output by region and location within the United States. Figure 2.7 maps the average annual permits per 1,000 population by county for the period 1988–1992.[24] The geographic variation is striking. On both coasts, and in the upper Midwest, many counties built five or more units per 1,000 population per year during this period, while most of the South and the Great Plains built less than one unit per year. Of course, these patterns are somewhat

Figure 2.7. *Average Annual Building Permits by County, 1990–95*

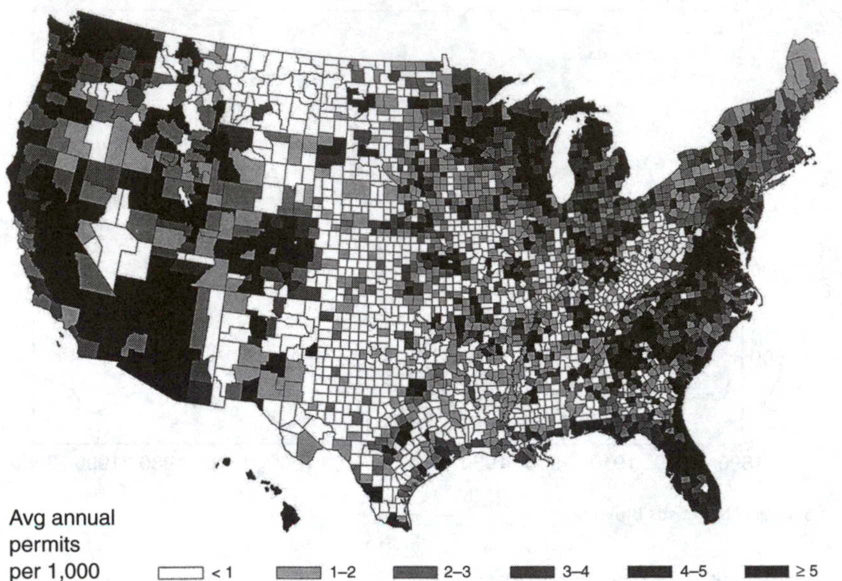

sensitive to choice of year; if we had displayed the early and mid-1980s, for example, the relative positions of the South and the upper Midwest would be more or less reversed.

Filtering and Supply from the Existing Stock

The great bulk of housing supply in any given period of reasonable length is from the existing stock. For example, according to the 1997 American Housing Survey (AHS), about 5 percent of all occupied housing units are four years old or newer. About 98 percent of housing occupied by households in the bottom income quintile is more than four years old. Unsurprisingly, the fraction of housing available from the existing stock decreases as we go up the income distribution, but even in the top income decile, about 92 percent of households live in units more than four years old.

In common parlance, as units "filter down," they pass from higher-income households (owners or tenants) to lower-income households. Units can also "filter up"—that is, pass from poor households to those with higher incomes—if a neighborhood is undergoing "revitalization" or "gentrification." Actually, there are at least three different definitions of filtering, which for convenience we label as follows:

1. "Income filtering," based on changes in the income of households living in the unit;
2. "Price filtering," based on changes in price per unit of housing services from a unit; and
3. "Quantity filtering," based on changes in quantity of housing services from a unit.[25]

There are at least three corresponding ways of measuring and analyzing filtering. These are to examine the following:

1. The incomes of changing occupants of existing housing units over time; do they "filter up" or "filter down?" (definition 1)
2. The price per unit of housing services for different parts of the housing stock (low quality vs. high quality); what determines the relative price of "poor" housing compared with "good?" (definition 2)
3. How quantity changes. What effect does new construction have on the amount of low-quality housing? What are vacancy rates like at the bottom of the market? How do units depreciate? (definition 3)

Weicher and Thibodeau's (1988) paper is motivated by an important policy question stemming from the third definition. Is publicly produced or subsidized housing a net addition to the stock, or does public construction merely replace private?

Weicher and Thibodeau test the quantity filtering hypothesis by dividing the housing market up into three related submarkets: the market for new units, the market for existing standard quality housing, and the market for existing substandard housing. They test quantity in the filtering model using two different data sources: the decennial censuses of 1960 and 1970; and several waves of the (then) Annual Housing Survey from the 1970s.

The essence of the Weicher-Thibodeau approach is to regress the proportion of substandard housing against the rate of new construction (adjusted for household formation), a vacancy rate measure, several cost variables, several demand-side variables, and the proportion of housing stock that was public or subsidized under the Section 221 program. The metropolitan area is the unit of observation. Short-run and long-run models are estimated.

Generally, the results suggest new construction at the high end reduces the number of substandard units one for one; and generally the number of public and subsidized units does not significantly affect the number of low-quality units in a given metropolitan statistical area (MSA). Weicher and Thibodeau (1988) interpret their results to suggest that "as higher-income households vacate existing standard quality housing to occupy new units, lower-income households can afford better quality housing, and ultimately there is less substandard housing" (37).

Another recent study has focused on price filtering (definition 2). Using household-level decennial Census and AHS data from the 1960s and 1970s, Rothenberg et al. (1991) used the method of hedonic indexes (discussed below) to analyze about three dozen MSAs. The predicted value from a properly specified hedonic model can be interpreted as an index of the quality/quantity of housing services, and, given expenditures, the price per unit of housing can also be estimated in each submarket. Rothenberg and colleagues used the hedonic results to assign sample units to one of ten quality submarkets (compared to Weicher and Thibodeau's three submarkets), by tenure (own vs. rent). They then aggregate by metropolitan area, so they can construct the proportions of households in each submarket, and the average price per unit of housing services in each submarket, by MSA.

Given these key variables, and a number of demand-side variables such as income and demographics, and a smaller set of supply-side variables,[26] Rothenberg et al. estimate a system of supply and demand relationships. The key innovation is the inclusion of cross-price terms as well as own-price; that is, demand and supply for housing in a given submarket depend not only on the price of housing in that submarket, but also on the price of housing in "nearby" submarkets (in quality and tenure), which are potential substitutes.

First they estimated a short-run model. On the demand side, the authors found the high-quality market most responsive to price, in general. Because of data limitations, Rothenberg et al.'s supply model is less well specified, but, as expected, supply effects are dominated by the size of the existing stock.

Rothenberg et al. estimated two "medium-run" (5- to 10-year) models as well. They found supply was responsive to changes in revenues and costs throughout the range of quality levels, although as expected, most supply-side adjustment at the high end was from new construction, while that from the low-quality levels was from filtering.

Supply from New Construction

We have already examined descriptive evidence on the supply of housing from new construction. Several papers have examined the responsiveness of the market for new construction more rigorously.

Muth (1960) is usually cited as the first econometric examination of the supply side of the U.S. housing market.[27] Muth regressed the real value of new construction against the relative price of housing and input prices; and also estimated an inverted model with housing prices on the left-hand side. In both cases, Muth found no significant relationship between price and quantity, consistent with elastic supply. However, Muth limited his investigation to the years between 1919 and 1934. Following Muth, Follain (1979b) estimated a series of similar regressions, using postwar data (1947) and examining issues of simultaneity and serial correlation. Follain found qualitatively similar results, consistent with elastic supply.

Several other papers that are not usually thought of as "supply elasticity papers" contain explicit or implicit estimates of such a parameter. Most of these papers have found or implied lower elasticities than Muth and Follain. Kearl (1979) reported an elasticity of 1.6 for new construction, and Huang (1973), 2.0 for starts. Topel and Rosen's (1988) research on starts found a long-run elasticity of 3.0 using quarterly data from 1963 to 1983. Poterba (1991) also presented data that seemed to indicate a rising supply price. In general, models and data that constrain "long run" adjustment to a few quarters or years characterize this set of papers. Also, the particular years chosen were, in at least the last two cases, periods when real housing prices were rising. Had they extended their estimation forward or backward in time they would have included declining prices as well, and would have surely estimated a larger price elasticity of supply.

Malpezzi and Maclennan (2001) consider four related tests of the price elasticity of supply, and present results from three of them for the United States and the United Kingdom, using data from the end of the 19th century to date. Here we briefly consider two models.

The first test is a simple one. If markets are elastic, then prices do not vary, at least in the long run. So a simple test of the price elasticity of new construction is whether there is a trend in the relative price of new construction.

The second model, first developed in Malpezzi and Mayo (1997b), follows Muth and Follain, taking advantage of some later suggestions of

Olsen (1987). Consider the following three-equation flow model of the housing market:

$$Q_D = \alpha_0 + \alpha_1 P_h + \alpha_2 Y + \alpha_3 D$$

$$Q_S = \beta_0 + \beta_1 P_h$$

$$Q_D = Q_S$$

All variables are expressed in natural logarithms. Among other advantages, we can then interpret coefficients as approximate elasticities. The variables are defined as follows:

Q_D = logarithm of the quantity of housing demanded
Q_S = logarithm of the quantity of housing supplied
P_h = logarithm of the relative price per unit of housing
Y = logarithm of real income
D = logarithm of population

The reduced form of the system can be found by equating supply and demand and solving for the observable variable, P_h, the price of housing. This yields the following:

$$P_h = \frac{\alpha_0 - \beta_0}{\beta_1 - \alpha_1} + \frac{\alpha_2}{\beta_1 - \alpha_1} Y + \frac{\alpha_3}{\beta_1 - \alpha_1} D$$

This expression shows that the coefficients of variables on the right-hand side are comprised of several elasticities; in econometric jargon, the structural parameters are not identified. But given an estimated total coefficient of income, and known or assumed α_1 and α_2, we can easily derive β_1, the supply elasticity.

We reviewed extensive literature on housing demand in the text above. This suggests estimating the simple reduced-form equations, and identifying the key underlying parameter of this investigation, the price elasticity of housing supply, based on parametric estimates of housing demand parameters from the literature. Recalling that all variables are in logs, and making the reduced form stochastic, we estimate

$$\beta_1 = \frac{\alpha_2}{\gamma_2} + \alpha_1$$

Thus, Malpezzi and Maclennan estimate the price elasticity of housing supply as

$$P_h = \gamma_0 + \gamma_1 Q + \gamma_2 Y + \gamma_3 D + \varepsilon$$

where γ_2 is the estimated reduced form coefficient of income and the parameters α_1 and α_2 are parametrically assumed. Since we do not know the elasticity with certainty, we can actually calculate β_1 by assuming the price elasticity of housing demand to lie in the interval –0.5 and –1, and assuming the long-run income elasticity of demand to be alternately 0.5 and 1.0. These values encompass most of the econometric estimates (Mayo 1981).[28]

For the prewar United States, Malpezzi and Maclennan calculate implied price elasticities of supply from the flow models as between 4 and 10, and postwar, between 6 and 13. In contrast, for the prewar United Kingdom the implied price elasticity from flow models is between 1 and 4; postwar it is between 0 and less than 1.[29]

The United States and the United Kingdom have many similarities, including a broadly similar legal and institutional framework for real property. However, there are a number of important differences. Among others, the United States has directed its financial system more toward housing, has greater tax advantages, and has a less restrictive planning and regulatory environment, particularly for single-family housing. This brief comparison is consistent with the notion that the supply responsiveness of the housing market is determined, in large part, by institutions and policies.

Finally, Mayer and Somerville (2000) have noted that new construction is a close approximation to the *change* in housing supply, rather than the housing supply itself. They therefore suggest that the appropriate elasticity regression has new construction as a function of house price changes, rather than house price levels. When they perform these regressions, they find a very low supply elasticity, which makes intuitive sense. As we already discussed, the vast majority of housing supply in the United States comes from existing units, the number of which changes little with changes in house prices.

Housing Units by Type, Age, and Quality

By one measure, owner-occupied and rental units are the same age: In 1990 the median age of a house, either owner occupied or rental, was 25 years. More than half of the entire U.S. housing stock is single-family owner occupied; very little owner-occupied housing is multifamily (figure 2.8). But while most rental housing is multifamily, more than one-quarter

Figure 2.8. *Occupied Housing Units by Structure Type and Tenure*

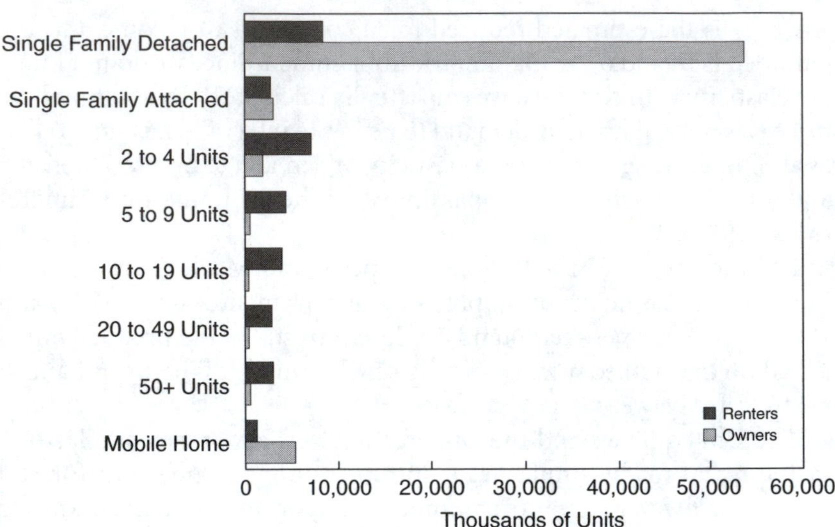

Source: 1997 American Housing Survey.

of rental housing (9 percent of the total housing stock) is single family. Surprisingly, little of the rental housing nationwide is in large buildings; only 8 percent of rental units are in buildings with 50 units or more. Of course, in large cities the proportion is substantially higher. Few single-family units are built for the rental market; most single-family rentals have changed tenure since construction.

Multifamily starts ran at a modest 100,000 to 200,000 units for the first half of the 20th century, except for a brief burst of close to 400,000 units per year during the 1920s.[30] Most of the postwar years saw private multifamily starts at around 400,000 to 600,000 per year; the years before 1973 were even more prolific for multifamily construction. In the 1990s, private multifamily starts were at their lowest level since the 1950s.

Increasing shares of new housing units are mobile homes, now known in many quarters as manufactured housing. Mobile home placements hit more than 500,000 per year between 1972 and 1973, and have since settled in at about half that amount.[31] The nation is approaching 6 million occupied units of manufactured housing, or more than 1 in 20.

We have already noted that in a given year most housing, in the United States as elsewhere, is supplied from the existing stock. There are more than 100 million units in the country, and new construction is usually well under 2 million, less than 2 percent of the housing supply. Most rental housing that is *not* multifamily was built for owner occupation but has since been converted to rental. Further, most owner-occupied units purchased are *not* new, but existing, as figure 2.9 illustrates. Sales of new single-family units have never topped 1 million, but in a good year, sales of existing single-family units approach 5 million.

So far we have focused on housing *units.* Units do not fully capture the state of the construction market. The average value of new units put in place is now 50 percent higher in real terms than 20 years ago. This mainly reflects the increasing quality of new construction. Figure 2.10 presents the real value of new construction compared with starts. While starts hit a peak in 1972 of about 2.4 million units and has trended down thereafter, the real dollar value of investment has climbed steadily throughout the postwar period. In particular, while the number of starts has dipped since its 1972 peak, the less closely monitored dollar value of new construction has continued to increase. Data on new construction tell about half of the "new supply" story. Spending on upgrading and maintenance and repair tells the other half. U.S. Commerce Department data show spending in excess of $100 billion *per year* on improvements, maintenance, and repair (see figure 2.10).[32]

Figure 2.9. *Single-Family Home Sales*

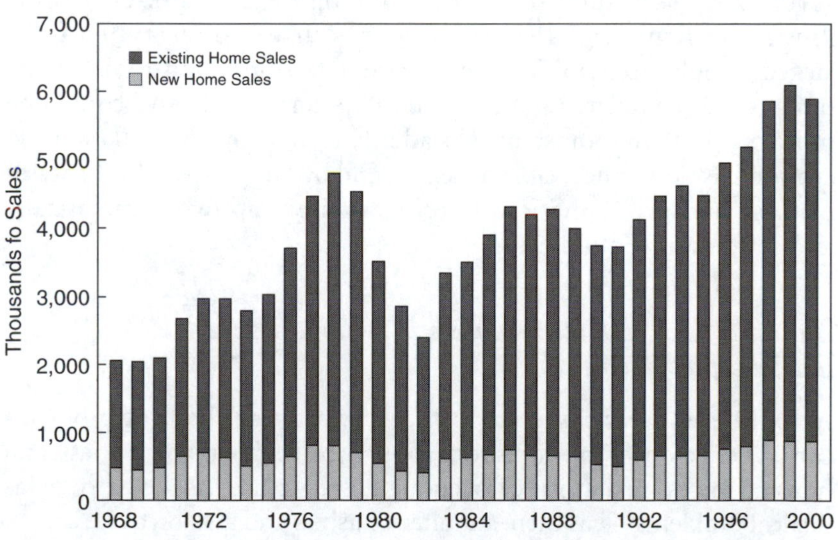

Source: U.S. Department of Housing and Urban Development.

Figure 2.10. *Residential New Construction Put in Place, 1966–1999*

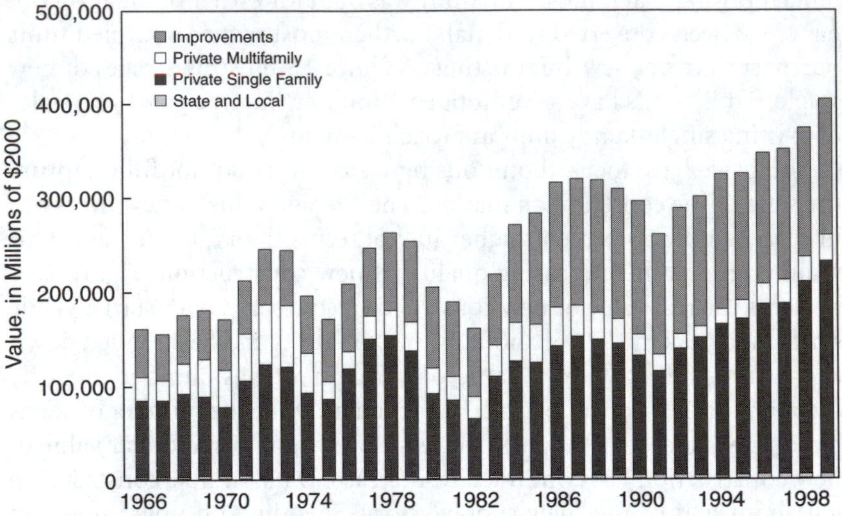

Source: U.S. Census Bureau.

This spending has resulted in substantial improvements in housing quality. Indeed, the postwar increase in housing quality, or its converse, the decline of inadequate housing, is startling. Many such measures exist (see Simonson 1980), but figure 2.11 presents some illustrative figures. In 1940 more than four out of every ten units lacked complete plumbing. Four decades later, only about 3 out of 100 units lacked complete plumbing. In 1940, one unit in five contained more people than rooms; four decades later, less than 5 in 100 were so crowded. By any conceivable measure, and by any conceivable analyses of these measures, American housing quality improved dramatically and continuously after 1945.

An Initial Look at Housing Prices: How to Measure and Interpret Them

At some level, every city, every town, every country's housing problems can be boiled down to two issues: Housing prices are rising too fast, and housing prices are not rising fast enough. Every place has these two paradoxical problems—has them simultaneously—and as soon as we can fix them both we can stop worrying about the housing market.

Figure 2.11. *Percent of U.S. Housing Units Meeting Quality Standards*

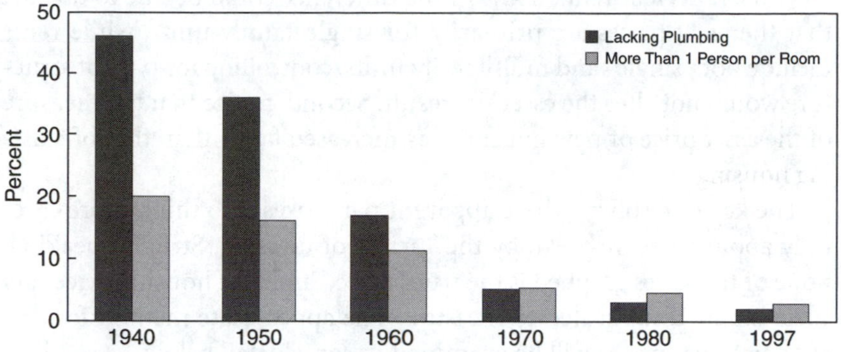

Sources: U.S. Census Bureau, American Housing Survey.

Figure 2.12 illustrates some recent, apparently contradictory results on housing prices. The top line in the figure represents the asset price (or value) of new housing, the middle line the asset price of existing housing, and the bottom line represents rent. All three are deflated by the overall consumer price index (CPI), so the lines represent different measures of the relative price of housing.

Figure 2.12. *Real Rents and Real House Prices in the United States, 1970–2000*

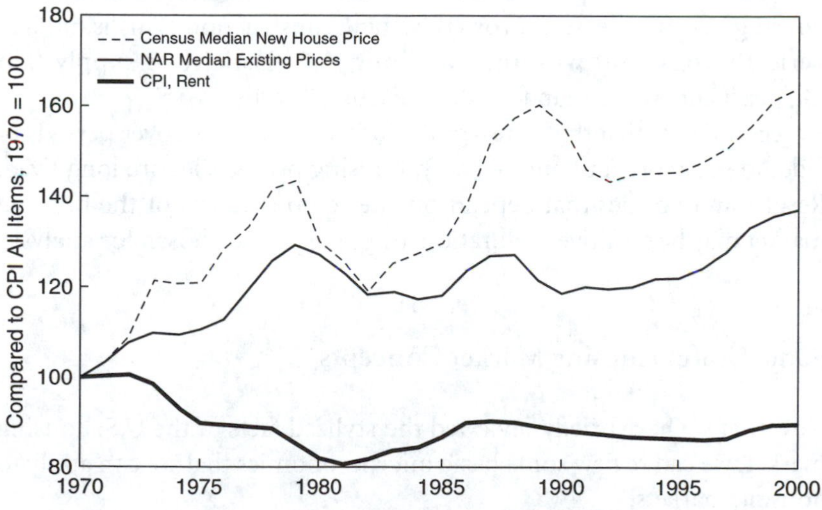

Sources: National Association of Realtors, U.S. Census Bureau, Bureau of Labor Statistics.
Notes: CPI = consumer price index; NAR = National Association of Realtors.

First, notice that while real asset prices rose over most of the last 25 years, rents fell. While some of the difference could be due to the fact that the asset prices are primarily for single-family units, while rents include both single- and multifamily units, controlling for type of structure would not alter the essential result. Second, notice that the measure of the asset price of new housing has increased faster than that of existing housing.

The key to resolving these apparent paradoxes is to think more carefully about what we mean by the "price" of housing. Strictly speaking, none of the series graphed is the true "price," and true housing prices are surprisingly complicated to measure. The appropriate method for discussing house prices will be examined in some detail below.

Another perspective on housing prices comes from examining them from a long-run perspective. We chose 1970 for a starting date for figure 2.12 because it was possible to find all three series back to that date. Few housing asset price series go back before 1963 (although the rental component of the CPI does go back further). Malpezzi and Maclennan (2001), following Follain (1979b) among others, constructed a measure of the relative price of new residential construction going back to the beginning of the 20th century. Figure 2.13 presents their index for the post–World War II period.

Notice two very interesting patterns in figure 2.13. First, in the very long run—over the postwar period—there is no discernible trend in housing prices, at least as proxied by new construction. This is, in fact, perfectly consistent with the high long-run elasticity of supply that Malpezzi and Maclennan found, as discussed earlier.

Second, note that there are significant trends in prices over periods of a decade or more. Put another way, housing price cycles are long lived. Results and policies that depend on the responsiveness of the housing market may be sensitive to duration and time period chosen for analysis.

Some Useful Housing Market Concepts

Now that we have briefly reviewed the stylized facts of the U.S. housing market, we can review some basic microeconomics that we can apply to housing markets.

Figure 2.13. *Relative Price, New Residential Construction Ratio of Two Implicit Price Deflators*

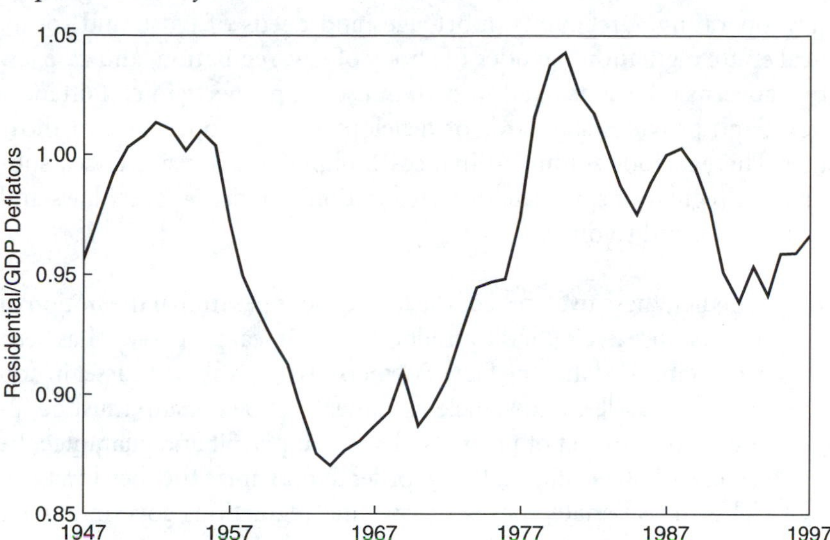

Source: Malpezzi and Maclennan (2001).

Property Rights

Until recently, property rights were taken for granted in most economic courses, and in most discussions of housing, at least in the United States. However, in much of the world, secure and well-defined property rights are only just emerging. This is particularly true in a number of Eastern European countries and in the countries comprising the former Soviet Union. In other parts of the world, notably parts of sub-Saharan Africa, property rights are very much in flux, as countries move (in fits and starts) from what might loosely be called "traditional" systems toward systems that are more heavily dependent on government as definer and arbitrator.[33] Even in the United States, where such rights are generally thought "well developed," it is useful to consider and analyze property rights more explicitly. Doing so aids clear thinking about issues such as tenure choice, land use regulation, and rent controls.

There are two areas of law—contract law and real estate regulation—that most concern the housing and real estate markets. Contract law deals with the many documents that facilitate the transfer of property and property rights, allocate those rights, and structure "deals." These include such items as contracts of sale, leases, easements and rights-of-way, operating agreements, mortgages and deeds of trust, and so on. Real estate regulation includes the body of law, regulation, and case law that governs the rights to allow certain uses of property in certain locations, and provides standards of development and operation of those uses. These include zoning ordinances, building and housing codes, subdivision regulations, private deed restrictions, environmental laws and regulations, and so on.

- Together, these two areas of the law render operational the notion of ownership, exercise, and transfer of rights in real property. It has been well established that the fact of ownership of a real estate asset in and of itself is useless and valueless. Rather, that ownership must be filtered through a set of property rights that permit and guarantee the exercise of ownership rights. In order to maximize the social value of rights in real estate, the set of laws and regulations governing their associated property rights must possess certain characteristics.
- They must be cleanly defined and assigned.
- They must be enforceable at a reasonable cost.
- They must have a clear process for adjudication and resolutions of disputes.
- The system must be widely accepted, which generally implies it must be seen to be "fair."[34]

External Costs and Benefits of Housing

One way housing is different from the "textbook" example of goods is that significant costs and benefits exist that are *not* incurred by individual suppliers or captured by individual consumers. Figure 2.14 presents a simple model of externalities in the housing market, from Malpezzi (1996a). Consider a single housing market in which (for the moment) all housing units are identical. Suppose that in the absence of regulation we observe supply S_1 and demand D_1, which are based on private costs and benefits for housing units; the market reaches equilibrium at point *A*. This equilibrium will be privately and socially efficient, unless some externality or other market failure is present. Suppose there are one or more externalities that raise the social costs of housing above their private costs. Examples could include costs due to congestion or changes in envi-

Figure 2.14. *Optimal Taxation and Regulation in the Presence of an Externality*

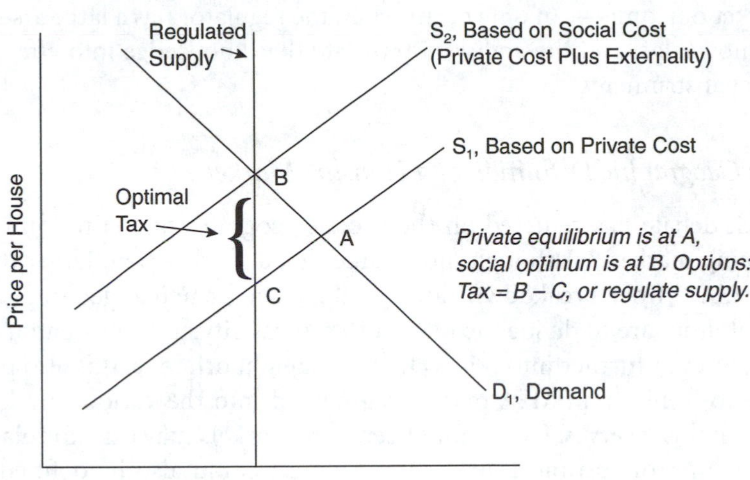

ronmental conditions. With the addition of such external costs, the social cost is denoted by S_2. Then, clearly *A* is "too much" housing at "too low" a price. If public agents were perfectly informed they could, in principle, regulate the supply of housing so that the socially preferable outcome, *B*, was reached. Alternatively, a tax could be imposed equal to the size of the externality—that is, equal to the difference between *B* and *C*.

Congestion, environmental costs, infrastructure costs, fiscal effects, and neighborhood composition effects are among the possible externalities, and the classic argument for government intervention in the market. Such externalities raise social costs of housing above private costs, and hence, in principle, require regulation. If such externalities are large, *and* are correctly measured by the regulating authority, *and* the specific policy instrument used to regulate is sufficiently precise, regulation can correct for these externalities.[35] So can taxation. But even if such externalities exist, departures from the preceding rather stringent requirements could leave society worse off in practice.

Externalities could also confer benefits to society, and these benefits can readily be added to the model. Let us consider external benefits as things that drive a wedge between the market demand curve, based on private benefits, and the social demand curve, which includes the externality.[36] Most real-world housing markets will have multiple externalities, so that successful regulation—regulation that on balance more or less corrects for market failure, rather than further worsening a suboptimal market outcome—can only occur when the regulator has a large arsenal of knowledge, and the ability to translate that knowledge into effective policy instruments.

The Geographic Definition of a Housing Market

Much debate has centered on the precise geographical definition of a housing market.[37] Although most agree that a market is no larger than an MSA,[38] finer breakdowns are possible. The principal geographical possibilities are to divide the MSA into central-city and suburban markets, or even further into census tracts or neighborhoods. It is also possible to think of an MSA market segmented into the various kinds of households it serves. For example, separate markets may exist for blacks and whites due to racial prejudice. Markets could also be defined in terms of housing quality.

Fundamentally, for a place to be defined as a housing market, it must be homogeneous in at least one dimension, and almost certainly in more than one. It is this homogeneity that allows different houses to be substitutes for one another. To define things negatively, if two houses are not substitutes, they are not part of the same housing market.

This is also a good place to note that, in this volume, when we examine individual housing markets, we will usually focus on urban housing markets.[39] However, most of our techniques, analyses, and conclusions are perfectly generalizable to rural as well as urban areas.[40]

Stocks and Flows; Capitalization

Another way housing market analysis extends simple textbook supply and demand is to assume that housing is an *asset* that yields a flow of services over time. This leads us to the basic concept of stocks and flows. Examples of stocks and their corresponding flows are legion; some are listed below:

Stocks	*Flows*
Wealth	Income
National Debt	Deficit
House Value	House Rent

The distinction between stocks and flows matters in several respects. For example, sometimes housing rents and asset prices move in tandem, and sometimes they move in different directions.[41]

Economists are careful in their use of the word "price." Rent is not really price, but an *expenditure*, comprising price and quantity, that is, Rent = Price times Quantity ($R = PQ$). What real estate brokers call "sales price" is not strictly speaking a price either, but the market value of a unit, or the present value of net rents (a "stock" or "asset" concept). Thus, when we analyze housing we refer to (1) the rental price per unit of housing services and (2) the quantity of housing services produced by a unit. The product of these is rent.[42]

Rents are translated into values or asset prices using the concept of present value. The relationship between rents and values is straightforward:

$$V = \sum_{t=0}^{T} \frac{R_t - C_t}{(1 + t)^t}$$

where V is the present value (a stock concept); R is rent (a flow concept); C_t is the recurrent cost of maintaining the unit, property taxes, and so on; i is the discount rate'; and t is the life of the asset.[43] In the special case where rents and costs are constant over time, and the time horizon is long,

$$V \cong \frac{R - C}{i}$$

This leads us naturally to our next question: How do we decompose value into its component parts, those of price and quantity?

Measuring Housing: The Price and Quantity of Housing Services

A necessary condition for housing market analysis is the ability to *measure* housing. How much "house" does a particular dwelling provide? How can we compare slum dwellings to those of the middle class? Those in Des Moines to those in Los Angeles? Apartments to single-family homes? Private to publicly provided units? How can we tell if a government program or regulation actually changes the consumption of housing, or its price, or some combination of the two? Thus, the need for measures of housing services is self-evident. The next few paragraphs will suggest some alternative measures. Some are based on expenditures (rents and values), and some are more direct measures of housing quantity/quality.[44] The reason we lump together our discussion of the quantity of housing services provided by a unit and its price in one place is that we never directly observe either one. Instead we observe *expenditures* like rent, (R), or house value, (V), which are the product of price and quantity. Algebraically, $R = PQ$, so we can extend our results from the preceding section:

$$V = \sum_{t=0}^{T} \frac{R_t - C_t}{\left(1+i\right)^t} \equiv \sum_{t=0}^{T} \frac{\left(P_t Q_t\right) - C_t}{\left(1=i\right)^t}$$

And again, in the limit, if each and every R_t and C_t is the same, as t approaches infinity this becomes:

$$V \cong \frac{R-C}{i} \equiv \frac{PQ-C}{i}$$

Measuring Price (and Hence Also Measuring Quantity)

Rents and values are relatively easy to measure and work with; sometimes we do not really have to be able to decompose expenditures into prices and quantities. For example, when measuring debt service capacity, or ability to pay rent, we do not often concern ourselves with how much of R is P and how much is Q. But in much housing market analysis it is important to measure prices, at least approximately.

Table 2.2 lists six general methods of measuring (or estimating) housing prices. We will discuss each method briefly in turn. Tables 2.3 and 2.4 present some representative price data for levels and changes for 30 large metropolitan areas. Examples are presented for each of the major methods.

The first type of measure is based on *simple medians* or *averages.* The most commonly used measures of this type include median sales prices for existing housing published by the National Association of Realtors (NAR) (column 2 of table 2.3), and the Census Bureau median house prices (column 1) and rents (columns 6 and 7). The method is, in general, self-explanatory. A big advantage of this type of measure is its simplicity, and the fact that comparisons over time and across markets are possible. The biggest disadvantage is that this type of measure does not usually control for differences in quantity of housing services, across markets or over time.[45]

(*text continues on page 38*)

Table 2.2. *General Categories of Price Measures*

Type of price measure	*Brief description*	*Uses time-series or cross-section?*	*Advantages*	*Disadvantages*
Simple medians or averages (e.g., NAR house prices, BLS Budget for Family of Four)	Self-explanatory.	Both, generally.	Simplicity.	Does not usually control for differences in quantity of housing services, across markets, or over time.
Laspeyres price indexes (e.g., CPI, Nation Income Accounts Deflators)	Take sample of units in base year. Revisit and appraise them over time. Compute percentage changes.	Generally, time-series only.	Widely available, at least for major markets.	Results may vary with "bundle" chosen; as prices change over time, typical bundle consumed changes in real life, not in the index.
Hedonics	Regress rent or value against characteristics of unit, location. Then use coefficients to predict rent or value for "standard" unit.	Most often cross-section, but can do time series as well.	Good theoretical and intuitive foundations.	Data requirements are very high.

(*continued*)

Table 2.2. *Continued*

Type of price measure	*Brief description*	*Uses time-series or cross-section?*	*Advantages*	*Disadvantages*
Repeat sales	Survey units that have sold twice. Compute percentage growth in sales prices over time.	Time-series only.	Based on actual transaction prices.	Most units are not sold in any given period; finding repeat sales to pair throws out lots of information. Units that sell are not necessarily representative of all units. Assumes relative values of attributes remain stable.
User Cost	Figure out what a "user" of the house really pays (or would pay), net of financing, taxes, maintenance, inflation.	Generally time-series (e.g., Hendershott and Shilling 1982) but can be cross section (e.g., Follain 1981, Green 1996).	Incorporates a model of what determines prices; accounts for effects of taxation, inflation, and maintenance on prices.	Hard to do well in cross-section.
Hybrid (combine two of the above methods)	Depends on which methods being combined.	Could be either	Can combine (e.g.) hedonic and repeat sales methods (as in Case and Quigley 1991), hedonic and user cost (as in Follain 1981).	Limited by data availability.

Table 2.3. *Housing Price Levels, Circa 1990, in Selected Large Metropolitan Areas*

Metropolitan area	*Census median value (1990 in $)*	*NAR[a] median house price (1990 in $)*	*MCG owner house price index (1990 in $)*	*Simple user costs versus property taxes and assumed rate of 0.14 ($)*	*Census median contract rent (1990 in $)*	*Census median gross rent (1990 in $)*	*MGC renter house price index (1990 in $)*
Los Angeles	226,400	212,800	205,594	32,649	570	626	674
New York	209,000	174,900	195,866	30,738	455	503	629
Chicago	111,200	116,800	96,082	17,099	425	491	513
Philadelphia	100,800	108,700	105,172	15,502	435	516	534
Detroit	68,300	76,700	62,184	11,254	363	455	451
Washington	166,100	150,500	145,022	24,802	623	667	649
Houston	64,300	70,700	56,025	9,947	339	406	404
Boston	186,100	174,200	174,392	27,790	581	656	623
Atlanta	89,800	86,400	74,712	13,411	441	529	466
Nassau	187,000	161,000	161,425	29,574	689	778	755
Riverside	133,900	132,100	110,238	19,548	494	562	492
Dallas	83,000	89,500	69,076	12,711	393	456	435
San Diego	186,700	183,200	155,932	27,142	564	611	582
Minneapolis	88,700	88,700	73,233	13,403	444	479	470
Saint Louis	70,000	76,700	66,417	10,499	320	415	420
Anaheim	252,700	242,400	197,568	36,624	728	790	747
Baltimore	101,200	105,900	96,880	15,269	399	490	480
Phoenix	85,300	84,000	72,183	12,478	394	465	415

(*continued*)

Table 2.3. *Continued*

Metropolitan area	*Census median value (1990 in $)*	*NAR[a] median house price (1990 in $)*	*MCG owner house price index (1990 in $)*	*Simple user costs versus property taxes and assumed rate of 0.14 ($)*	*Census median contract rent (1990 in $)*	*Census median gross rent (1990 in $)*	*MGC renter house price index (1990 in $)*
Oakland	224,400	—	187,045	32,655	585	642	630
Tampa	71,300	71,400	66,323	10,556	377	448	403
Pittsburgh	55,600	70,100	52,930	8,945	289	366	347
Seattle	136,700	131,500	113,977	20,260	459	516	493
Miami	86,500	89,300	88,851	13,177	422	493	506
Cleveland	74,100	80,600	69,410	11,348	332	406	404
Newark	191,400	187,000	166,737	29,901	513	583	632
Denver	87,800	86,400	73,409	13,267	377	431	411
San Francisco	332,400	259,300	267,412	47,802	663	709	761
Kansas City, MO	66,500	74,100	53,046	9,989	346	425	379
San Jose	289,400	—	257,084	41,865	715	773	743
Sacramento	136,700	136,700	121,010	19,897	465	531	492

Source: Malpezzi, Chun, and Green (1998).

a. NAR = National Association of Realtors.

Table 2.4. *Housing Price Changes, Circa 1990, in Selected Metropolitan Areas*

Metropolitan area	*CPI percentage change in residential rent, renters, 1990–91*[a]	*CPI percentage change in owners' equivalent rent, 1990–91*[a]	*Percentage change in NAR nominal median house price, 1990–91*[b]	*Percentage change in agencies' nominal repeat sale house price, 1990–91*[c]
Los Angeles	2.9	2.8	2.9	−0.7
New York	3.5	3.9	−0.8	0.8
Chicago	4.6	4.5	12.2	4.7
Philadelphia	4.0	4.2	8.9	2.2
Detroit	1.7	2.6	5.1	4.7
Washington	3.0	3.6	4.1	2.2
Houston	9.0	7.2	4.7	5.0
Boston	0.6	1.3	−2.4	−1.1
Atlanta	0.9	1.5	3.4	2.3
Nassau	—	—	−1.1	0.9
Riverside	—	—	2.5	—
Dallas	4.3	3.7	−1.3	3.3
San Diego	1.8	3.3	2.3	−0.4
Minneapolis	1.9	1.6	2.7	3.1
Saint Louis	0.9	1.9	3.5	2.9
Anaheim	—	—	−1.1	—
Baltimore	3.7	4.4	4.0	4.5
Phoenix	—	—	1.8	3.6
Oakland	—	—	—	−0.4
Tampa	2.9	3.1	−0.1	2.5
Pittsburgh	2.9	4.1	5.8	6.5
Seattle	6.7	8.3	8.8	3.3
Miami	3.5	3.0	4.9	4.9
Cleveland	6.3	4.5	6.9	6.6
Newark	—	—	−4.4	1.4
Denver	2.8	2.7	3.1	5.6
San Francisco	3.6	3.9	−0.3	−0.9
Kansas City, MO	4.2	2.4	3.4	2.3
San Jose	—	—	—	−0.5
Sacramento	—	—	0.7	−1.2

Notes: — = not available.

a. Bureau of Labor Statistics.

b. National Association of Realtors.

c. Fannie Mae Foundation and Freddie Mac Foundation.

Not surprisingly, inspection of table 2.3 suggests that these medians vary greatly across metropolitan areas. Even if we grant that simple medians mix price and quantity, we also know from a number of studies that quantity varies less than price in such a sample. Simple medians, however, while imperfect, do include valuable information.

NAR data are available quarterly for about 100 metropolitan areas. They are limited to single-family units, as reported from multiple listing service databases. Alternative median housing "prices" (loosely speaking) are decennial census median rents and values. These have the disadvantage of only being available in census years, but are available by state, county, and metropolitan area in widely available printed reports, and in even finer breakdowns in other reports and computer databases.[46] Even a quick perusal of small-area data shows tremendous regional variation in rents and values. For example, the median census value for the country as a whole in 1990 was $78,000. But many counties in the Great Plains had medians below $30,000, while many counties on the coasts had medians greater than $100,000. In fact, a dozen counties actually had medians above $250,000.[47] Patterns for rents were roughly similar if not quite as variable. The median gross rent in 1990 was $300, but 28 counties had medians of over $700.

An important point is that rents and values tend to be higher in urban areas, where incomes tend to be higher; so higher prices and rents would not necessarily be as much of a burden. Still, while there is some moderation of regional effects, the same general patterns hold. Examining some 3,100 counties, the median of 3,100 ratios of median house price to median income was 2.1. But 16 counties had ratios greater than 6.0, and 20 had ratios less than 1.0. We will return to this simple but basic ratio later.

In our final initial examination of regional variation, in figure 2.15 we map the real growth (or decline) in house values by county from 1980 to 1990. In the median county, real house prices declined by 1 percent per year over the decade. Seventy percent of all counties posted median declines; but 28 counties had real increases greater than 7 percent per year. Note the startling declines in many counties, especially in the Great Plains.

The second type of measure mentioned in table 2.2 is the *Laspeyres price index.* The best known example is the CPI, which attempts to measure the overall cost of living. Laspeyres indexes are constructed as follows: (1) take a sample of units in some base year; (2) revisit them over time, and appraise; and (3) compute percentage changes.[48] More formally, Laspeyres indexes are constructed as:

Figure 2.15. *Change in County Median House Value (Owners), 1980–90.*

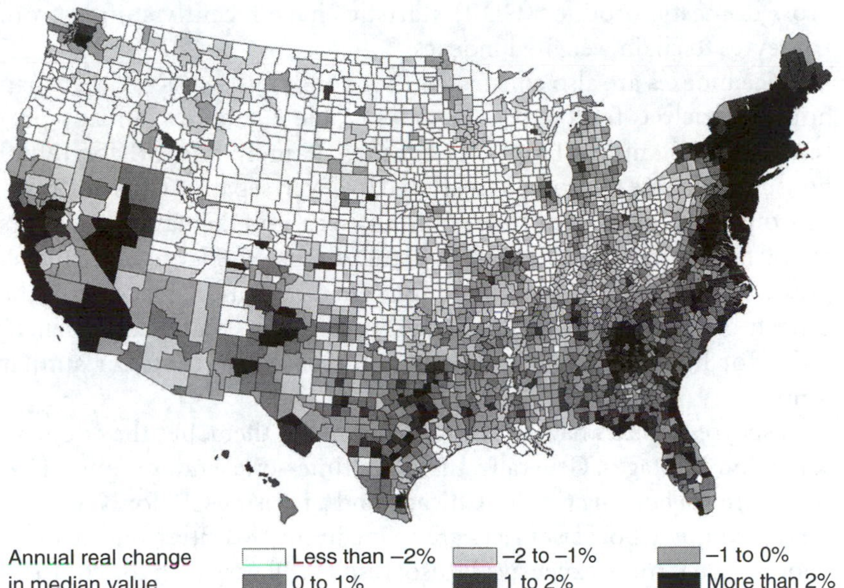

$$I_t = \frac{P_t Q_0}{P_0 Q_0} \cdot 100$$

where I is the index, P is the price per unit of housing services, Q is the quantity of housing, and subscripts denote time. Time, 0, is the base year or period, and time, t, is any year, forward (positive t) or backward (negative t). Thus the index is just the ratio of what is spent in time t to what's spent in time 0, holding constant the "bundle," or set of goods, purchased in time 0. The Laspeyres index generally overstates pace changes, because it fails to allow for substitutions.

Laspeyres indexes are the most commonly found indexes, but others exist. The converse of Laspeyres is the Paasche. The *Paasche price index* is constructed in a fashion similar to the Laspeyres index, except that instead of pricing a bundle, Q_0, based on the initial period's typical consumption, the Paasche index uses a bundle based on the final period's consumption. So-called *Fisher* and *Divisia* price indexes are essentially averages of Laspeyres and Paasche indexes. *Chain weighted* indexes are price indexes whose bundles change rapidly over time. The official U.S. gross domestic product (GDP) statistics have recently shifted from Laspeyres to chain weighted indexes.[49]

Price indexes are also constructed for goods and services other than housing, such as food and retail sales. Table 2.4, above, already presented some familiar Laspeyres indexes, namely the CPI for rental housing for some metropolitan areas. However, separate CPIs are available only for a handful of metropolitan areas, and the national indexes are by far the most widely reported and discussed. Figure 2.15, above, presented the rental CPI, adjusted for general inflation. Since 1985, the Bureau of Labor Statistics (BLS) has also used a "rental equivalence" index for homeowners; that is, an index based on rents for similar units.[50]

Laspeyres indexes have much to recommend them, but they do have some disadvantages. Generally, these are time-series indexes only. That is, if there is a housing CPI for Chicago and a housing CPI for New York, we can compare how fast prices are rising in the two cities, but we don't know which is more expensive.[51] Also, results will vary with the choice of "bundle." We want to hold the bundle fixed, but actually, as prices change over time, the typical bundle consumed changes in real life, even if not in the index.[52]

Time-series price indexes have to be presented and interpreted with care, especially for long time series. As an example, consider the all-item CPI from 1913 to date. Since 1967 is the base for this index, the initial value in 1913 was about 30. A 10 percent rise in prices around 1913 would thus appear as a rise of about 3 in the CPI. A 10 percent rise around 1993, when this CPI was around 433, would appear as a rise of 43. We have the same percentage increase in prices, but when one examines or graphs the numerical values of the index, the recent price increase *appears* to be more than 14 times as great!

There are two ways to better depict the true behavior of prices over time. One way is to simply present year-to-year percentage changes, rather than rely on index values. The other way is to use a logarithmically scaled graph of the index. Each has its advantages. Percentage changes are easy to explain to audiences unfamiliar with logs, and show clearly how price volatility changes over time. Logarithmically scaled graphs show how prices rise in a cumulative fashion, but without misleading the reader into thinking that recent price increases are *so* much faster than earlier changes.

Another useful trick with these indexes is to simply divide one by the other to show *relative prices.* More precisely, if I^H is our housing index and I^A is all goods and services, the real housing price index I^R is defined as

$$I^R = \frac{I^H}{I^A} \cdot 100$$

If we consider the CPI for rent, for example, figure 2.15 uses the broad-based implicit price deflator to adjust the rental CPI and show how real rents have changed over recent years.

Hedonic Indexes

This section discusses the estimation of so-called "hedonic regressions" for housing and how they can be used to construct price indexes and to examine demand and supply relationships. First, we present an introductory and intuitive explanation of hedonic price estimation. Then we present an empirical example.[53]

Hedonic equations provide one way to decompose expenditures on housing into measurable prices and quantities so that rents for different dwellings or for identical dwellings in different places can be predicted and compared. A hedonic equation is a regression of expenditures (rents or values) on housing characteristics, and will be explained in some detail below. The independent variables represent the individual characteristics of the dwelling, and the regression coefficients may be transferred into estimates of the implicit prices of these characteristics. The results provide us with estimated prices for housing characteristics, and we can then compare two dwellings by using these prices as weights. For example, the estimated price for a variable measuring number of rooms indicates the change in value or rent associated with the addition or deletion of one room. It tells us in a dollar and cents way how much "more house" is provided by a dwelling with an extra room.

Once we have estimated the implicit prices of measurable housing characteristics in each market, we can select a standard set of characteristics, or bundle, and price a dwelling meeting these specifications in each market. In this manner we can construct price indexes for housing of constant quality across markets. In a similar fashion we can use the results from a particular market's regression to estimate how prices of identical dwellings vary with location *within* a single market (e.g., with distance from the city center) or even to decompose the differences in rent or house values into price and quantity differences. Some simplified examples will make these procedures clear.

The hedonic regression assumes that we know the determinants of a unit's rent:

$$R = f(S, N, L, C), \text{ where}$$

R = rent (or we can substitute V, value, if estimating hedonic equations for homeowners or using sales data);
S = structural characteristics;
N = neighborhood characteristics;
L = location within the market; and
C = contract conditions or characteristics, such as utilities included in rent.

This method is best illustrated by example. But first we need to discuss some preliminaries, such as how to define the market (choose our sampling frame), how to pick a particular functional form for the regression, and general principles of variable construction.

Choice of Functional Form

There is no strong theoretical basis for choosing the correct functional form of a hedonic regression (see Halverson and Pollakowski 1981 and Rosen 1974). Follain and Malpezzi (1980), for example, tested a linear functional form as well as a log-linear (also known as semilog) specification. But they found, as detailed below, the log-linear form had a number of advantages over the linear form.

The log-linear form is written

$$\ln R = \beta_0 + S\beta_1 + N\beta_2 + L\beta_3 + C\beta_4 + \varepsilon$$

where $\ln R$ is the natural log of imputed rent; S, N, L, and C are structural, neighborhood, locational, and contract characteristics of the dwelling, respectively;[54] and β_1 and ε are the hedonic regression coefficients and error term, respectively.

The log-linear form has five things to recommend it. First, the semilog model allows for variation in the dollar value of a particular characteristic so that the price of one component depends in part on the house's other characteristics. For example, with the linear model, the value added by a third bathroom to a one-bedroom house is equal to the value it adds to a five-bedroom house. This seems unlikely. The semilog model allows the value added to vary proportionally with the size and quality of the home.

Second, the coefficients of a semilog model have a simple and appealing interpretation. The coefficient can be interpreted as approximately the percentage change in the rent or value given a unit change in the independent variable. For example, if the coefficient of a variable representing central air conditioning is .219, then adding it to a structure adds about 22 percent to its value or its rent. Actually, the percentage interpretation is an approximation, and it is not necessarily accurate for dummy variables. Halverson and Palmquist (1980) show that a much better approximation of the percentage change is given by $e^b - 1$, where b is the estimated coefficient and e is the base of natural logarithms. So a better approximation is that central air will add exp $e - .219 - 1 = 24$ percent.

Third, the semilog form often mitigates the common statistical problem known as heteroskedasticity, or changing variance of the error term. Fourth, semilog models are computationally simple, and thus well suited to examples. The one hazard endemic to the semilog form is that the antilog of the predicted log house price does not give an unbiased estimate of predicted price. This can, however, be fixed with an adjustment (see Goldberger 1968). Alternatives to the linear and semilog forms exist, but we will not detail them here.[55] Finally, we note that in our example below, the independent variables are mostly dummy (or indicator) variables. This allows us a fair amount of flexibility in estimation.

Example: A Hedonic Regression for Washington, D.C., Renters

This section presents the results of estimating the model just described to the Washington, D.C., metropolitan area. The model is described in great detail in Malpezzi, Ozanne, and Thibodeau (1980). The estimates are presented in table 2.5. The usual measure for how a functional form fits the data in a regression sample is R-squared, or the percentage of variation in the dependent variable explained by the model. In our example this statistic is .715. In other words, roughly speaking, the regression model explains about 72 percent of the total observed variance in the natural logarithm of contract rent (the dependent variable).

Let us examine some of the explanatory variables and their coefficients to illustrate some points about the specification and interpretation of these models. Most of the variables represent characteristics of the structure. The bathroom variables are coded as three dummy (zero-

(*text continues on page 47*)

Table 2.5. *Hedonic Regression (Renters), for the Washington, D.C., Area*

Dependent Variable: Log of Contract Rent
Degrees of Freedom: 5,481
R-Squared: 0.72

Variable name	*Coefficient*	*Standard error*	*t-statistic*	*Prob* < $\lvert t \rvert$	*Variables label*	*For dummy variables: exp{b}-1*
INTERCEPT	4.8573	0.0283	171.39	0.0001	Intercept	
B1	0.1151	0.0148	7.77	0.0001	Bath Dummy 1.5	0.1220
B2	0.1994	0.0141	14.15	0.0001	Bath Dummy 2	0.2207
B3	0.4030	0.0221	18.27	0.0001	Bath Dummy GT 2	0.4963
R1	–0.0817	0.0117	–6.97	0.0001	One Room	–0.0784
R3	0.0397	0.0074	5.40	0.0001	Three Rooms	0.0405
RG4	0.0238	0.0032	7.33	0.0001	Rooms When GE4	
BED0	–0.1995	0.0122	–16.33	0.0001	No Bedrooms	–0.1809
BED2	0.1703	0.0076	22.31	0.0001	Two Bedrooms	0.1856
BED3	0.2576	0.0140	18.43	0.0001	Three Beds	0.2938
BEDG4	0.0823	0.0050	16.35	0.0001	Number Beds When GE 4	
ELEVP	0.1309	0.0165	7.95	0.0001	Elevator Present	0.1398
SFATT	0.0278	0.0138	2.02	0.0436	Single-Family Attached	0.0282
SPDET	0.0540	0.0171	3.15	0.0016	Single-Family Detached	0.0555
DUPLEX	–0.0086	0.0164	–0.53	0.5991	Two Units	–0.0086
NGT50	0.0582	0.0168	3.47	0.0005	More than 50 Units	0.0600
AGE1	–0.0033	0.0018	–1.80	0.0712	Age of Structure	

AGE1SQ	0.0000	0.0001	–0.37	0.7141	Square Age	
DAGE	0.0888	0.0640	1.39	0.1652	Dummy Old Structure	0.0929
RHEAT	–0.1255	0.0267	–4.70	0.0001	Wall or Room Heat Flue	–0.1179
ROOMAC	0.0969	0.0083	11.62	0.0001	Room Air Conditioner	0.1018
CEMTAC	0.2190	0.0113	19.43	0.0001	Central Air Conditioner	0.2448
NORAD	0.0205	0.0137	1.49	0.135	Rooms without Heat	0.0207
POOR	–0.2575	0.0237	–10.89	0.0001	Wabsnt + Sabsnt + Nobath + Shared + Nheat	
NOPRIVCY	–0.0716	0.0140	–5.12	0.0001	Pass Tru Br to Room and or Bath	–0.0691
NOUT	–0.0586	0.0221	–2.65	0.008	No Outlets	–0.0569
BADHALL	0.0000	0.0080	0.00	0.9972	Bad Hall Light	0.0000
DFECT	–0.0053	0.0034	–1.58	0.1139	Bleak + Rleak + Cracks + Holes + Plaster + Rats	
CLOT	–0.0256	0.0018	–14.42	0.0001	Length of Tenure	
CLOTSQ	0.0007	0.0001	7.00	0.0001	Square Length of Tenure	
DLOT	–0.1392	0.0532	–2.62	0.0089	Dummy for Old Tenants	–0.1299
CROWDS	–0.0167	0.0107	–1.57	0.1161	Persons per Room	
BLACK	–0.1815	0.0080	–22.56	0.0001	Black Dummy	–0.1660
SPAN	–0.0248	0.0201	–1.23	0.2183	Spanish Dummy	–0.0245
LLBLG	0.0542	0.0194	2.79	0.0053	Landlord Lives in Building	0.0557
NHUTNC	0.0955	0.0133	7.21	0.0001	Non Heat Utility Included	0.1002
HEATINC	0.1031	0.0142	7.26	0.0001	Heat Included in Rent	0.1086
FURNINC	0.1297	0.0229	5.67	0.0001	Furniture Included in Rent	0.1385
PARKINC	0.1473	0.0166	8.89	0.0001	Parking Included in Rent	0.1587
EXCELN	0.0731	0.0094	7.75	0.0001	Excellent Neighborhood Rating	0.0759

(continued)

Table 2.5. *Continued*

Variable name	*Coefficient*	*Standard error*	*t-statistic*	*Prob < |t|*	*Variables label*	*For dummy variables: exp{b}-1*
GOON	0.0382	0.0079	4.84	0.0001	Good Neighborhood Rating	0.0389
POORN	0.0065	0.0152	0.42	0.6709	Poor Neighborhood Rating	0.0065
ABANDON	–0.0742	0.0112	–6.63	0.0001	Abandoned Housing, Enumerator	–0.0715
LITTER	–0.0031	0.0083	–0.37	0.7113	Litter in Neighborhood	–0.0031
NOSHOPS	–0.0209	0.0083	–2.53	0.0115	No Convenient Shopping	–0.0207
Q	0.0041	0.0015	2.72	0.0065	Time Trend	
QHEAT	0.0016	0.0018	0.88	0.3776	Time Trend w Heating	
CC1	0.1150	0.0137	8.40	0.0001	Primary Central City	0.1218
MONTGOM	0.0298	0.0140	2.13	0.0333	Mongomery County Dummy	0.0302
PRINCEG	–0.0010	0.0134	–0.08	0.9395	Prince George's County Dummy	–0.0010
ALEXARL	0.0473	0.0144	3.29	0.001	Alexandria/Arlington Dummy	0.0484

one) variables: B1 for one and one-half baths; B2 for two baths; and B3 for more than two baths. The omitted category is units with one bathroom (our sample eliminates units with no baths). As an approximation, we can see that having one and one-half baths adds about 12 percent to rent (compared to one bath); having two baths adds about 22 percent to rent (compared to one bath); and having two or more baths adds about 50 percent to rent (compared to one bath).

Even with the Halverson and Palmquist correction, the coefficient estimates may or may not accurately reflect the actual value of the characteristic in question. Whether or not they do so depends mainly on what, if any, omitted variables there are missing from the equation, and whether or not these omitted variables are correlated with the included variables. For example, if a variable, such as square footage, is omitted because it is not in the data set, and it is highly correlated with the set of bath dummies, we might find that the coefficient estimates of baths overestimate the actual "price" of a bathroom.

We may use similar methods to examine the other coefficients. Note that the room variables—R1, R3, and RG4—are slightly different from the bathroom dummies. First, the omitted category is two rooms, not one. Thus the coefficient of R1 is less than zero, suggesting (as we would expect) that a one-room unit rents for less than the omitted category, a two-room unit. Three-room units rent for more. Note that since RG4 is a continuous variable *when rooms are greater than four* (i.e., is not a dummy),[56] to get the price of four rooms relative to two rooms we must multiply the coefficient, 0.2378, by four (0.2378×4; see table 2.5 for coefficients). To get the price of six rooms, multiply the coefficient by six, and so on.

The variables AGE1 and AGE1SQ are both negative, although AGE1SQ is not statistically significantly different from zero. This suggests that rents decline with the age of the unit, as expected. Buildings with an elevator command a premium of about 14 percent. Single-family attached and single-family detached units command a premium, relative to the omitted category of structures with 3 to 49 units. Duplexes rent for about the same amount as 3- to 49-unit structures; the coefficient is negative, but it is not significant. Individual units in large buildings with more than 50 units rent for a premium in the Washington MSA market. Most of the coefficients of the various quality and condition variables, such as ROOMAC, CENTAC, NOUT, and so on, have reasonable and expected signs.

Contract conditions also affect prices. Consider the coefficients for length of tenure (in years), CLOT and CLOTSQ. The negative coefficient on CLOT suggests that the longer a tenant lives in the unit, the less he or she pays; but the positive coefficient on CLOTSQ suggests that this discount for length of tenure begins to flatten out over time. The negative coefficient for the CROWDS variable, persons per room, suggests that units with more tenants rent for less, presumably because they depreciate faster. The dummy variables for both black and Spanish household heads suggest that housing in minority neighborhoods is discounted in Washington.[57] Utility variables and neighborhood variables also behave more or less as expected; that is, units with additional utilities included in contract rent command higher rents; units where tenants express the strongest satisfaction with the neighborhood also command higher rents.

The hedonic method also yields estimates of inflation in the price of rental housing. The variable Q, which is the time trend during the year of the survey (1974), increases at about .04 percent per month, suggesting annual inflation in rents in Washington of about 5.5 percent during the year the survey was carried out. The coefficient for QHEAT was not significant, suggesting that rents did not rise significantly faster in units that had heat included in the rent. The final set of variables, CC1, MONTGOM, PRINCG, and ALEXARL, are locational variables. The first variable is a dummy for living in the central city (the District itself); the second, Montgomery County, Maryland; the third, Prince George's County, Maryland; the fourth, Alexandria or Arlington, Virginia. The omitted category is the rest of the Washington, D.C., MSA. Taken as a whole they are highly significant. On balance, renters in the District pay a premium over the rest of the MSA, once we control for the quality of housing.

Uses of Hedonics

Having discussed how to estimate hedonic equations, we now discuss a few uses. We will also return to hedonic models, and to these applications, in later chapters.

Appraisal

Hedonic techniques are often used in real estate appraisals (although the term "hedonic" is not always used by appraisers). In appraisal work, it is common to limit the sample of houses to a small group of homogenous units, located in one neighborhood or small area. Generally the data set contains sales (transactions) data rather than the occupant self-appraisals found in the AHS. But the basic techniques described above remain the same.

Price Indexes

We may use hedonic results to compute place-to-place price indexes for a constant quality dwelling. Once we estimate coefficients with a separate regression for each market (city or town) we can predict the rent for the same unit in each market using the following steps:

1. Picking a set of independent variables that describes the unit to be priced. This is called the bundle.
2. Multiplying each coefficient by the value chosen for this particular bundle, and summing them, for each regression in turn.
3. Exponentiating this sum to get back to dollars, because the original regressions were log-linear (at least in our example), and then making the appropriate adjustment to get an unbiased estimate of dollar value.

Of course, hedonic regressions can be used in a similar fashion to compute time-series indexes for one or more markets, if we have a series of samples separated in time. Table 2.3 presented some place-to-place indexes from Malpezzi, Chun, and Green (1998). Other indexes can be found in Thibodeau (1992, 1995).

Program Analysis

Hedonic estimates can be used for program analysis in two quite distinct ways. In one approach, hedonics are used to predict market rent for subsidized units, rent-controlled units, or any other units whose price is subject to government intervention. In the other approach, first stage hedonic equations are followed by second stage estimation of a system of supply and demand equations for individual characteristics.

The central finding of two papers by Butler (1982) and Ozanne and Malpezzi (1985) is that, as long as a sensible set of about 10 basic unit characteristics are included, hedonic regressions of reduced rank have similar predictive power to regressions with more complete sets of characteristics (40 or 50). On the other hand, individual coefficient estimates *do* change.[58]

The central implication of these results can be expressed simply.[59] On the one hand, because prediction *is* robust, hedonics can be reliably used when prediction is the point of the exercise, as it would be in market valuation of subsidized housing units, for example. On the other hand, analysis of individual coefficient estimates, including characteristic demand analysis, is more difficult, and, in particular, more sensitive to specification problems.[60]

Repeat Sales Price Indexes

Repeat sales indexes are estimated by analyzing data where all units have sold at least *twice*. Such data allow us to annualize the percentage growth in sales prices over time. These are time-series indexes in their pure form. They do not provide information on the value of individual house characteristics or on price levels. They have the advantage of being based on actual transaction prices, and in principle allow us to sidestep the problem of omitted variable bias. However, units that sell are not necessarily representative of all units. Sometimes it's difficult to tell whether a unit retains the same characteristics across time. For example, remodeling could change a house's characteristics.

The best way to understand how repeat sales indexes work is to look at an example. Figure 2.16 shows a graph of 17 properties that sold twice in the Shorewood Hills neighborhood of Madison, Wisconsin, in the late 1980s and early 1990s. Each property is numbered from 1 to 17, and each property appears twice. The y-axis is the logarithm of the selling price of the unit.

We can think of the repeat sales estimator as an attempt to measure the average slope of the lines in figure 2.16, year by year. In a classic paper, Bailey, Muth, and Nourse (1963) illustrate how to compute this using regression methods and a larger sample.[61]

Figure 2.16 *Example of Repeat Sales*

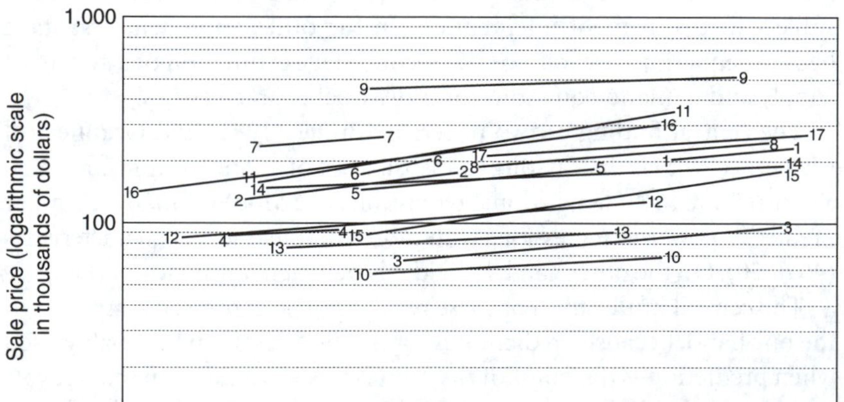

One way to motivate the actual technique used to construct the repeat sales index is to start by reconsidering the hedonic model. Consider a simple semilog hedonic equation

$$\ln P = X\beta + \beta_1 D_1 + \beta_2 D_2 + \beta_3 D_3 + \beta_4 D_4$$

where P is the value or rent for the unit, and where the vector X includes all the relevant characters, including a constant term; and the time dummies D_i represent periods that follow the initial base case period.[62]

The vector X represents a list of housing and neighborhood characteristics that would enter a hedonic equation. The vector D is a series of dummy variables representing the time periods under consideration. These could be months, quarters, or years, depending upon the type of data at hand.

Consider a house, "*A*," that sells in periods 2 and 4 (period 0 is the base year). In period 2, we calculate:

$$\begin{aligned}\ln P_2^A &= X\beta + \beta_1 D_1 + \beta_2 D_2 + \beta_3 D_3 + \beta_4 D_4 \\ &= X\beta + \beta_2 D_2\end{aligned}$$

since D_1, D_3, and $D_4 = 0$. And of course, by similar reasoning, in period 4:

$$\ln P_4^A = X\beta + \beta_4 D_4$$

Then, by subtraction, we find:

$$\begin{aligned}\ln P_4^A - \ln P_2^A &= X\beta + \beta_4 D_4 - X\beta - \beta_2 D_2 \\ &= \beta_4 D_4 - \beta_2 D_2\end{aligned}$$

This is for a representative housing unit that sells twice. Given a sample of such units, we want, in effect, the "average" β_4 and β_2. (Recall that regression is, in effect, estimating a series of *conditional means.*) Clearly, by subtraction, the characteristics vector drops out, as do the dummy variables for periods in which no transaction takes place.

Table 2.6 illustrates with the sample data. The first two columns of table 2.6 contain the first and second sales prices from our repeat sales sample. The third column is simply the difference in the natural logarithm of these prices. The next two columns record the dates.

Let us, for simplicity, consider time to be represented in years. The base year is 1986. Then let our dummy variables represent 1987, 1988, and so on through 1992. Notice the coefficient for β_2 is negative if the unit is first sold in period 2 and positive if it is last sold in period 2, but the magni-

Table 2.6. *Repeat Sales Price Index: Example*

						Matrix of time dummy variables (1986 is base year)						
Number	*First sale price ($)*	*Second sale price ($)*	*Difference in log prices*	*First sale date*	*Second sale date*	*1986*	*1987*	*1988*	*1989*	*1990*	*1991*	*1992*
1	200,000	232,000	0.148	Jun-91	Sep-92	0	0	0	0	0	–1	1
2	131,000	180,000	0.318	May-87	Jul-89	0	–1	0	1	0	0	0
3	66,500	95,100	0.358	Nov-88	Aug-92	0	0	–1	0	0	0	1
4	85,000	90,000	0.057	Mar-87	May-88	0	–1	1	0	0	0	0
5	145,000	186,000	0.249	Jun-88	Nov-90	0	0	–1	0	1	0	0
6	175,000	215,000	0.206	Jun-88	Apr-89	0	0	–1	1	0	0	0
7	240,000	261,566	0.086	Jul-87	Oct-88	0	–1	1	0	0	0	0
8	186,250	244,500	0.272	Aug-89	Jul-92	0	0	0	–1	0	0	1
9	455,000	506,000	0.106	Jul-88	Mar-92	0	0	–1	0	0	0	1
10	58,200	69,000	0.170	Jul-88	Jul-91	0	0	–1	0	0	1	0
11	157,000	340,000	0.773	Jun-87	Aug-91	0	–1	0	0	0	1	0
12	85,000	127,500	0.406	Sep-86	May-91	–1	0	0	0	0	1	0
13	75,900	87,900	0.147	Sep-87	Jan-91	0	–1	0	0	0	1	0
14	149,800	195,000	0.264	Jun-87	Sep-92	0	–1	0	0	0	0	1
15	88,500	186,000	0.743	Jun-88	Sep-92	0	0	–1	0	0	0	1
16	144,000	302,000	0.741	Apr-86	Jun-91	–1	0	0	0	0	1	0
17	220,000	265,000	0.186	Aug-89	Dec-92	0	0	0	–1	0	0	1

tude of β_2 stays the same in either case. Thus, we can simply construct a dummy variable that imposes this restriction upon the estimation. That is, we construct a dummy variable that takes on the value −1 if it is the first sale, +1 if it is the second sale, and 0 if no transaction took place during the period. Then we simply regress the difference in log prices against this matrix of rather unusual dummy variables. Notice that we suppress the constant term in the regression because it drops out in the subtraction of the two characteristic vectors X. Then the coefficients of each of these dummies yields an estimate of the changing price between the base period (here in 1986) and succeeding periods.

A few points can be briefly made about interpretation. First of all, taking the logarithmic approximation at face value, an estimate of the annual price change can be computed by subtracting one year's coefficient from the next period. Secondly, if we wish to interpret these as percentages, we should make the Halverson and Palmquist (1980) correction discussed above.

Another possible refinement is to consider that the variance of these housing prices will generally increase over time. In today's econometric parlance, such prices are not *stationary.* Case and Shiller (1987) suggest refining the Bailey, Muth, and Nourse model to mitigate such problems. The model we have just described is used as a first stage, and the residuals from this first-stage model are used to construct weights that can be used to correct for heteroskedasticity using *generalized least squares.*

- Repeat sales indexes are currently much discussed in the literature because they have the following advantages. No information is required on the characteristics of the unit (other than that an individual unit has not significantly changed its characteristics between sales).
- The method can be used on data sets, which are potentially widely available and collected in a timely manner, with great geographic detail, but do not have detailed housing characteristics. For example, Case and Shiller's original work used data collected by the Society of Real Estate Appraisers. Much of the current research in this area has been undertaken by Fannie Mae and Freddie Mac, who have the advantage of large data sets with price data from a huge number of transactions nationwide.

The repeat sales method has a number of shortcomings as well, including the following:[63]

- Even at its best, the method only yields estimates of price *changes.* No information on price levels, or place-to-place price index, is derivable from the repeat sales method. Of course, the repeat sales method can be combined with some other method; that is, to update earlier estimates of price levels constructed using some other method.
- Because only a few units transact twice over a given time period, the repeat sales method uses only a fraction of potential information on the housing market.
- Units that transact frequently may be systematically different from units representative of the stock as a whole. How big this problem is depends partly on the purpose of the index. It certainly would be less of a problem if the purpose of the index were to track the prices of units that transact.
- The method implicitly assumes that there is no change in the quality or quantity of housing services produced by the unit between periods. Of course, this assumption is always violated to some degree. Those who construct these indexes spend a lot of time weeding out units that have been upgraded using, for example, collateral data on building permits, or the limited structural information that may exist in the data set in use.
- The method also assumes that the coefficients on the underlying hedonic model remain constant: this is what allows the house characteristics to drop out of the model. But this assumption may also be questioned. For example, as families have gotten smaller, so too has the value of bedrooms, holding all else equal. Thus the hedonic coefficient for bedrooms in 1990 was almost certainly different from the coefficient in 1960, regardless of the particular market.

Table 2.4 (above) presents some repeat sales index results for selected metropolitan areas. Stephens et al. (1995) show that while the fit is not perfect, repeat sales indexes are perhaps surprisingly similar to results to the crude NAR index constructed using simple medians. In fact, the overlying trends in prices are remarkably similar. What varies most across type is the *volatility* of the index. That suggests that in applications where volatility is important, such as portfolio choice models, the choice of index method becomes more critical. Clearly this is an area ripe for future research.

Hybrid Indexes

Finally, *hybrid* indexes combine elements of two or more methods into one index. Such methods seek to take advantage of the strengths while minimizing the weakness of the constituent indexes. These could be time series, cross section, or both. For example, we can combine hedonic and repeat sales methods, or hedonic prices and user cost.[64] These methods are somewhat complicated, and have heavy data requirements.

The essence of most hybrid models is that they "stack" repeat sales and hedonic models, and then to estimate the two models imposing a constraint that estimated price changes over time are equal in both models. In effect, such methods are weighted averages of the hedonic and repeat sales, and have the advantage of making use of all available information.

Knight, Dombrow, and Sirmans (1992) use seemingly unrelated regressions as a way to get more efficient coefficient estimates than the coefficient estimates obtained by the Bureau of Labor Statistics (BLS). But this procedure requires tedious matching of similar observations across years.

User Cost

The idea behind user cost is simple: Determine what a "user" of the house really pays (or would pay), net of financing, taxes, maintenance, inflation, and so on. User cost measures are most often time series but can be cross section.[65] User cost incorporates a model of what actually *determines* prices, and accounts for the effects of taxation, inflation, and maintenance on prices.

One advantage of this measure is that it requires us to study the determinants of rents and prices. The user cost of housing capital is based on a theory of long-run determination of equilibrium rents (of housing and of other capital).[66] User cost is the cost to use a unit of housing capital each period. For a renter, user cost is the rent he or she pays. For owners of housing capital (landlords and homeowners) it's more complicated. Let us consider a landlord.

Assume the landlord is interested in maximizing profit (π), and incurs costs (C) each period. The landlord sets out to maximize profit, as shown:

$$\max \pi = R - C$$

where R is his or her rent/revenue, and C is user cost. In a competitive rental market, C includes normal profit, and excess profits π are zero, so rent will equal user cost in a competitive equilibrium. But what, in turn, determines this cost?

We begin with the simplest possible set of assumptions: no taxes, inflation, or any other complication. Assume a unit of value, V, is completely financed, with a mortgage that lasts forever at rate *i*. Then the landlord's user cost is simply

$$C = iV$$

In long-run competitive equilibrium, rents will equal landlord's user cost.[67]

Now suppose the unit depreciates at rate *d* and requires a constant level of maintenance, *m*, proportional to the value of the property. Let *g* be the rate of price appreciation. Assuming that the unit does indeed appreciate, positive appreciation lowers user cost. Finally, add property taxes at an effective rate *T*. Our expanded user cost is

$$C = \left(i + d + m + T - g\right)V$$

Next consider the nominal interest rate as the sum of expected inflation and the real rate, *r*, that is, where nominal rates adjust immediately to changes in expected inflation, $E[\theta]$:

$$i = r + E\left[\theta\right]$$

If *gr* is expected *real* appreciation, we have

$$R = \left[\left(r + E\left[\theta\right]\right) + d + m + T - \left(gr + E\left[\theta\right]\right)\right]V$$

In this simple model, θ drops out, and we are left with the result that the cost of capital is unaffected by inflation. *In this case,* inflation's increase in interest charges is just offset by the increased expected nominal appreciation.

So far the model could apply equally well to homeowners and landlords. Let us now focus on landlords. Adding income taxes at rate *t*, with deductibility of mortgage interest and maintenance expenses, with depreciation tax allowance δ, and with taxation of nominal capital gains at ordinary rate *t:*

$$\begin{aligned} C &= \left[\left(r + E\left[\theta\right]\right)\left(1 - t\right) + T\left(1 - t\right) + d - \delta\left(1 - t\right) + m\left(1 - t\right)\right. \\ &\quad \left. - \left(gr + E\left[\theta\right]\right)\left(1 - t\right)\right]V \\ &= \left[\left(1 - t\right)\left(r + T + m - gr - \delta\right) + d\right]V \end{aligned}$$

The first thing many readers will notice is that the term in brackets is in effect what real estate investors call a "cap rate," that is, the ratio between stock price, *V*, and flow price, *R* (which is equal to *C* in equilibrium). Note that even this simple version of the model permits us to see possible effects of policy changes. For example, if marginal tax rates, *t*, fall, user costs, and hence rents, will rise—as long as $r + T + m$ is larger than $\delta r + \delta$, and as long as V is fixed (more on this later).

Further refinement of the user cost model is possible. For example, we have implicitly assumed capital gains taxes are paid on accrual, and we have not accounted for financial leverage (the effect of the *size* of the mortgage). But the simple model developed here is sufficient to explain the concept.[68]

Now we have a tool to examine the effects of such macroeconomic shocks as tax changes and changes in expectations on rents and values. Many studies have applied this theory to the determination of rents, and to the price of owner-occupied housing. For example, de Leeuw and Ozanne (1981) developed a user cost formulation and use it to clarify how different tax treatments of owner-occupied and rental housing drive a wedge between their user cost, at least in the short run. Other studies have applied user cost to explain market behavior, as for example, Hendershott and Shilling's analysis of how changes in the relative user cost of rental and owner-occupied housing affect tenure choice over time.

In the real world, elements of user cost do not necessarily change one at a time and independently. For example, around the time of the major tax reform in 1986, a number of analysts predicted, given tax changes, that user cost of rental housing—and hence rents—would rise. Others suggested these changes would be more or less offset by declines in interest rates and asset prices, so the net effect of the 1986 tax reform on user costs and rents would be small.[69] In retrospect, the latter view proved correct.

Follain, Hendershott, and Ling (1992) present some recent user cost calculations and compare them to the real rental CPI and changes in the rental CPI during the same period. The correlation between the level of rents and the user cost expression is very low (0.17). Interestingly, the correlation between user cost and *changes* in real rents is much higher (0.69). Why would this be the case, when user cost is a theory of the determination of rent *levels?*

Three possible explanations come immediately to mind. First, our measures of user cost may be imperfect. In particular, user cost is a function of *expected* inflation, generally and in house prices. There is no generally accepted way to measure these expectations. Common procedures are to use some weighted average of past values (adaptive expectations), use realized values in future periods (perfect foresight), or use some ad hoc regression model to "forecast" expected inflation. Second, the model as discussed so far assumes instantaneous adjustment of units. Such an assumption is doubtful on at least two counts. First, most tenants have leases. Second, even when leases come due, Malpezzi, Ozanne, and Thibodeau (1980), among others, have documented the existence of substantial discounts for long-term tenants. Thus, we would expect to see user costs affect rents only with significant lags.

The first panel of table 2.7 shows the results of regressing the log of rents against the log of Follain, Hendershott, and Ling's user cost measure (1992).[70] Results are broadly consistent with the argument just made about lags. Contemporaneous user cost appears to have no statistically significant effect on rents; but lagged a year or even two, the effect *is* significant.

The third explanation harkens back to the assumption, discussed above, that all other things are equal. Rent is equivalent to the user cost expression times the asset price of the unit. What if, in fact, the changes in taxes, financing terms, expected inflation, and so on change asset prices? We noted above that the user cost expression can be interpreted

Table 2.7. *Rents, Housing Values, and User Cost*

I. Dependent Variable: Log of Real Rent (CPI)
Sample: 1978–1990

	Coefficient	*Standard Error*	t-*Statistic*	*Prob* > |t|
Log User Cost	–0.015	0.025	–0.6	0.560
Log User Cost (–1)	0.052	0.025	2.1	0.074
Log User Cost (–2)	0.082	0.022	3.7	0.006
Autoregressive Term	0.347	0.125	2.8	0.024
Constant	4.734	0.045	105.9	0.000

Adjusted $R^2 = 0.90$

II. Dependent Variable: Log of Real Housing Value (NAR)
Sample 1978–1990

	Coefficient	*Standard Error*	t-*Statistic*	*Prob* > |t|
Log of Real Rent	1.409	0.400	3.5	0.010
Log User Cost	–0.062	0.030	–2.1	0.076
Log User Cost (–1)	–0.084	0.036	–2.3	0.052
Log User Cost (–2)	–0.048	0.039	–1.2	0.256
Autoregressive Term	0.394	0.120	3.3	0.013
Constant	–1.232	1.896	–0.6	0.537

Adjusted $R^2 = 0.80$

Source: Authors' calculations, Bureau of Labor Statistics data.

as a capitalization rate; that is, the rate at which rents, *R*, are discounted into asset prices, *V*. That is, to re-express

$$V = \frac{R}{i}$$

as $R = iV$. Taking logarithms, the equation is $\ln V = \ln R – \ln i$.

The bottom half of table 2.7 presents a least squares regression of the log of National Association of Realtors (NAR) house value against the log of the real rent CPI, and the log of the discount rate, lagged up to two years. Broadly, increases in real rents are associated with increases in values; and increases in the discount rate from the user cost model are associated with decreases in value. However, F-tests reject the hypotheses that the coefficients of rents and user cost are 1 and −1, respectively.

The estimated values of these relationships may depart from their theoretical values because the theory is incomplete; or because the data used for the test are deficient. On the second point, in particular, we note the following:

- The difficulty of measuring expected future price increases, as discussed above;
- The short time span of our data, only 13 years (a particular problem given the use of lags);
- The use of NAR median house value data as a proxy for the true asset price of rental housing, which is not readily available.

Thus, our simple examination of some time series user cost data is instructive but not conclusive. Blackley and Follain (1996), probably the best recent time-series study, also find a weaker link between rent and user cost than many economists expect. However, their study also has some data problems, especially the lack of an independent asset price series for rental housing.

An alternative approach is to examine the user cost model across metropolitan areas. Capozza, Green, and Hendershott (1997) provide an empirical test that demonstrates the asset pricing model of house price determination, that is,

$$V = \frac{R}{uc}$$

that works well across cities and across time. This means that if user cost is not explaining rents, it *is* being capitalized into house prices. This is consistent with the fact that the total amount of housing services is inelastically supplied over one to several years. Mayer and Somerville (2000) show that this is in fact the case. Malpezzi and Maclennan (2001), while finding elastic long-run housing markets, also find large cycles in prices over a decade or more, suggesting the market may be inelastic over the relevant range for these models.

Like the other price measures, user cost has its pros and cons. Among the advantages of the user cost measures are the following:

- User-cost measures provide a conceptual way of looking at prices, allowing us to think about the effect of, for example, tax and financial changes on the price of housing.
- User-cost measures can actually be derived from optimizing models of homeowners and landlords.[71]
- User-cost measures show quite clearly how the ultimate cost to a homeowner or consumer can be quite different from the apparent asset price of the housing unit. This is essential for understanding issues such as tenure choice.

Of course, there are limitations and problems with the user-cost method as well. Among these we include the following:

- User-cost measures have not often been available on a disaggregated geographic level. However, there is no reason in principle that such measures could not be constructed at the MSA level, for example.[72]
- User-cost results will be somewhat sensitive to the exact specification. For example, the user cost measure can be sensitive to assumptions about the fraction of a unit an owner finances. Generally some marketwide average or some simple rule of thumb is applied, but the leverage (and hence user cost) of individuals will vary.
- Of all the components of user cost, probably the most problematic—and the one that often drives results—is expected appreciation. Expected is a key word. In an ad hoc manner, most studies use some adaptive expectations model and operationalize it using some moving average of previous house prices. However, very little is actually known about how expectations are formed in the housing market. Since results are quite sensitive to this component, developing better models of house price expectations would revise measures of user cost enormously.

Appendix 2.1: Data Sources for Housing and the Economy

This appendix describes some of the data sources for studying U.S. housing markets, and for studying the economic context in which these markets function. Of necessity, this section will only highlight some of the most common and most useful sources.

During the past several years there has been tremendous progress in making data available through the Internet, including the World Wide Web. Our discussion here focuses on traditional, mainly printed, sources, although we have included a few web sites. Any comprehensive list of Internet addresses would become outdated within a year or two of publication, partly because addresses change often. Most traditional paper sources are available in some electronic form now, and can normally be found using search engines if the title of the original work is known.

Also, note that many electronic sites contain mainly recent data. Serious analysis often requires time series or panel data. We expect a lot of historical data to make its way to the web over the next few years, if it has not done so already.

With these caveats, we suggest any reader not familiar with the following web sites investigate them:

- The U.S. Census Bureau's web site, http://www.census.gov;
- The federal government's general statistical fact-finder, http://www.stat-usa.gov;
- Our own web site at the University of Wisconsin's Real Estate Department, http://www.bus.wisc.edu/realestate, which contains many links to other data sites.

General References

For those seeking data on housing and the economy in the United States, one of the best places to start is the annual *Statistical Abstract of the United States,* published by the U.S. Census Bureau.[73] The Census Bureau likes to refer to this as "The Nation's Fact Book," and is not far off the mark. However, most of the data in the *Statistical Abstract* are for a limited number of years and/or places, and there is often very little explanation of exactly what the figures represent. A superb companion to the *Statistical Abstract of the United States* is the two-volume *Historical Statistics of the United States from Colonial Times to 1970,* produced by the Census Bureau in the bicentennial year, 1976. This two-volume set not only contains historical series on many of the data described in the *Statistical Abstract,* it has invaluable references, methodological summaries, and descriptions of the data in each chapter. The chapters are arranged by topic. The chapter on construction and housing would be of particular interest to students of the housing market, but there are other chapters on population, prices, national income and wealth, and financial markets and institutions, which are equally valuable.

Neither of the sources described in the preceding paragraph is very useful for tracking recent trends in the economy or the housing market, particularly on a monthly or quarterly basis. For this purpose the Bureau of Economic Analysis's *Survey of Current Business* is an invaluable reference.[74] Published monthly, the *Survey of Current Business* presents national income accounts data and other useful data, such as income by state.

The annual publication of the Council of Economic Advisers, *The Economic Report of the President,* is another useful compendia of statistics for the United States. *The Economic Report of the President* includes a helpful appendix that contains data (primarily annual with some quarterly and monthly) on a wide range of economic series, including limited data on housing markets. Another good source of information is the U.S. Department of Housing and Urban Development's *U.S. Housing Market Conditions,* a quarterly review that focuses mostly on data for the housing market—starts, permits, interest rates, "affordability indexes," and so on. The quarterly *Construction Review,* published by the Commerce Department's Industry and Trade Administration (ITA), also pulls together housing data from many different sources. *Construction Review* includes data from the United States and from other countries. The ITA is converting the review to an online publication, available at http://www.ita.doc.gov.

In recent years, the Census Bureau and other government agencies have cut back substantially on data collection and publication. Some private-sector publishers have filled the publishing void, producing volumes that extend now-discontinued series such as *Historical Subsidies* and *Handobook of Labor Statistics.* See, for example, Gaquin (2001), Jacobs (2001), Kurian (2001), and especially Simmons (2001).

Seasonality

Many economic series have regular patterns within a year. For example, in the Midwest, housing sales in January are typically less than half of what they are in July. Normally, housing starts always dwindle in the winter months and grow in the spring. In order to make meaningful comparisons of month-to-month changes, it is necessary to account statistically for these seasonal effects. One method is to take a moving average that smoothes out the seasonal affects. Another method is to use regression techniques with dummy variables for months. A third technique, which is a little more complicated than we would like to describe here, has been developed by Census statisticians. Called the "X11" technique, it is not a secret stealth fighter, but rather a somewhat complicated algorithm for removing seasonality in the data. Most of the quarterly or monthly housing that the government data reports is "seasonally adjusted at annual rates." It represents what a year would look like if the month reported were typical. Figure A.2.1 illustrates with monthly housing starts data that is seasonally unadjusted and adjusted.

Current Dollars vs. Constant Dollars

Many of our aggregate statistics and prices are expressed in dollar amounts. Clearly, we need to account for general price inflation in order to make comparisons over time. The most common method of doing this is to divide the housing price index by some general price index. The most commonly used index is the Consumer Price Index (CPI) published by the Bureau of Labor Statistics. However, for various reasons the CPI is actually not the best index to use for deflating most

Figure A.2.1. *Monthly Housing Starts*

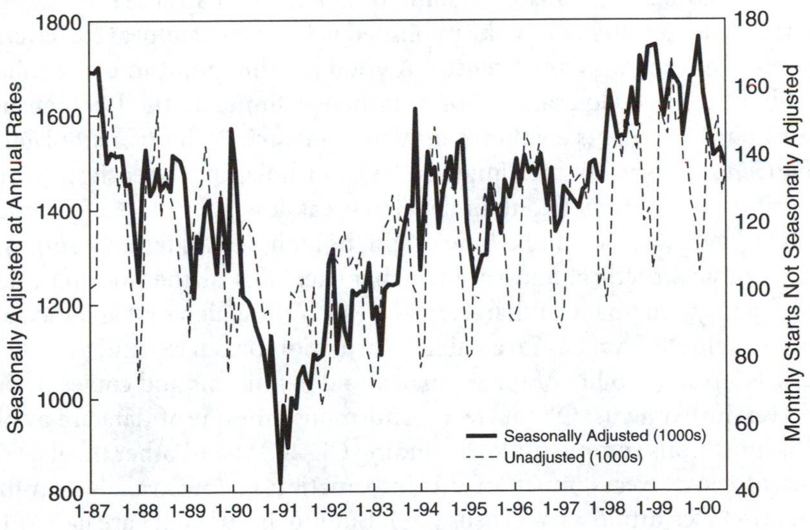

Source: U.S. Department of Commerce.

series.[75] The Commerce Department's "implicit price deflators" are generally superior. They are subject to fewer biases than the CPI; most important, they allow for substitution between goods as relative prices change. They generally also cover a wider range of goods and services, since many goods and services actually produced in an economy are not purchased by end-consumers.

Measures of the Housing Stock

The Decennial Census

The benchmark data on the U.S. housing stock are from the decennial census. Every 10 years, the U.S. Census Bureau collects detailed information on the number and location of housing units, as well as some information on the value of the unit if owner-occupied, the rents and utility payments for rental housing, selected measures of condition such as number of rooms, presence or absence of basic plumbing, and so on. Details of the census can be found in the U.S. Department of Commerce's *Census Catalogue and Guide.* Another invaluable data source, especially for hands-on analysis of census data, is Myers (1992). Postwar censuses have generally asked a short list of questions to all enumerated households, including limited information on the housing unit. There is also a so-called long form, which is administered to a sample of 5 percent of enumerated households.

Census data are available in numerous ways. Perhaps the most familiar to many researchers are the published volumes that appear for several years after each decennial census. A good starting point to get familiar with the census is to examine some of these volumes. In the 1990 census, for example, there is a volume entitled *Summary Population and Housing Characteristics* for the United States as a whole, and for each state and territory. These books contain detailed breakdowns by place of population by age, sex, race, and ethnic origin; household and family composition; basic structural and vacancy characteristics of the housing unit; occupancy and financial characteristics (such as median rent and median house value), as well as invaluable information on survey and sampling procedures, reliability of the estimates, and definitions and copies of the survey instruments. Of course, an enormous amount of data are available in various computer files, including CD-ROM and other media. For recent census years, much of this information is now available on the Internet (see http://www.census.gov). But much early data are harder to find or are still unavailable on the web site. Also, the printed volumes often include more useful tabulations broken down by metropolitan area. At least for the present, analysis of housing market changes will require some familiarity with printed versions and older media.

The American Housing Survey

From time to time, the Department of Commerce supplements the census effort with a special-purpose survey called the American Housing Survey. Begun in 1973, the AHS was originally an annual survey (and was once known as the Annual Housing Survey) but became a biannual survey in the early 1980s. The AHS currently surveys about 50,000 housing units/households located throughout the United States. Separate metropolitan American housing surveys are carried out to obtain larger samples for 40 large MSAs. Before the budget cutbacks in the 1980s, 60 metropolitan areas were surveyed, and the sample sizes per MSA ranged from 5,000 to 15,000. Today the largest MSA samples have 3,000 observations. The AHS is a valuable complement to the decennial census both because the AHS is conducted more often and because it has many more detailed questions about housing conditions and financing, albeit sometimes at the expense of geographic coverage. Documentation of the AHS includes many published volumes, which cover national data and information for selected large metropolitan areas; see especially Hadden and Leger (1990) and the online documentation available at http://www.huduser.org.

Data Formats

Both the decennial census and AHS data come in published form, where the user takes whatever format the Census provides as given. But they also come in a number of computerized formats, which permit more flexible analysis of the data. The Census provides two different household-level data sets, called PUMS (Public Use Microdata Sample). One is a 1 percent sample of the population and the other is a 5 percent sample. The AHS similarly provides microdata on its 50,000 household observations. Both these formats give analysts great flexibility in creating their own tables, and undertaking, for example, regression analysis. However, due to Census Bureau confidentiality requirements, the locational information associated with each record in the file is limited. Details vary with each file and with the year the file was generated, but generally the rule is that the census will not identify a location that permits an observation to be placed within some geographic area containing fewer than 100,000 people. While it does safeguard confidentiality, the rule greatly complicates many analyses. A particular problem is that one can rarely identify smaller towns in many of these surveys. Even in larger cities, one can usually only imprecisely identify the metropolitan area from which an observation comes.

The decennial census data are also available in computer format in a number of "semi-aggregated forms." They are referred to as "STF files" for Summary Tape Files (even though they are now available on CD-ROM rather than tape). These data provide medians and averages of key census data by census tract, county, and block.

There are four types of STF files.[76] STF1 includes selected tabulations on population and housing characteristics for counties, places, census tracts, block groups, and blocks. STF2 is similar to STF1, but has more detailed breakdowns by race, including Hispanic origin. STF2 also includes separate data for Native American and Alaskan native areas. However, STF2 does not include breakdowns for block groups or blocks. STF3 includes population, housing, and economic characteristics. The geographic breakdown is similar to STF1. However, STF3 also includes data by ZIP Code. STF4 is similar to STF3, but does not include block groups or blocks, and repeats tables by race and ethnic origin. Using the STF files in practice is somewhat complicated, and the reader is referred to Myers (1992) once again for an excellent discussion.

We have found over the years that analysis of the household-level data from the census and the AHS databases is often the best way to answer interesting questions about housing markets. However, learning to use these data sources entails a fair amount of up-front work. Generally they are not available in user-friendly form, such as spreadsheet or Dbase files (although the STF data are in Dbase format). As a result, analysts must write programs in more sophisticated statistical packages such as SAS or SPSS in order to analyze the data. While not inherently difficult, getting started is often somewhat time-consuming. Once again, Myers (1992) provides a wealth of practical information on how to analyze these data, especially in chapter 12.[77]

Other Measures of the Stock

While the census provides useful decennial benchmarks, and the AHS provides a wealth of stock information for recent years, longer-time-series data are more limited. One of the useful sources of time-series data on the housing stock in the aggregate is produced by the Department of Commerce's Bureau of Economic Analysis under the title *Fixed Reproducible Tangible Wealth in the United States;* see Katz and Herman (1997). Issued from time to time by the Bureau of Economic Analysis, this volume is the basic reference on the capital stock of the United States, including the stock of housing. Stock estimates are provided net and gross, and in current and constant prices. Data are presented for nonresidential structures as well as housing, and other forms of capital such as plant and equipment. These data are available on an annual basis from 1925. Unfortunately, there is almost no geographic detail to this data. Estimates of the real estate capital stock by location can be found in Hartzell, Pittman, and Downs (1994) and in Malpezzi, Shilling, and Yang (2001).

Flow Measures of Housing Output

Consider the following stages of residential construction. First, some unit of local government must authorize a housing unit and issue a permit.[78] Then a housing unit is started. Data may also be collected on the housing unit as it is under construction. Finally, the housing unit is completed; then it enters into inventory and is sold. The units may remain vacant. If the unit contains apartments or other rental units after it is sold it may or may not be taken by a tenant; that is, "absorbed." Units may be rented or owned. Each of these stages in the early life of a housing unit generates data and a corresponding Current Housing Report from the Census.

Permits

Housing Units Authorized by Building Permits is a monthly report issued by the Census Bureau (Current Construction Report C-40, *Building Permits*). This bellwether report presents data on privately owned housing units authorized in permitted issuing places, month by month and annually, by metropolitan area, and by many smaller jurisdictions (some data are available down to the level of individual permit-issuing places). The permit data include information on the number of housing units by size class (single family, duplex, three and four units, and valuation of the proposed units by the same breakdown). Information since the 1960s is available in paper form; the data for recent years are also available on the web. Among available flow measures, permit data generally have the greatest degree of geographical disaggregation. Permit data are also subject to less sampling error than many of the other measures. Of course, not every unit that obtains a permit is eventually built; but about all of them are. When looking at monthly or quarterly data, it should be kept in mind that these are prospectively built units, not units yet completed.

Housing Starts

Every month the Census Bureau samples a number of permit-issuing places and visits governments and developers to generate estimates of the number of housing units actually started. The starts data available generally have less geographic detail and somewhat higher sampling variability than the permits data. The starts data are available on a monthly basis in Current Construction Report C-20, *Housing Starts.* The data are broken up by type of structure (single family, duplex, three and four units, five units or more), inside and outside the MSA, and the four major geographic regions. The C-20 report also includes data on new mobile home placements and shipments. The aggregate data also break out whether the units were built for sale or for rent. Although data on housing starts are less geographically disaggregated, they have been kept since 1880. Permits data, on the other hand, are only readily available for years since the 1960s.

Value of New Construction Put in Place

This is quite literally the dollar value put in place over a given period. For an individual project, this includes the value of the various inputs. While ultimately the *value of new construction put in place* (VNCPP; see Census report C-30, *Construction Put in Place*) becomes equivalent to *completions,* VNCPP is much more a measure of the pipeline. As a consequence, it is particularly useful to those who are studying the effect the construction industry has in the aggregate economy during any particular period. The data are broken out by private and public construction and include many types of buildings that are not residential. Residential buildings are broken out into three categories: single-family units, new housing units of two or more units, and improvements to existing units. There are data on a wide range of nonresidential buildings, including industrial, office, hotels, and so on; farm nonresidential; utilities; and public construction, both buildings and various components of infrastructure. Data are presented in both current and constant dollars, on a monthly and annual basis. Generally, little geographic detail is available.

Housing Completions

Housing completions are provided monthly in a format similar to *starts* in Construction Report C-22, *Housing Completions.* Housing completions data have been collected since only 1968.

New One-Family Houses Sold

Construction Report C-25, *New One-Family Houses Sold,* provides data on the number of houses actually sold each month, and some regional detail. The report also contains data on the sales price, median, and average, as well as the median number of months on the market at the time of sale. There is also limited information on the type of financing.

Other Market Conditions

Market Absorption of Apartments

Housing Report H-130 presents data on absorption of apartments and newly constructed buildings with five or more units. The data include information on the total number of unfurnished apartments completed in each period and rented within three months, six months, and twelve months. There is limited information on the geographic area, including whether the building is inside or outside of a central city; whether it is inside or outside of an MSA; and whether it is located in the Northeast, South, Midwest, or West.

A companion report, H-131, *Characteristics of Apartments Completed,* also provides data on apartments built and absorbed, but has more details as to price range. The report also contains some data on features such as parking availability, air-conditioning, utilities, and so on. However, the level of geographic detail is again disappointingly small.

Housing Vacancies and Home Ownership

The current Housing Report H-111, *Housing Vacancies and Home Ownership,* presents data from the Current Population Survey and focuses on rental and homeowner vacancy rates. Data are available quarterly since 1960. Data are also broken out by type of structure and rent level. This publication also includes data on homeownership rates for the United States annually from 1965 to date. Homeownership rates are also broken out by age of householder. The level of geographic detail is again disappointing, with the most disaggregated tables being presented for four major regions.

Other Census Data Sources

Among other general Census sources, two that are particularly useful are the *State and Metropolitan Area Data Book* and the *County and City Data Book.* These are published approximately every five years on a rolling horizon. As of this writing, the latest *State and Metro Area Data Book* available is for 1991; the latest *County and City Data Book* available is for 1994. Each book presents basic economic and social data, including selected housing data, by state and metropolitan area, and by city and county, respectively. Data are also available in computerized format. We find the Department of Commerce's *USA Counties* CD-ROM especially useful.

Many other publications on income and population are also relevant for studying housing markets. Several are listed here, including the Bureau of Economic Analysis's *Local Area Personal Income;* Current Population Reports Series P-60, *Consumer Income: Measuring the Effects of Benefits and Taxes on Income and Poverty; Census of Construction Industries;* the Bureau of Labor Statistics' *Handbook of Labor Statistics;* and the *Monthly Labor Review.* The Bureau of Labor Statistics also publishes consumer price index data. *CPI Detailed Report* contains price indexes for selected metro areas, including separate shelter components.

Housing Prices

National Income Accounts Measures

One source of house price information in the aggregate is the National Income Accounts deflator for new construction, available from the Bureau of Economic Analysis's web site, http://www.bea.doc.gov. However, the residential construction deflator has limitations. First, it is a national aggregate, when much of the time we would prefer a price measure for a metropolitan area or other more disaggregated level. Second, it is really a cost-based price measure, based on the cost of construction, including land development costs, but excluding the cost of raw land. When possible we prefer to measure housing prices using transactions, that is, based on actual buying and selling in the marketplace. The great advantage of the new construction deflator is that it is available from approximately 1880. See Malpezzi and Maclennan (2001) for details of and use of such deflators.

Census Price Indexes

One set of transaction-based price indexes commonly used is the *Census Median* and *Average House Price Indexes.* These have already been discussed briefly, as they are presented in the *New Houses Sold* report described above. The new single-family home price has been available on an annual and quarterly basis since 1963. One limitation of this index is that it does not by itself account for differences in the quality of new houses over time. Generally, housing size and quality have improved since 1963, so these house prices tend to overstate relative house price inflation. Recognizing this, the Census has presented a parallel *Constant Quality Price Index* since 1978. Generally, the geographic distribution of these indexes is limited to an aggregate index for the United States and indexes for the four major census regions.

Another set of parallel price indexes is the *Median Prices of Existing Single Family Dwellings.* These have been available in the aggregate for the United States and for the four major census regions since 1968. They are originally constructed by the National Association of Realtors and are available for HUD's *Housing Market Statistics* at http://www.huduser.org.

One source that addresses the limited geographic disaggregation of these price indexes is the benchmark decennial census data. For the census years we have median house prices (from 1950) and median rents (from 1940) for each MSA, as well as for many smaller jurisdictions, cities, and places. These data have their own limitations: They are available only for every 10 years, and the median statistic does not control for housing quality. The latter problem can be addressed using the method of hedonic indexes, as Malpezzi, Chun, and Green (1998) do for the 1990 census. To our knowledge no one has yet constructed such constant quality price indexes *over time* using decennial census data.

National Association of Realtors Data

Another source of house prices is the National Association of Realtors (NAR) survey data. We have already mentioned that HUD and Census report NAR's national and regional data, but NAR also provides data for a sample of large MSAs. These data are median prices from local Board of Realtor Multiple Listing Services. Generally, these data are available on a quarterly basis for a panel of large MSAs, beginning in 1979. While they are not adjusted for quality differences between MSAs, or within MSAs over time, Stephens et al. (1995) suggest that the data are surprisingly close to more sophisticated indexes, at least over periods of several years.

Repeat Sales Indexes

Another source of price data is repeat sales price indexes as described above. Case and Shiller (1989, 1990) and Stephens et al. (1995) present basic results for a limited number of locations. The private firm Case-Shiller-Weiss and a collaboration of the research departments of Fannie Mae and Freddie Mac have produced such indexes for a wide range of MSAs and even smaller areas. However, the small area indexes are proprietary, and not readily available for research purposes. Freddie Mac, HUD, and the Office of Federal Housing Enterprise Oversight publish price indexes by state from 1985 to date. Unfortunately, the geographic boundaries defined by states are not the most natural definition of a market, but these indexes are still useful.

Other Indexes

Another set of available price indexes comes from Malpezzi, Ozanne, and Thibodeau (1980), who constructed constant quality price indexes for 59 metropolitan areas using Annual Housing Survey data from the 1970s. These indexes were later updated and expanded in a number of useful ways in Thibodeau (1992, 1995). Thibodeau (1992) contains a wide range of price indexes for the 59 metropolitan areas for which AHS data are available. Indexes are constructed inside and outside central cities, for high- and low-quality housing, and for three to four different time periods for each MSA. Thibodeau's volume also gives a clear discussion of the various issues involved in price index construction across MSAs. Updated versions of some of these indexes can be found in Thibodeau (1995).

Most of the price indexes mentioned so far have been focused on single-family units (the NAR data, the repeat sales indexes), or on a mix of unit types (e.g., Thibodeau). De Leeuw (1993) published an experimental price index for multi-family housing.

Financial Variables

The most commonly analyzed single financial variable related to housing is the mortgage interest rate. However, analysis of interest rates is slightly complicated by the fact that contract terms and points vary. Freddie Mac's *Secondary Mortgage Markets* presents data since 1972 on both FHA and conventional loans, including average interest rates and average points paid by year for loans of varying maturity. Analysis of adjustable rate mortgages (ARMs) is even more complex; given the different products in the market, Freddie Mac also produces an ARM index, published in HUD's *U.S. Housing Market Conditions.*

Data on residential delinquencies and foreclosures are available from the Mortgage Bankers Association.

A valuable yet underutilized resource is the annual database produced by the National Association of Realtors on *The Home Financing Transaction.* The database is collected by requesting nearly 2,000 experienced residential brokers to complete a detailed form on the last two financial transactions in which they have participated. Data include date of transaction, location of transaction, sales price, down payment, mortgage amounts (first and second), interest rates, points charged, and any buy down of the mortgage. If any of the loans are adjustable rate loans, data on frequency of interest rate adjustment, type of index, caps (both per period and over the life of the loan), treatment of negative amortization, and other terms are also described. Information on the income and composition of the borrowing household, and the quality and structure of the housing unit are also included.

Cost Indexes

Several sources publish public construction cost indexes for housing and real estate. The first is the Department of Commerce's *Composite Cost Index.* This is a weighted index of construction costs that is available on a monthly basis. Historical data are available from 1915.

The American Appraisal Company produces an index, usually known as the *Boeckh Index,* which is available on a monthly basis. Historical data are available from 1915. The data are broken out by metropolitan area, structure type, and type of material.

McGraw-Hill publishes the *Engineering News Record Indexes.* These monthly indexes are also available from 1915. However, these have less geographic detail than the *Boeckh* indexes.

There is no generally accepted land price index for the United States. The Department of Agriculture publishes time-series data on the price per acre of farm real estate (including structures), which is often used as a proxy for rural land costs, but this is available by state only. For those interested in urban land prices, it is a crude proxy for urban land prices at the fringe. Another source of land price data, albeit for only one metropolitan area, is Homer Hoyt's pathbreaking *One Hundred Years of Land Values in Chicago.* The FHA publishes estimates of land price data used for single-family homes for metropolitan areas, but coverage is somewhat spotty with respect to both location and time. Finally, the Urban Land Institute publishes land price data for selected metropolitan areas roughly every five years; it has done so since 1975. (See Black and

Hoben 1985.) While probably the best data available, even those at ULI regard this data as only indicative at best.

Appendix 2.2: Some Simple International Comparisons

How does the United States compare to other countries in terms of housing? Table A.2.1 presents some basic demographic and economic data, and a few key housing market indicators, for the United States and several dozen other countries. The data are preliminary and come from an ongoing World Bank/United Nations Development Programme research project on "Housing and Urban Development Indicators." These first data from the project have been collected for a large city from each of the 53 countries (see Angel 2001; Angel and Mayo 1996; and Mapezzi and Mayo 1997a). The market chosen to represent the United States is Washington, D.C.

The first column of table A.2.1 presents World Bank estimates of gross national product (GNP) per capita in 1993 U.S. dollars. Cities are ordered by GNP per capita as reported by the World Bank. Notice that the per capita GNPs of Germany, Norway, Sweden, Japan, and Finland exceed that of the United States, $21,790. However, these numbers are unadjusted for prices faced by consumers in each country. When GNP is adjusted to reflect local price differences for what economists call "purchasing power" parity (PPP), the United States' per capita income remains the highest in the world. One of the largest elements in the PPP correction, as it happens, is housing prices. Thus, for example, Japan has a very high unadjusted GNP per capita; but part of this is due to very high housing prices. If one adjusts for the higher prices Japan pays, relative to international norms, its PPP or "real" product is lower relative to other countries than if measured in terms of unadjusted GDP.[79]

While most of the cities represented in table A.2.1 are the largest in their respective countries (Washington being one notable exception), the populations of these cities range from more than 10 million in Paris or Seoul to fewer than 400,000 in Lilongwe, Malawi.

Of greater interest for our present purpose are the indicators related to housing markets. Column 3 presents a simple indicator, floor area (in square meters) per person. The United States' lead in this indicator is clear, with 69 square meters (about 700 square feet) per person. The contrast with Japan is notable. Although real incomes in Japan are only

(*text continues on page 78*)

Table A.2.1. *Basic International Housing Indicators, 1993*

Country (city)	*Country GNP per capita (US $)*	*City population (in millions)*	*Floor area per person (m2)*	*Housing production per 1,000*	*Owner occupancy (%)*	*Ratio of house price to income*
Tanzania (Dar es Salaam)	110	1.6	5.0	14.8	27	1.9
Malawi (Lilongwe)	200	0.4	6.6	9.3	33	0.7
Bangladesh (Dhaka)	210	5.2	3.7	8.0	30	6.3
Madagascar (Antananarivo)	230	0.9	5.1	1.9	36	3.3
Nigeria (Ibadan)	290	5.7	9.0	2.1	62	3.6
India (New Delhi)	350	8.4	8.6	4.1	48	7.7
Kenya (Nairobi)	370	1.4	5.1	2.7	29	1.0
China (Beijing)	370	7.0	9.3	13.3	8	14.8
Pakistan (Karachi)	380	8.2	7.1	na	83	1.9
Ghana (Accra)	390	1.4	10.4	2.6	28	2.5
Indonesia (Jakarta)	570	8.2	10.2	7.1	56	3.5
Egypt (Cairo)	600	6.1	12.0	10.5	32	6.7
Zimbabwe (Harare)	640	1.5	7.0	7.7	45	2.8
Senegal (Dakar)	710	1.6	8.1	3.4	57	3.0
The Philippines (Manila)	730	7.9	12.0	5.7	48	2.6
Cote d'Ivoire (Abidjan)	750	1.9	7.9	7.8	21	1.4
Morocco (Rabat)	950	1.1	6.0	6.5	46	6.7
Ecuador (Quito)	980	5.3	8.6	9.3	79	2.4
Jordan (Amman)	1,240	1.3	10.0	12.5	75	3.4
Colombia (Bogota)	1,260	4.9	8.8	6.0	62	6.5

(continued)

Table A.2.1. *Continued*

Country (city)	*Country GNP per capita (US $)*	*City population (in millions)*	*Floor area per person (m2)*	*Housing production per 1,000*	*Owner occupancy (%)*	*Ratio of house price to income*
Thailand (Bangkok)	1,420	6.0	16.5	18.5	68	4.1
Tunisia (Tunis)	1,440	1.6	6.5	7.8	67	6.1
Jamaica (Kingston)	1,500	0.6	15.3	11.3	41	4.9
Turkey (Istanbul)	1,630	7.3	17.0	6.6	60	5.0
Poland (Warsaw)	1,690	1.7	17.4	1.9	35	10.8
Chile (Santiago)	1,940	4.8	15.9	6.2	80	2.1
Algeria (Algiers)	2,060	1.8	8.5	2.7	45	11.7
Malaysia (Kuala Lumpur)	2,320	1.2	18.6	8.6	59	5.0
Mexico (Monterrey)	2,490	2.5	8.6	6.0	83	3.7
South Africa (Johannesburg)	2,530	8.7	11.1	7.0	64	1.7
Venezuela (Caracas)	2,560	3.8	16.0	3.9	65	2.0
Brazil (Rio de Janeiro)	2,680	6.0	19.4	4.9	62	2.3
Hungary (Budapest)	2,780	2.0	23.5	3.0	45	6.6
Czechoslovakia (Bratislava)	3,140	0.4	23.2	6.8	14	6.5
Republic of Korea (Seoul)	5,400	10.6	18.8	7.2	40	9.3
Greece (Athens)	5,990	3.1	24.5	6.4	55	3.8
Israel (Tel Aviv)	10,920	1.3	24.8	3.8	80	5.0
Spain (Madrid)	11,020	4.8	24.4	4.9	74	3.7

Singapore	11,160	2.7	20.0	6.4	90	2.8
Hong Kong	11,490	5.8	7.1	14.2	43	7.4
United Kingdom (London)	16,100	6.8	31.9	2.6	58	7.2
Australia (Melbourne)	17,000	3.0	50.7	8.2	73	3.9
The Netherlands (Amsterdam)	17,320	0.7	23.8	7.6	9	4.8
Austria (Vienna)	19,060	1.5	31.0	4.4	17	4.7
France (Paris)	19,490	10.7	32.4	5.0	43	4.2
Canada (Toronto)	20,470	3.8	41.1	7.3	60	4.2
U.S.A. (Washington, D.C.)	21,790	3.9	68.7	6.6	61	3.9
Germany (Munich)	22,320	1.3	35.0	5.0	17	9.6
Norway (Oslo)	23,120	0.5	42.0	6.9	74	5.5
Sweden (Stockholm)	23,660	1.5	40.0	5.6	45	4.6
Japan (Tokyo)	25,430	8.2	15.8	11.0	40	11.6
Finland (Helsinki)	26,040	0.8	30.4	13.3	63	3.7

Source: World Bank (unpublished tables).

slightly lower than U.S. incomes, Japanese living space per capita is less than one-fourth that of Washington, D.C. Most European markets also have low floor areas per person compared with the United States. The highest market after the United States is Australia, with 51 square meters. At the low end of the scale, people in countries such as Tanzania and Kenya make do with an average of about 5 square meters.

The next column gives a quick look at the number of housing units built per thousand population in a typical year. Not surprisingly, this measure of output varies less with respect to income and more with respect to population growth. The fastest rates of housing production can be found in cities like Dar es Salaam, Beijing, Bangkok, and Hong Kong. Among the developed cities, Helsinki and Tokyo have very rapid rates of construction.

The next column still presents data on the percentage of households that own their dwellings. Exactly what ownership means varies from country to country, but we can see that the United States ranks very high among developed countries. But it is not the highest: Melbourne and Oslo have higher homeownership rates than Washington, as does Helsinki. Note the very low rate in Amsterdam; many European cities have large stocks of social or public housing, and renters have stronger rights of tenure in these places.

The final column is an important leading indicator of housing market conditions, the ratio of house price to income. In the United States, the ratio's typical value for most markets is between 2 and 3; Washington's value of 3.9 is quite high even for the United States. But note that it is fairly low compared with the cities of many other developed countries, especially Tokyo's value of 11.6. Other cities that have notably high ratios include Seoul, Algiers, Warsaw, and Beijing. A number of analyses, such as Malpezzi (1990), Renaud (1989), and Angel and Mayo (1996) argue that this ratio is an excellent overall measure of the performance of the housing sector, and that it is closely related to things such as the policy and regulatory environment.

NOTES

1. For comparison, food is about 16.4 percent and medical care 16.9 percent. Data are from *Statistical Abstract of the United States 1996* (table 695, total expenditures, divided by population). Until the late 1980s, medical care was a smaller proportion of expenditure than housing.

2. A *competitive market* is characterized by many buyers and sellers. In particular, if more of a good is demanded, additional producers enter the industry; if less is demanded, or if some producers are less efficient, they leave the industry (go bankrupt). See Olsen (1969). Recent research on so-called *contestable markets* highlights the key role of "entry and exit" in reaching efficient market outcomes. See Baumol (1982).

3. Green, Malpezzi, and Vandell (1994) show how the Korean government's attempt to fix housing problems by intervening in the production process has, in fact, made housing problems in Korea worse. Moreover, the accumulation of these interventions means that any attempt to implement market reforms will require a painful transition period.

4. Other things do matter, of course. Prices, taxes, tastes, and the level of education are some of the other demand determinants we will discuss later.

5. For example, Mankiw and Weil (1989) (about which more in chapter 4); Peeks and Wilcox (1991b); Green and Hendershott (1996); and Mayo (1981).

6. For example, Borsch-Supan (1986), Hendershott and Smith (1985), Haurin, Hendershott, and Kim (1990), and Green (1996).

7. Immigration is the hardest component of population change to predict, especially over a medium or long time horizon. These projections assume fairly stable immigration, which may or may not be realized.

8. A few analysts have suggested that these trends might lead to a reduction in long-run demand for housing, most notably the well-known study by Mankiw and Weil (1989), which is discussed in detail in a later chapter. Green (1996) discusses the effects of household composition on tenure choice.

9. The pre- and postwar volatility of income is currently a subject of debate. This is due partly to the fact that during wars and depressions national income accounts are less reliable, and the fact that prewar U.S. data is less reliable in general. See Malpezzi and Maclennan (2001).

10. The formulation is quite general, so we can refer to price elasticities of demand, elasticities of supply, etc. Each is a ratio of the percentage change in some outcome, to a percentage change in some determinant.

11. We briefly discuss a few of these studies; the reader is referred to three classic survey articles, by de Leeuw (1971), Mayo (1981), and Olsen (1987).

12. EHAP was a large social policy experiment undertaken by the Department of Housing and Urban Development (HUD) and a number of think thanks. See Bradbury and Downs (1981), Struyk and Bendick (1981), and Sa-Aadu (1984a) for summaries of the program. See Fallis, Hosios, and Jump (1995) for an updated discussion.

13. Selectivity bias arises when the sample used for estimation (here, recent movers) is systematically related to one or more endogenous variables.

14. By the definition of elasticity, if $0 < \varepsilon_Y^D < 1$, then rents rise with, but more slowly than, income, and the rent-to-income *ratio* falls as income increases. If $\varepsilon_Y^D = 1$, then the rent-to-income ratio is constant. If $\varepsilon_Y^D > 1$, then the ratio increases with income. See Malpezzi and Mayo (1987) for a more detailed discussion of the difference between demand in cross section and demand in the very long run, and evidence that in the former $\varepsilon_Y^D < 1$, generally, while in the very long run, $\varepsilon_Y^D > 1$, at least over a range of developing countries studied.

15. See, for example, the well-known film *It's a Wonderful Life*. The movie was made during the Depression, and its premise is that a small-town thrift institution that extends

mortgage credit not only provides opportunities for homeownership and increased housing consumption, it also ensures social stability and economic growth. For a slightly more dispassionate view, see Struyk (1977).

16. However, as we will discuss later, there are large indirect subsidies, primarily through the tax code and to some extent the financial system.

17. Details of regimes in selected cities are discussed in U.S. Department of Housing and Urban Development (1991) and Malpezzi (1993).

18. Most U.S. tenure choice papers assume there is a private rental and a private homeownership market, and that households choose one or the other. Public housing tenants and other subsidized tenants are either ignored or dropped from the analysis. There is a largely separate literature on participation in public housing programs, which we discuss later.

19. See Struyk (1975), Li (1977), Bruegemann and Peiser (1979), Ihlanfeldt (1980), Johnson (1981), Hendershott and Shilling (1982), and Boehm (1993).

20. Li (1977), Green (1996), and Gyourko, Linneman, and Wachter (1999).

21. Green (1997) shows that housing investment leads the business cycle but is not led by it.

22. For additional recent research on the supply side of the housing market, see the January 1999 special issue of the *Journal of Real Estate Finance and Economics,* including DiPasquale (1999), Blackley (1999), and Somerville (1999), among others. See also Lee (1999) and Mayo and Sheppard (1996).

23. *Statistical Abstract of the United States 1996,* tables 1198 and 1175.

24. Housing starts, used above and widely cited in the press, are only available for a sample of locations. Permits have a much wider geographic coverage. Over several years these measures are very highly correlated. See also McDonald and McMillen (2000).

25. For examples of income-filtering studies, see Ratcliff (1949) and Zais and Thibodeau (1983); for price filtering, see Grigsby (1963), Lowry (1960), Olsen (1969), and Weicher and Thibodeau (1988). For quantity filtering (depreciation), see Malpezzi, Ozanne, and Thibodeau (1987), Shilling, Sirmans, and Dombrow (1991), Knight and Sirmans (1999), and Rydell (1976), among many others. Much of the recent literature on filtering is theoretical, including works such as Anas and Arnott (1991), Braid (1984), and Sweeney (1974). Two notable empirical studies are by Weicher and Thibodeau (1988) and by Rothenberg et al. (1991).

26. The two supply-side variables (other than price) are population growth rates from prior periods, and vacancy rates. It's somewhat unusual to specify population growth as a supply-side variable.

27. Among previous studies, some of which were cited by Muth, see Blanck (1953) and Grebler, Blank, and Winnick (1956).

28. Mayo (1981) reviews demand elasticity. Malpezzi and Maclennan (2001) also show that if the estimate of coefficient γ_2 is unconstrained, there are regions in which the transformation into price elasticity space is not "well behaved." If the coefficient of income in the reduced form is negative, a naive interpretation of the results would be a downward sloping supply curve for housing. Since coefficients are estimated, if negative coefficients are obtained, Malpezzi and Maclennan reject this interpretation on theoretical grounds. Rather, they interpret this as most consistent with perfectly elastic supply. In some other cases, a parameterized estimate of the supply elasticity could be, by naive

arithmetic, "less inelastic than perfectly inelastic." On similar grounds, Malpezzi and Maclennan argue such results imply supply elasticities of effectively zero.

29. Malpezzi and Maclennan also estimate elasticities from a related stock adjustment model. Results are somewhat different. Postwar stock adjustment elasticities are lower in both countries. They range from slightly more than 1 to 6 for the United States, and from 0 to less than 1 for the United Kingdom. The divergence between stock and flow model results appears surprisingly high. More work on the relationship between the stock and flow models could prove particularly fruitful.

30. The Census Bureau only began to identify the planned tenure of new units in 1974, so we are limited by the data in examining rental starts precisely. But since most single-family homes are *originally* built for owner occupation, and most multifamily is built for rental, this should give a good view of broad trends.

31. See figure 2.8, above. Wallis (1991) presents a journalistic overview of such housing, and Boehm (1995) provides a more rigorous examination.

32. Some indirect evidence suggests the maintenance data are severe underestimates. Consider the difference between net and gross depreciation of the housing stock as a crude estimate of such recurrent expenditures. (This implicitly assumes constant returns to scale in maintenance and repair expenditures.) The only credible estimate of gross depreciation is that of Rydell et al. (1981). Using Housing Assistance Supply Experiment data they estimated gross depreciation of 6 to 8 percent per year. Malpezzi, Ozanne, and Thibodeau's (1987) review of net depreciation estimates ranged from about 0.5 percent to 2 percent per year, with their own estimates at the lower end of the range. Thus, we would expect roughly 4 percent of the nation's $8.6 trillion housing stock to be a rough estimate of maintenance. This implies expenditure of $300 billion or more *per year.*

33. A more detailed discussion, focusing on the development of real estate property rights in formerly socialist economies, may be found in Malpezzi and Vandell (1993) and in Pejovich (1990).

34. This only scratches the surface of this fascinating topic. On property rights generally, see, for example, Ackerman (1975), Barzel (1989), Demsetz (1964, 1966, 1967), Jaffe and Louziotis (1996), and Pejovich (1990). On property rights in land, see Bromley (1989) and Hallett (1988).

35. We are also abstracting from who exactly bears these costs; for the moment, assume we tax "winners" and compensate "losers" so as to share costs "fairly." And note that governments may decide that some externalities, such as a preference for racial segregation, are not "legitimate."

36. Studies of housing's external benefits include Green and White (1997), Glaeser and Sacerdote (2000), Newman and Harkness (2000), and Haurin, Parcel, and Haurin (2000).

37. Schnare and Struyk (1976), Murray (1978), de Leeuw and Struyk (1975), Rothenberg et al. (1991), and Goodman and Thibodeau (1998).

38. Metropolitan Statistical Area. MSAs are defined by the Census Bureau, and are comprised of one or more central cities of 50,000 or more population and the surrounding counties economically linked to the central city.

39. Although many metropolitan areas, as defined by the census, contain some rural areas, most rural areas are nonmetropolitan. Occasionally we focus on state-by-state comparisons.

40. Still, rural markets per se are woefully understudied. See Reeder et al. (1987), Belden and Wiener (1999), Vandell (1997), and Tin (1993) for exceptions.

41. See DiPasquale and Wheaton (1992b), and Renaud, Pretorius, and Pasadilla (1997), as well as the discussion of user cost later in this chapter.

42. If we can or will assume that all units in our analysis are the same—that all yield the same *Q*—then rent can be interpreted as a price. If we are not willing to make such an assumption, we can use hedonic indexes to "standardize" the quantity of housing services. More about hedonic price and quantity indexes will be presented later.

43. Real estate texts often omit costs in the present value expression, on the understanding that *either* rents are measured net of costs *or* the discount rate used has been appropriately adjusted.

44. In this chapter we will not distinguish between the quantity of housing services provided by the unit and its quality. Sometimes it is a useful distinction, but it is not an important one for the present purpose.

45. The Census Bureau does publish a "quality adjusted median," but only for the United States and its four major regions.

46. See appendix 2.1 for a brief discussion of reporting formats for census data; Meyers (1992) has a more detailed discussion. The Census Bureau's web site, http://www.census.gov, is the gateway to a host of housing and economic data.

47. These and many other county-level data are mapped on our web site at http://www.bus.wisc.edu/realestate.

48. If units have changed substantially since the last visit (e.g., if a room has been added to a house), the data are adjusted using independent census estimates of the value of the change.

49. Microfoundations of the different indexes can be found in Diewert (1991). A discussion of the recent and forthcoming changes in U.S. indices generally can be found in Greenlees and Mason (1996). See Rogers, Henderson, and Ginsburg (1993), Case, Pollakowski, and Wachter (1991), and Ptacek and Baskin (1996) for a discussion of housing price indexes in particular.

50. Initial rent for a unit that has just entered the CPI sample is based on the owner's imputation (i.e., the owner's estimate of what the unit would rent for in the current market). BLS then matches the owner-occupied units to a separate sample of rental units with similar characteristics and locations. BLS then uses an estimate of the rent changes for the matched rental units to estimate changes in the imputed rental cost for owner-occupied units. As of this writing, BLS is making changes to this procedure (Ptacek and Baskin 1996). The matching process will be replaced with a simpler weighting scheme to apply to the renter sample that proxies for owner-occupied units. Before 1985 BLS used measures based on asset prices and mortgage interest rates, plus operating costs. Such an approach confounded consumptions and investment demand, which is counter to the aims of a Consumer Price Index.

51. All cities start with a base value of 100; there is no way to compare from place to place. Also, statements about relative time trends of different series are often extremely sensitive to choice of base year.

52. The bundle does in fact change; it has to, because houses typically available in 1913 and those typically available in 1995 are just very different. The problem is quite general, and even more extreme; how does one handle computers, a component of

today's bundle, or buggy whips from yesterday's? Price index specialists spend a lot more time than we will agonizing over how to compute a true "constant utility" price index, among other issues. We will not discuss these in much detail, but they are interesting issues. See, for example, Koutsoyiannis (1975, 40–45).

53. See, in addition to the references listed below, Rosen (1974), Pollakowski (1982), and Sheppard (1999) for more detailed discussions of hedonic price indexes.

54. Without loss of generality, we have written one of each, when there will usually be several; or, if you like, consider each (*S, N, L,* and *C*) a *vector.*

55. An example is the general transformation suggested by Box and Cox (1964), or the translog model of Christensen, Jorgenson, and Lau (1973). See Halverson and Pollakowski (1981) for additional detail.

56. That is, it takes on a zero if you have one, two, or three rooms and takes on the value of the number of rooms if and only if that number is greater than or equal to four.

57. We will discuss racial differences in the housing market in detail in chapter 4. For now, note that since Washington is a highly segregated city, the coefficient of race is driven by the fact that some whites are willing to pay a premium for segregated housing. See Follain and Malpezzi (1981).

58. The changes are both statistically significant and large enough to matter in policy analysis based on coefficients, except for coefficients of variables likely to be uncorrelated with omitted characteristics (e.g., date of interview, which yields estimates of housing price inflation).

59. Specifically, the two-step model depends on reliable coefficients from the first-stage regression to compute implicit prices of characteristics for the second-stage demand equation. If the first-stage coefficients are unstable, the second stage is unlikely to yield robust demand estimates.

60. Characteristic demand models are subject to a number of other specification and identification issues. See Follain and Jimenez (1985) for a review.

61. The method was later refined by Case and Shiller (1987), who took steps toward mitigating the heteroskadacity problems endemic to this technique.

62. For notational simplicity we suppress error terms. Careful consideration of house-specific errors and their "drift" over time is a hallmark of Case and Shiller's (1987) treatment.

63. In addition to the references on repeat sales above, see Shiller (1991), Gatzlaff and Hawrin (1997), Clapp and Giaccotto (1992, 1994, 1999), and Gatzlaff and Ling (1994). We also recommend the excellent review of repeat sales issues contained in Wang and Zorn (1997).

64. See Case and Quigley (1991), Quigley (1995), or Hill, Knight, and Sirmans (1997) for examples of the former, and Follain (1982) for an example of the latter.

65. Examples of time series include Hendershott and Shilling (1982) and Blackley and Follain (1996). Cross-section examples include table 2.4 of this volume, as well as Follain (1982), Green (1996), and Capozza, Green, and Hendershott (1996).

66. Among early rigorous user cost analyses, see Diamond (1978), de Leeuw and Ozanne (1981), and Hendershott and Shilling (1982). Pozdena (1988), chapter 6, presents a nice introduction.

67. If entry and exit are deterred (e.g., by regulation), rents may exceed user cost.

68. For a fuller development, see Hendershott and Shilling (1982).

69. Brueggeman and Thibodeau (1986) are an example of the former; Hendershott (1990) and Follain and Ling (1988) are examples of the latter.

70. Intercept and first-order autoregressive terms are also included. The former is familiar but the latter may not be. Autoregressive models are designed to mitigate problems of serial correlation, that is, when the regression assumption that errors are independently distributed over time appears to be violated. The presence of serial correlation may be interpreted as evidence of omitted variables in the model. These issues are discussed in any econometrics text, for example, Goldberger (1991).

71. See Hendershott and Shilling (1982) for example.

72. Follain (1982) and Green (1996) are examples of such studies.

73. Most Census publications, except where otherwise noted, are listed in the bibliography under U.S. Department of Commerce, Bureau of the Census.

74. The Bureau of Economic Analysis is also part of the U.S. Department of Commerce.

75. For example, the CPI is infrequently adjusted for changes in consumer spending patterns. Also, since housing makes up 29 percent of the CPI, we are, to some extent, dividing the housing index by itself.

76. This discussion is based on Myers (1992, 76–78).

77. See also HUD's codebook for the American Housing Survey 1973–1993 for details.

78. Actually about 95 percent of all locations in the United States require permits; about 5 percent do not. The Census Economics and Statistics Administration is always struggling to adjust data for this undercounting.

79. See Kravis, Heston, and Summers (1982) for details.

3

A Brief Review of Housing Policies and Programs

General Aspects of Housing Policy

Objectives of Housing Policy

Before we can fairly evaluate U.S. housing policy, it is necessary to enumerate some of its objectives. Among the many objectives that can be articulated are the following:

- Ensuring a minimum level of housing quality;
- Increasing the supply of housing by stimulating new construction, maintenance, and improvement of the existing stock;
- Stabilizing rents and asset prices;
- Stabilizing construction and business cycles;
- Maintaining incentives for savings and investment;
- Reducing crowding;
- Encouraging homeownership;
- Reducing racial and economic segregation; and
- Fostering community development.

Reducing the rate of inflation and increasing the consumption of nontradable goods are other possible macroeconomic objectives. Income redistribution can be either an explicit or implicit objective.

Public and Private Roles in the Housing Market

In the United States the private sector provides the great bulk of housing—owner occupied and rental—for high- and low-income households. The U.S. public sector provides housing units directly through public housing, but compared with the public housing equivalents in many European countries, for example, it is a residual sector, and only a minority of low-income U.S. households live in such units. More low-income households (but still a minority of all U.S. low-income households) receive some kind of housing subsidy to purchase private accommodation. Of about 34 million renter households in the United States, about 14 million (41 percent) are in theory eligible for some kind of housing assistance because of their low incomes.[1] About 6 million, or 18 percent of renter households, receive assistance; 1.9 million are in public housing, about 1.7 million are in projects that are in public programs managed by the private sector, and most of the rest of these subsidized households receive rent certificates or vouchers.

Many authors have cited budget figures over the past decade to support their contention that the federal government has reduced its support of housing. These figures are for *on-budget* expenditures (tax, finance, and other off-budget expenditures are something else, and we will discuss them later). Figure 3.1 shows the most common source of confusion on this issue. Real federal *budget authority* for housing fell from a high of roughly $70 billion (1987 dollars) in the late 1970s to a current level of around $12 billion per year. During the late 1980s such budget authority fell under $10 billion per annum.

But budget authority is in effect a multiyear promise to spend money in the future. Budget authority figures are affected by several quirks in budgetary procedures, the most important of which is that different programs require budget authority of varying duration. Programs such as public housing require the U.S. Congress to authorize expenditures for as many as 20 years into the future, while vouchers and other demand-side programs require only 5-year budget authority.[2] To date, as previously authorized subsidies have come due, Congress and the president have cooperated in rolling them over, but recently this automatic rollover has been challenged.

A much better measure of actual spending on housing is *outlays*. Figure 3.2 presents these figures. Real outlays on housing have increased virtually every year since data were first collected in 1962. While the rate of increase was incremental during the 1980s, only since 1995 have outlays stagnated in real terms.

Figure 3.1. *Real Federal Housing Budget Authority*

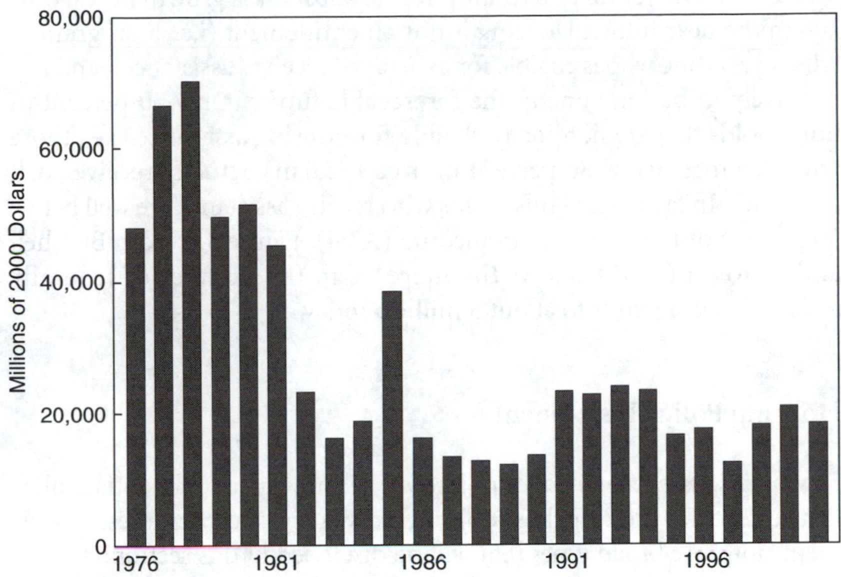

Source: Office of Management and Budget.

Figure 3.2. *Real Federal Housing Outlays*

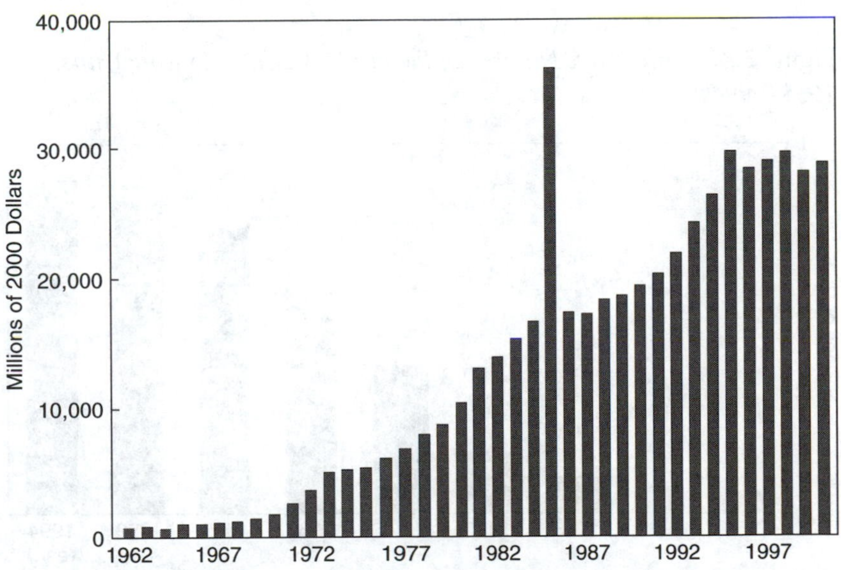

Source: Office of Management and Budget.
Note: 1985 spike due to one-time failure to roll over certain debt.

Even if recent stagnation proves to be a temporary phenomenon, it is unlikely that there will be a resumption of substantial growth in real outlays in the near future. Housing is not an entitlement (i.e., a program in which everyone who is eligible for assistance receives assistance), and it is not likely to become one in the foreseeable future. Only 30 percent of households that are nominally eligible for housing assistance (i.e., those with incomes below 80 percent of area median) actually receive such assistance. In fact, most households who receive assistance are well below 50 percent of the area median income (AMI). Figure 3.3, from Burchell and Listokin (1995), shows the increase in the number of federally assisted housing units to about 5 million today.

Housing Policy Instruments

Having discussed some policy objectives, we now turn to potential policy instruments for meeting those objectives. We may categorize these instruments into five broad types that will be discussed in this section:

- Defining and enforcing property rights;
- Subsidy and direct public provision;

Figure 3.3. *Cumulative Number of Federally Assisted Housing Units, 1955–1994*

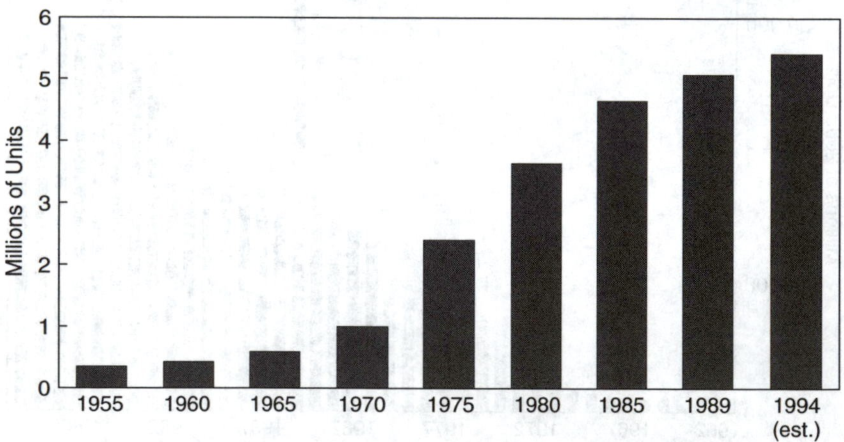

Source: Listokin (1991); 1994 estimate based on CBO data.

- Taxation;
- Finance;
- Regulation.

Property Rights

We have already discussed property rights in chapter 2, where we noted that until recently property rights in housing were not often analyzed, and in fact are generally taken for granted. The radical restructuring of housing markets in a number of other countries, especially former Communist countries, has highlighted this area and led to a range of research.[3] At the same time, recent research by Green and White (1997) has shown the role property rights can play in improving a wide range of social outcomes. In this chapter we will discuss the other interventions at greater length. Among them are subsidies and direct public provision, which will be discussed first and at greatest length, followed by taxation, finance, and regulation.

Housing Subsidies: Demand Side or Supply Side?

The largest debate in American housing policy since the 1930s has been the choice betwen supply-side and demand-side subsidies. That is, should we subsidize houses, or should we subsidize people?

Two sentences can summarize American housing policy since the 1930s: From the 1930s to the 1960s the federal government focused on subsidizing units. Since the 1970s there has been a shift to subsidizing people. As Michael Teitz puts it,

> We have moved away from the assumption embodied in public housing, that the primary way to approach the problem of supplying adequate and affordable housing for the poor should be the construction and supply of housing specifically for their use. In its place, we have assumed instead that the object of policy should be to ensure that the poor participate in housing markets in much the same way as other groups in society, and that public programs should support that participation (Teitz 1991, 2).

Teitz uses "we" to mean the federal government and the large proportion of analysts who study federal housing programs. While Teitz's comment is a fair statement of general trends, three salient points should be kept in mind:

- While there is no doubt that a general shift from supply-side to demand-side subsidies has taken place in the past few decades, there are still cogent arguments that can be made for a mix of supply-side and demand-side subsidies (as well as counters to some of the arguments).
- Despite the shift to demand-side programs, supply-side programs do exist, ranging from those that maintain and manage existing stocks of public housing to new supply-side programs such as the Section 42 Tax Credit program.
- Much of the analysis of recent housing programs (such as the Experimental Housing Allowance program) is implicitly designed to increase the welfare of recipient households in a static sense. More recently, additional objectives have been put forward that are more dynamic, as housing policy is beginning to be driven by such objectives as fostering economic independence and self-sufficiency for recipients. Policies need to be reexamined in light of these new—or rather, newly emphasized—objectives.

Rental assistance programs fall into two categories: direct and indirect. Direct assistance programs include public housing and various explicit subsidy programs. Indirect assistance programs are off-budget items, mainly tax expenditures.[4]

Public Housing

U.S. public housing is publicly constructed and publicly owned and is rented to tenants at highly subsidized rates. About 1.5 million U.S. households live in public housing, or less than 2 percent of the population.

Compared with Europe's, U.S. public housing is much more targeted to low-income households. Currently only households with incomes below 50 percent of the area median are eligible.[5] As a result, the sector is viewed (accurately) as a residual form of tenancy. Virtually all public housing tenants are poor. Public housing tenants are not ethnically representative of the U.S. population. Slightly more than 50 percent of public housing tenants are black, and 12 percent are Hispanic.

The oldest major rental program in the United States, public housing was enacted in 1937. The units are owned and operated by local public housing authorities (PHAs), which are creatures of local governments.[6] The federal government pays the capital cost of the units. Initially, rents the PHAs charged were meant to cover operating costs, but since the

1960s rents have instead been set as a percentage of income (currently 30 percent). The federal government pays the difference between rents and estimates of operating costs.

Many public units are in very poor condition. In the public consciousness, public housing is identified with large-scale Bauhaus-inspired tower blocks. In fact, most units are in smaller-scale buildings. But both large- and small-scale units have problems associated with concentrating low-income households in easily identifiable "projects."[7]

Since the Nixon and Carter administrations, government has been shifting money away from public housing to other programs. No new units have come on line since the early 1980s except those that were already in the pipeline. Yet the existing stock of public housing is too big to be ignored.[8] Current controversies include how much government should spend rehabilitating these units, the role of tenant management, and whether the units can and should be sold to tenants.

Section 202

Enacted in 1959, Section 202 of the Housing Act authorizes the federal government to finance rental (or cooperative) housing for the elderly and handicapped. Nonprofit corporations develop the units. Tenants are eligible for Section 8 subsidies or vouchers in addition to the supply-side financial subsidies.

Generally, housing programs like Section 202 that are aimed at the elderly and handicapped enjoy broad political support. Even Ronald Reagan used the construction of an Elderly Public Housing Project as a photo opportunity. However, the program is not terribly large. About 150,000 units have been constructed since 1959, and current activity is modest.

Section 221 (d)(3)

Section 221(d)(3) provided shallow interest-rate subsidies to nonprofit or limited-dividend developers of low- and moderate-income rental housing. The program began in 1961, and the pipeline closed in 1968, after some 126,000 units were completed. The program is currently very controversial because it is in a transition period. In the original contracts with developers, the federal government required units to remain low- to moderate-income rentals for 20 years, after which the units could be sold or redeveloped. During the 1980s and 1990s, many of these contracts expired. Housing activists point to a significant short-run reduction in the low-income stock as these units converted to market rate. Housing developers point to the adverse incentive effects of abrogating previous contracts permitting developers to sell or redevelop these low- to moderate-income apartments. In the current budget climate, the federal government is reluctant to purchase the units from developers at market prices to keep them in the low-income stock. According to the Joint Center for Housing Studies' latest *State of the Nation's Housing* (1999), between 1995 and 1998 the number of rental units receiving supply-side subsidies fell by 65,000 (out of about 4.5 million total such units). About half of these losses were apparently due to owners that chose to move their units to market price as their Section 8 and similar contracts expired.

The Joint Center estimates that more than one million supply-side subsidy contracts will expire over the next five years. Of course, many owners would re-sign if contracts are made available, but it is hard to forecast how much money the federal government will make available for supply-side extensions, or how many landlords, if offered the option to re-sign, will decide to move to market instead. Those who believe demand-side subsidies are generally superior may view this as an opportunity to convert households living in these units to housing vouchers.

Section 236 Rental Program

Although similar in some respects to Section 221(d)(3), which it succeeded in 1968, Section 236's projects generally have deeper interest-rate subsidies and are more focused on for-profit developers. During its operation from 1968 to 1973, Section 236 financed approximately 530,000 units. As 221(d)(3) participants did, the owners contracted to rent the units to for low-income households for 20 years. As with 221(d)(3), this time limit has or will expire soon for many projects, so the Section 236 program units face the same issues as the 221(d)(3) units.

Section 8 New Construction and Substantial Rehabilitation

In 1974 the Nixon administration undertook a wide-ranging revision of federal housing policies. These so-called Section 8 programs had four major components: a new construction program, a substantial rehabilitation program, a "moderate" rehabilitation program, and a program that used existing private-market units.

The New Construction and Substantial Rehab programs are clearly supply-side programs. The government contracts with a private developer/

landlord, who builds or rehabilitates units to be rented out to eligible households.[9] The government pays the difference between 30 percent of tenant income and the so-called "fair market rent" (FMR) for the unit. For new construction units, the FMR is roughly the 75th percentile of rents for private new construction in the metropolitan area, generously indexed.[10] Many Section 8 units also benefited from other programs, such as Section 202 or tax-exempt bond financing.

Because new private rental construction in most U.S. markets is for upper-middle-income households, and the FMR is near the top of this distribution, per unit program costs are quite high. In the 1980s this program was cut back substantially, but only after a long political struggle. Provisions allowing developers to earmark projects for elderly and/or handicapped tenants strengthened the political support for this program. Since many elderly have low incomes and are widely perceived to be excellent tenants by developers/landlords and by neighbors, projects so earmarked had strong political support, in contrast to general low-income housing.

Section 8 Existing

Section 8 Existing was the first large housing allowance program in the United States. Eligible low-income tenants are certified by PHAs and may search for private rental units that meet the program's physical standards.[11] Landlords are paid the difference between 30 percent of the tenant's adjusted income and the FMR.[12] Existing FMRs are calculated differently from new construction/substantial rehabilitation FMRs and are usually not too different from area median rents. Still, the FMR causes problems. For example, an FMR is calculated over a wide geographical area, so it may be generous in outlying suburbs but inadequate in the city. Section 8 Existing tenants cannot live in a unit that rents for more than the FMR, even if they would be willing to pay the additional rent themselves.

Other issues relate to the physical standards that the unit has to meet; some households might rationally trade off lower physical quality for better location. Because the government limits households' contribution to 30 percent of income no matter what the rent for the unit, households have no incentive to shop for units below the FMR. In fact, they have every incentive to collude with landlords in agreeing to a rent at the FMR even for units that would rent for less in the private market. Another set of issues relates to leases. The government in effect becomes a third party to Section 8 leases, and consequently Section 8 tenants generally have more rights and are harder to remove for cause than market tenants. Until recently, Section 8 had a "take one, take all" rule: Landlords were not legally required to accept Section 8 tenants, but landlords who took even one such tenant were legally obligated to take all who applied. This rule was recently removed, and HUD has been trying to make vouchers more attractive to private landlords.

While the Section 8 program is usually thought of as a demand-side program, in fact it is somewhat more complicated. Given the way subsidies are calculated, to the extent program rents (FMRs) exceed market rents, the program has a substantial supply-side subsidy element in it. Moreover, the physical quality standards, tenants' inability to pay more than FMR, and the disincentive for tenants to shop for units below the FMR mean that tenant benefits per dollar of program expenditure are smaller than they could be. Still, most housing economists consider the program more efficient than public housing and new construction programs.

Housing Vouchers

Housing vouchers were the centerpiece housing program for the Reagan and Bush administrations, and remained so for the Clinton administration. Like Section 8 Existing benefits, vouchers are housing allowances, but with several important differences. The voucher check goes to the tenant, not the landlord; tenants may pay more than FMR if they choose high-quality units; and they may keep the savings they reap if they shop for and obtain a cheaper unit. Like Section 8 Existing used to be, the voucher program is subject to the "take one, take all" rule, as well as to lease terms that landlords find restrictive. Recent legislation is merging Section 8 Existing and vouchers into a single program, modifying the "take one, take all" rule, and relaxing rules on leases somewhat.

Most economists like vouchers because they are generally more efficient than other programs (higher tenant benefit per dollar spent), as detailed below. But in the United States, political support is generally stronger for programs tied more closely to the consumption of specific goods (housing, food, and medical care) than for income support. The Reagan and Bush administrations pushed vouchers through a suspicious Congress, and *increased* the number of people receiving housing assistance when compared with previous administrations. Still, the number of households assisted remains limited: Like other housing programs, the voucher programs are *not* entitlement programs. No new vouchers were authorized between 1995 and 1998; the 1999 Clinton administration budget for 2000 requested an additional 50,000 vouchers for use in the Welfare-to-Work program, and another 50,000 mainly targeted to the homeless, elderly, and disabled.

Other Subsidies

The federal programs described above are high profile and important, but they do not exhaust the range of available subsidies. State and local governments have substantial rental subsidy programs.[13] Also, tax expenditures on housing—rental and owner occupied—generally dwarf on-budget expenditures. Tax expenditures are discussed below.

Another type of subsidy is derived from the states' ability to raise money through tax-exempt bonds. States may legally issue bonds exempt from federal (and, usually, state and local) taxes, for any public purpose. Because the interest on these bonds is not taxable, they have a lower nominal interest rate than taxable bonds. Historically, "public purpose" has been elastically defined, and over the past 20 years states have often issued such public bonds and passed the lower rates on to favored private enterprises.[14] Sometimes these enterprises include providers of rental housing.

The advantage to state and local governments from these programs is that the federal treasury pays most of the cost of the program. Economists and the federal treasury dislike these programs because they have large revenue costs relative to any benefits,[15] and because of a belief that markets are better allocators of capital than government officials are.[16]

Summary of Rental Subsidies

Many housing advocates assert that housing subsidies were cut back under the Reagan and Bush administrations. This is not really correct, as shown above in figure 3.2. It is true that the number of units produced under public housing and under assisted private construction (Section 8 new construction) fell; that modest increases in total assistance were channeled into the Section 8 Existing and voucher programs; and that the long-term outlook for maintenance of vouchers at their current level is unclear as of this writing. Still, it is difficult to make a case that a reduction in federal spending on housing worsened housing problems in the 1980s.

The first column of table 3.1 shows the current stock of federally assisted housing, by major program as of 1996 (the latest year for which data are available). The second column shows the corresponding "flow," or net change in the number of units for selected programs, between

Table 3.1. *Federally Subsidized Housing Units: Stock and Flow*

Type of housing	*Stock of units, 1996*	*Change in number of units, 1985–96*
Public Housing	1,326,000	–36,000
Section 236	447,000	–83,000
Section 8 New	897,000	259,000
Section 8 Mod Rehab	106,000	–14,000
Sec. 8 Existing/Vouchers	1,346,000	549,000
Section 42 LIHTC	332,000	332,000
Other	360,000	—

Source: U.S. Department of Housing and Urban Development.
Notes: — = not available; LIHTC = Low Income Housing Tax Credit.

1985 and 1996. The difference between the stock of programs, with large numbers of units still in supply-side programs such as public housing, and flow, where recent activity was mainly demand side, is arresting. Despite the dearth of a new supply of public housing and of additional Section 8 new construction units over the past decade, together these programs account for more than 2.2 million subsidized units today, far more than the demand side of the Section 8 Existing and voucher programs (1.3 million). Thus, it is not surprising that two major policy issues today are the management and maintenance of public housing and the disposition of Section 8 new construction and Section 236 units as their contracts come due.

The supply of inexpensive housing (particularly single-room occupancy [SRO] units) *has* been decreasing. This seems to argue for a resumption of the supply-side programs. On the other hand, the vacancy rate of the lowest cost housing is not unusually low. Perhaps this reflects a spatial mismatch between low-cost housing and jobs for low-skill workers. In any case, the history of supply-side programs suggests that the per unit cost of these programs is so high that it would be less costly to provide demand-side subsidies to enable low-income households to rent middle-cost private units.

Subsidies to Owner-Occupied Housing: Section 235

The bulk of subsidies to owner-occupied units are provided through the tax code, so we defer our discussion of them to the next section of this chapter. However, it is necessary to at least review an important and very problematic homeowner subsidy program from the 1960s and 1970s, namely the Section 235 program. The Section 235 homeownership assistance program, established in 1968, was basically an interest rate subsidy tied to a new (or substantially rehabilitated) housing unit. The developer or redeveloper applied first, and then the individual household moving into the unit also had to qualify for the subsidy. The subsidy took the form of a below-market loan. Specifically, the Section 235 subsidy was the lesser of two numbers:

- the difference between 20 percent of monthly income and the total monthly payment for the mortgage, mortgage insurance, taxes, and hazard insurance; or
- the difference between monthly mortgage payments and mortgage interest premiums, and the payment to principle and interest at a 1 percent interest rate.

The key problems with Section 235 were related to the extreme depth of the subsidy and the moral hazard and adverse incentives built into the program. The latter stem from the fact that the bulk of the subsidies were captured by developers and financial institutions that had no direct stake in the outcome of a loan after signing, because repayment was guaranteed by the government.

Severe problems with this program led to a moratorium in 1973. U.S. Department of Housing and Urban Development (1974) reviewed the Section 235 program and found developers had strong demand for units given the deep mortgage subsidies available (see also Mitchell 1985). However, only about 2 percent of income-eligible households were ever assisted by the program, and those tended to be more lower-middle-income than households near the bottom of the income distribution.

HUD's evaluation of Section 235 noted that there were strong incentives for units under the program to be priced above market price in order to capture part of the subsidy for the developer, although no empirical evidence was presented. For a typical participating household, the subsidy was about one-eighth of the average family's income. Since there was usually no household equity in the unit, it was not surprising that the default rates for Section 235 units often hit 30 or 40 percent in selected metropolitan areas. In the words of HUD's evaluation, "abuses and fraud are an inherent and demonstrable danger of such an incentive structure" (1974, 105).

The government's evaluation of the Section 235 program found, among other things, that most participating households were lower-middle income rather than low income. The evaluation found that subsidies received by recipients increased as family income went up. Taking transfer and production efficiency together (see discussion above), the government evaluation found Section 235 resulted in only an 82-cent benefit to the recipient per dollar spent by the government. However, this calculation did not incorporate the high costs of default, some of which became more apparent after the evaluation was completed. Other issues raised were the actuarial soundness of the insurance fund for Section 235, which became insolvent as foreclosures rose in the 1970s. On balance, given this experience, it is not surprising that the Section 235 program was discontinued in 1973, after less than five years of operation.

Efficiency of Rental Housing Subsidies

Housing economists make distinctions between *production* efficiency, *consumption* efficiency, and *administrative* efficiency. Production efficiency refers to the economic value of the unit compared with the cost of producing it. Consumption efficiency refers to the value the *tenant* places on the unit compared with its market value. Administrative efficiency refers to the amount spent on program management and administration rather than the program itself.

Sources of potential production inefficiency in public housing include inappropriate locations, wages that exceed labor's marginal productivity, incorrect factor proportions, high administrative costs, off-budget financing costs, tax breaks, and higher maintenance costs. All of these problems reflect the absence of market discipline. Private developers will go broke if they consistently build units whose market value is less than cost; public developers (e.g., PHAs) may not, or at least they may defer the inevitable longer than private developers.

Production inefficiency would not exist if public developer/landlords were as efficient as those required to operate in an idealized market environment. The idealized textbook market has input and output prices that reflect marginal productivity and costs. The real-world private sector may contain hidden subsidies (e.g., in finance or taxation) or hidden costs (e.g., regulation costs). This careful analysis is necessary to reveal true relative efficiencies between the public and private sectors. Public-sector landlords have no obvious a priori comparative advantages over private ones, and in fact postwar experience around the world suggests the reverse. The rental market does not generally have great economies of scale, and most private rental markets have many participants and reasonably open entry and exit. Thus it can be argued that, if the private rental market cannot meet demand because of problems in land or financial markets, for example, or because of an inappropriate regulatory framework, these problems should be attacked directly. In this light, supply-side programs can be viewed as a distinctly second-best solution.

Consumption inefficiency implies that the tenants value the housing less than the market does, or that their consumption is constrained by the requirements of the program. This is a particular problem with public rental housing, because the product is very standardized while demand is not. Cash is the most consumption-efficient transfer, because people will only buy things they value as much as or more than the market price. A priori, policies and programs that rely on private landlords might be expected to provide a wider range of options and to reduce consumption inefficiency.

Empirical evidence suggests that public housing is rarely a very efficient way to increase housing consumption or welfare. In the most complete study to date, Mayo (1986) reported that the consumption efficiency of U.S. public housing is about 86 percent (ratio of benefits to costs) and that its production efficiency is only 43 percent (ratio of value to costs). This would yield a total program efficiency of 37 percent (0.86 × 0.43). Another study, by Olsen and Barton (1983), took a narrower view of production efficiency: It reported that U.S. public housing cost 14 percent more than it was worth. Tables 3.2 and 3.3 present key results from selected empirical studies of U.S. housing programs.

Production and Administration Efficiency

Perhaps the most careful analysis of production efficiency to date remains Mayo et al. (1980b), summarized in Mayo (1986). Mayo and his colleagues, and others such as Muth (1973), developed formal models of production and efficiency. A summary of the results of these models follows. First, it is argued that public supply-side agents make incorrect decisions about housing factor inputs because they act based on the "wrong" prices of these inputs. For example, Muth and others have noted that public housing location decisions are not generally based on market considerations; in early years of the program, units had to be built on cleared slum land, which may not have been the optimal location for such units.

Table 3.2. *Estimated Production Efficiency in Major U.S. Housing Programs*

Program	*Study*	*Production efficiency (%)*
Public Housing	Schnare et al. (1982)	49
Public Housing	Mayo (1986)	50
Public Housing	Olsen and Barton (1983)	86
Section 236	Mayo (1986)	61
Section 236	Mayo (1986)	74
Section 8 New Construction	Wallace et al. (1980)	71
Section 8 New Construction	Schnare et al. (1982)	74 to 85
Section 8 Rehab	Schnare et al. (1982)	85 to 100
Section 8 Existing	Wallace at al. (1980)	74
Section 8 Existing	Leger and Kennedy (1990)	93
Housing Allowance	Mayo (1986)	88
Housing Vouchers	Leger and Kennedy (1990)	93

It is also often argued that public housing, especially in its early years, had a "capital-intensity bias" because capital costs were subsidized more heavily than maintenance and repair costs. Muth has also argued that when supply-side programs are financed using, for example, tax-free bonds, the result is again a procapital, antimaintenance bias. Since these distorted prices lead to the wrong decisions about location, trade-offs between initial capital and maintenance trade-offs, and so on, such price distortions will be translated into a significantly higher cost per unit of housing services delivered.

In a sense the whole rationale for supply-side subsidy programs is to short-circuit normal market discipline. That is, the argument is that due to some externality (see chapter 2) or other market imperfection, the result produced by the market is socially inferior to a result that could be produced by government intervention. But accepting the existence of market failure does not imply that we need to ignore production efficiency in devising a solution. Ideally, we would choose the least costly supply-side (or other) intervention required to meet our social objectives, that is, to correct the market imperfection. Of course, such a solution places very high demands on the government's ability to monitor market failure and devise appropriate correction programs.

Production inefficiency may also occur when the supply-side agents provide the wrong mix of housing characteristics and location. Public agents may, for example, produce units with large amounts of interior space and low quality; renters might prefer smaller, higher-quality units. A counter argument is that the supply-side agents are in fact responding to another case of market failure, because the private market may be impeded from providing modest-quality units of sufficient size for some types of low-income families.

The Possibility of "Crowding Out"

Research by Murray (1983, 1999) and Swan (1973) generally suggests that increases in public housing construction eventually lead to a reduction in the supply of private units, but that the degree of "crowding out" varies with program type.

Murray (1983) used quarterly data from 1961 to 1977 to test these hypotheses. Between 1961 and 1977, about 1.9 million subsidized housing starts were undertaken, of which 1.2 million were conventionally financed. Overall, these subsidized starts were about 7 percent of the total output during the period. Murray also differentiated subsidized housing starts by their source of financing. About 60 percent of the subsidized starts during this period were financed with conventional mortgages and presumably competed directly with unsubsidized starts for lenders' dollars. The other 40 percent of subsidized starts were publicly financed.

Murray's econometric results from structural supply and demand models indicated that "conventionally financed moderate income housing starts [have] no effect on the stock of housing, even in the short run" (1983, 596). However, government-financed starts that were targeted to low-income and elderly households did have positive net effects in the short run; that is, crowding out was less than one for one. According to Murray's supply equation, the supply curve for unsubsidized starts shifted about 1 unit to the left for every 100 subsidized units built, and the demand curve shifted about 79 units to the left. Taken together, the new short-run equilibrium level of unsubsidized starts was about 27 units lower for every 100 subsidized units. The weighted average of these effects suggests that for every 100 subsidized units started, unsubsidized units are reduced by 72 units in the short run and 85 units in the long run.

Recently, Murray (1999) revisited this issue. In his second paper, Murray had the advantage of more disaggregated data and a longer time span (from 1960 to 1987 for some series, and from 1935 to 1987 for others).

Murray's prior work focused on the effect of subsidized starts on unsubsidized starts; in this paper he notes that what we are truly interested in, in the long run, is the effect of programs on the *stock* of housing. The best interpretation of Murray's most recently published econometric estimates is that, in the long run, conventionally financed subsidized housing crowds out other housing one for one. On the other hand, *public* housing does not exhibit a statistically significant crowding-out effect. Murray's evidence suggests that unsubsidized housing and public housing grow together in the long run. This evidence suggests public housing units and private market units are not particularly good substitutes, but units produced by the private sector with supply-side subsidies are largely substitutes for private unsubsidized housing.

Consumption Efficiency

More is known about consumption efficiency than about production efficiency. Table 3.3 presents this key result from selected empirical studies of U.S. housing programs. The table shows that consumption efficiency is generally higher for allowances and other demand-side subsidies, as expected.

Table 3.3 shows measures of consumption efficiency broadly by program type. The first and largest group of study results presented is for public housing, the program type in which the government is most directly involved in choosing the size, quality, and location of the hous-

Table 3.3. *Estimated Consumption Efficiency in Major U.S. Housing Programs, by Study*

Program	*Study*	*Consumption efficiency*
Public Housing	Mayo (1986)	86
Public Housing	Clemmer (1984)	67
Public Housing	Hammond (1983)	64
Public Housing	Olsen and Barton (1983)	58
Public Housing	Kraft and Olsen (1977)	73
Public Housing	Murray (1975)	66
Mitchell-Lama Public Housing (NYC)	DeSalvo (1975)	55
Section 236	Mayo (1986)	74
Section 8 New Construction	Mayo (1986)	63
Section 8 New Construction	Schwab (1985)	63
Section 8 Existing	Mayo (1986)	82
Section 8 Existing	Sa-Aadu (1984a)	61
Housing Allowance	Mayo (1986)	93
Housing Allowance	Cronin (1982)	91 to 100

ing. At the other extreme are housing allowances where households have greater choice. Details of allowances vary, but they are generally close to today's housing voucher/Section 8 Existing certificates programs.[17]

Each of the studies cited in table 3.3 used a different data set and/or a different method. Studies generally followed some variant of the consumer's surplus technique outlined in appendix 3.1. Given these differences, direct comparisons must be made with caution. Even given this caveat, table 3.3 supports the relative efficiency of demand-side programs. The average consumption efficiency of supply-side programs in the table is 67 percent; the average for demand side is 83 percent. Further, in each study that examined one or more programs of each type, demand-side programs were judged more efficient.

Program Participation

Each of the consumers' surplus measures in table 3.3 is conditional on participating in a given housing program, but households must choose to participate. Understanding participation rates is thus essential to understanding the true efficiency of a program.

Given the deadweight losses and transaction costs, it is not surprising that programs that require higher physical standards for eligible housing units have lower participation rates. The determinants of participation were carefully studied as part of the Experimental Housing Allowance Program.[18] Participation rates have varied widely with program design. For example, in the so-called "Demand Experiment" in Pittsburgh and Phoenix, 30 percent to 90 percent of eligible households participated; the main determinant of different participation rates was the stringency of quality standards. In the program variant containing no housing standards there was 90 percent participation.

Generally, if program participation is low, consumer's surplus measures, such as those in table 3.3, must be considered overestimates of the program's consumption efficiency vis-à-vis the larger target population. In effect, if participation rates are low, then those who participate are a self-selected sample of households that happen to value units similar to those offered in the program. The sample households are not necessarily representative of target households overall.

Housing Subsidies and Poverty

To what extent do housing subsidies reduce poverty? Let us begin with a reminder of three main points. First, the findings above suggest that programs with few standards are close to income transfers and have the biggest direct effect on poverty. Second, programs with high standards do not have high participation rates. Finally, there is little integration of housing subsidies with other assistance. As Newman and Schnare (1990) point out, "as welfare reform moves to a higher priority on the nation's legislative agenda, housing is conspicuous by its absence" (389). "Housing" and "welfare" planners and reformers seem curiously out of touch with each other. According to Newman and Schnare, of a total of 8 million assisted households, 4.6 million households receive income assistance only; 2.1 million receive housing assistance only; and 1.3 million receive both income and housing assistance. Newman and Schnare find that the relationship between need and any combination of benefits appears random.[19]

Privatization of Public Housing

Three kinds of issues have been relatively neglected in the now large literature on privatization. First, when should services be privatized, or, more precisely, what criteria should govern changing services from public to private? Second, what concomitant regulatory changes are required for the new delivery system? Third, how can the privatization or other change be implemented? Malpezzi (1990) discusses these issues in general and presents an analytical approach using the example of publicly provided housing. Here we will recount recent U.S. experience in the privatization of public housing, basing our discussion on a review by Rohe and Stegman (1992).

Privatization of public housing was one of the centerpieces of the 1990s' Homeownership Opportunity for People Everywhere (HOPE) program.[20] As of this writing, few public housing units have been sold. One demonstration project privatized about 1,300 units in 17 PHAs. This demonstration project is the basis of Rohe and Stegman's evaluation of the proposals.

On the face of it, privatizing public housing would not be easy in this country. Unlike their counterparts in Great Britain, the best-known housing privatizer, virtually all public housing tenants in the United States are poor, with a median income of $6,571 in 1989, and with 35 percent of households reporting *no* wage or salary income.[21] Many observers would also point to the poor physical and neighborhood conditions of some public housing units. But according to survey results reported in

Casey (1992), objective measures of public housing conditions suggest they are not much worse than those for all renters, and public housing tenants' opinions about the quality of their housing are even better than those of private renters.[22]

The first important point noted in Rohe and Stegman's article is that none of the PHAs attempted to privatize large high-rise units. A few cities targeted some townhouse complexes, but most focused on scattered single-family units. Each PHA had some latitude to design its own privatization program. Most appraised units at market value, then offered them to tenants at a discount, typically 30 to 50 percent. All PHAs set minimum incomes for participation, ranging from $7,500 to $17,000; note that all minimums were above the median income for public housing. All had restrictions on resale, with recapture provisions for capital gains. [23] HUD encouraged PHAs to arrange private financing rather than to tap public sources. When private financing was made available, it was generally with a PHA guarantee to buy back any defaulted mortgage.

With these provisos, over four years about 320 of the 1,300 units were sold. Four PHAs failed to sell a single unit, including the two PHAs targeting the largest townhouse complexes. On the other hand, six PHAs sold 90 percent or more of their targeted units. Rohe and Stegman pointed to several recurrent problems. First, many PHAs did not sustain their commitment to the program, often because of top-level management instability at the PHA. Drawing qualified buyers to the program was difficult, partly because of residents' low incomes, but also because few potential buyers had satisfactory credit histories. Finally, many tenants apparently preferred to remain as public housing tenants; if their incomes fell (e.g., because of layoffs), their rents would also fall. As homeowners, tenants would bear greater financial risks if their income fell.

In a few cases, PHAs wanted to sell off entire projects. HUD prohibited involuntary relocation, however, and PHAs who tried to sell multifamily projects had problems with holdouts.

In sum, it appears that scattered-site single-family projects in stable neighborhoods with tenants that have above-average rental incomes are good candidates for privatization. The more problematic units are not. Whether the privatization is a net plus or minus depends largely on whether the government's goal is to divest itself of units that run well, so it may concentrate on the most problematic stock; or whether further "residualization" of U.S. public housing is itself a potential new problem.

Taxation of Housing

We begin by considering how housing would be taxed under an ideal income tax. First, consider housing like any other asset that yields a return.[24] Economists commonly feel that if income is adopted as the basis of taxation, real income from whatever source derived should be subject to tax, but that income should be measured after the costs of producing it have been subtracted, as "net" income. Both recurrent income (from wages and capital) and capital gains would be subject to tax, but only *real* (i.e., inflation-adjusted) capital gains would be taxed.

Table 3.4 presents a stylized view of such a scheme. The first column is our "ideal" system. If we could not or would not tax the income from an asset, it follows that we should not permit the deduction of the costs of producing the (untaxed) income. The second column presents this "second best" solution.

How does the U.S. income tax system compare to these ideals? The last three columns of table 3.5 present a stylized but reasonably accurate view of how we tax three different kinds of capital: rental housing (and nonresidential real estate, which is broadly similar in its tax treatment); owner-occupied housing; and other capital (plant and equipment).

The bottom line of table 3.4 is clear. The U.S. tax code has generally favored investment in housing and other real estate over investment in plant and equipment over the past 20 years. Within real estate, owner-occupied housing has been favored, relative to other real estate.

For rental housing, table 3.5 suggests that net rental income and *real* capital gains be taxed as ordinary income. Offsetting deductions would be permitted to landlords for the costs of doing business, including maintenance and repair, interest payments, property taxes, and net economic depreciation of the unit. "Extra" taxes, including implicit taxes such as rent control, would not be imposed.

These same principles suggest that, in the case of owner-occupied housing, current costs (including interest payments, maintenance and repairs, net depreciation, and property taxes and rates) would be deducted from taxable income. Imputed rent (i.e., the rent that the unit would command in the market) would be taxed, and the real portion of capital gains would be taxed. Owner-occupants' imputed rental income is not taxed in the United States, and our tax system permits most households to defer, if not escape, capital gains taxation. Unlike owners of rental housing capital, owner-occupants are not permitted to deduct

Table 3.4. *Simplified Summary of Taxation of Income from Capital*

	Ideal	*Second best*	*Rental housing, nonresidential real estate*	*Owner-occupied housing*	*Plant and equipment*
Current Income	Fully taxed.	Untaxed.	Taxed.	Imputed rent is not taxed.	Generally taxed twice, once as corporate income and again when distributed to shareholders.
Capital Gains	Real capital gains are fully taxed.	Untaxed.	Nominal capital gains taxed on realization.	Effective taxation is rare.	Nominal capital gains taxed on realization.
Opportunity Cost of Equity	Deductible.	Not deductible.	Not deductible.	Not deductible.	Not deductible.
Interest	Deductible.	Not deductible.	Deductible.	Deductible.	Deductible.
Maintenance and Recurrent Expenses	Deductible.	Not deductible.	Deductible.	Most are not deductible.	Deductible.
State and Local Taxes	Deductible.	Not deductible.	Deductible.	Deductible.	Deductible.

Table 3.5. *Percentage Itemizers, Average Mortgage Interest Deduction, Marginal Tax Rates, Average Federal Income Tax Liability, and Mortgage Interest Tax Expenditure by Income Class, 1997*

		Average mortgage interest deduction				*Average tax benefit from mortgage interest deduction*				
Income	*Percentage itemizers*	*All households*	*Itemizers only*	*Marginal income tax rate (%)*	*Average income tax liability*	*All households*	*Itemizers only*	*Total tax benefits from mortgage interest deduction (in thousands of $)*	*Percentage of total tax benefits*	*Percent of itemizers*
Less than $20,000	6.9	$83	$1,203	9.6	–$243	$8	$116	244,971	0.6	6.1
$20,000–$40,000	22.5	$685	$3,044	16.2	$1,977	$111	$493	3,337,858	7.5	19.7
$40,000–$60,000	50.3	$2,201	$4,376	22.9	$4,991	$504	$1,002	10,092,460	22.7	29.3
$60,000–$100,000	73.8	$3,989	$5,405	28.3	$7,800	$1,129	$1,530	10,809,170	24.3	20.5
$100,000–$120,000	85.9	$5,498	$6,400	28.3	$11,170	$1,556	$1,811	7,273,806	16.4	11.7
$120,000–$140,000	85.9	$6,630	$7,718	28.9	$14,590	$1,916	$2,231	3,983,144	9.0	5.2
$140,000–$160,000	83.7	$6,476	$7,737	31.3	$19,980	$2,027	$2,422	1,958,894	4.4	2.4
$160,000–$180,000	89.3	$5,645	$6,321	31.3	$23,788	$1,767	$1,979	933,240	2.1	1.4
More than $180,000	89.3	$11,134	$12,468	35.8	$43,843	$3,986	$4,464	5,822,901	13.1	3.8
Total	34.4	$1,704	$4,953	18.0	$4,051	$445	$1,292	44,456,445	100.0	100.0

Source: Green and Reschovsky (1998).

maintenance and repair expenditures, nor do they receive a depreciation allowance, but they are permitted to deduct mortgage interest payments and property taxes. The net effect is to raise the after-tax cost of rental relative to owner-occupied housing capital.

Not all homeowners benefit from the mortgage interest deduction. Elderly households that have paid off their mortgages and households residing in areas with low house prices and low state and local taxes often do not itemize their deductions. Currently, the value of the standard deduction for a married couple is $7,500. Thus, if a homeowner's total deductions are less than $7,500,[25] the owner will not itemize his or her deductions, and therefore will receive no benefits from the mortgage interest deduction.

Why do we have such a system? Capozza, Green, and Hendershott (1996) posit that an important reason is that measuring income from owner-occupied housing is difficult because owners do not receive cash rents. The mortgage interest deduction is allowed anyway because it places debt on a level playing field with equity. In the idealized table above, debt and equity would be treated equally.

Income Tax Treatment of Rental Housing

Because the current tax treatment of rental housing is in many respects a reaction to perceived problems with the tax treatment prior to reforms in 1986, we will briefly discuss the prior treatment. This will be followed by the post-1986 treatment, and potential changes in the near future.

General Tax Treatment before 1986

During the 1970s, rental housing was generally treated like other productive investments. Current income was taxed at ordinary rates; capital gains, at somewhat preferential rates.[26] Costs of producing rental housing were deductible, including interest expense and depreciation, whose allowance was based on a 25- to 32-year useful life, with the possibility of taking larger or "accelerated" deductions in the earlier years of the investment.[27] Depreciation applied then, as it does now, to structures only, not land.

In 1981 Congress passed the Reagan Economic Recovery Tax Act (ERTA), which slashed marginal tax rates from 70 percent to 50 percent. Most significantly for rental housing, the depreciation allowance was calculated using a useful life of 15 years,[28] and accelerated methods of calculating the deduction moved the deductions forward.[29] The net effect was to make rental housing a very favorable investment relative to, say, plant and equipment.

Tax Treatment of Rental Housing Since 1986

Three tax changes made by the Tax Reform Act of 1986 (TRA) had particularly strong effects on rental housing. First, TRA reduced marginal rates from 50 percent to 28 percent, reducing incentives for tax shelters.[30] Second, the act lengthened the depreciation period from 18.0 to 27.5 years and abolished accelerated methods.[31] Third, in response to "abusive" shelters (common under ERTA 1981), income from rental housing was deemed "passive" income, and accounting losses (due to remaining depreciation and other costs) could only be used to offset "passive" income.[32]

Passive activity is any activity involving a trade or business in whose operations the taxpayer does not "materially participate" on a regular and continuous basis. Most rental activities are treated as passive, even if the material participation test is met. (Under current rules, small landlords with incomes under $100,000 per year who materially participate can claim losses up to $25,000.) It could be argued that, given the current low inflation and low tax rates, significant passive losses should be rare; but alternately, taxing gains while not permitting full deduction of losses increases financial risks. Moreover, because current negative pretax real estate earnings as reported to the IRS closely track actual losses, the passive loss rules may be unnecessarily punitive.

Regarding the reduction in depreciation allowances, empirical work such as Malpezzi, Ozanne, and Thibodeau (1987) suggests that the allowances are still above economic depreciation. Unlike the case with some previous changes in depreciation, pre-TRA owners were not "held harmless"; that is, those who paid prices founded on expectations of generous depreciation allowances were out of luck.

Because the "user cost of capital" framework suggests that these increases in tax liabilities will be passed on in higher rents, a number of authors predicted big increases in rents after the reform. In the aftermath of TRA, rents have remained fairly stable; in fact, the biggest increases in user cost and in rents appeared in the early 1980s, during generous tax treatment, rather than after 1986.

Tax Credits

There are special tax credits for developers of low-income housing. In conjunction with the TRA, the Low Income Housing Tax Credit (LIHTC, also known as Section 42) was designed to provide incentives for private sector production of low- to moderate-income housing. The credits provide a mechanism for funding a wide range of projects, including new construction, substantial rehabilitation, moderate rehabilitation, acquisition, and repair by existing owners. Over the first three years of the program, about $6 billion worth of funding was made available, aiding 300,000 units of low-to-moderate income housing. Program activity then increased, as the nonsubsidized multifamily market declined. In recent years, tax credit units have made up 40 to 50 percent of total multifamily construction.

The Low Income Housing Tax Credit provides 70 percent[33] of the cost of new construction or 30 percent of the acquisition cost of existing low-income housing, in return for limits on rents charged. The credits are allocated over a ten-year period based on the Applicable Federal Rate (AFR). Nominally, the value of the credit is 9 percent annually for the 70 percent credit and 4 percent annually for the 30 percent credit. For acquisition of existing rental housing, the applicable credit is also 4 percent.

In order to be eligible for these credits, the developer must decide between two rental options for the unit. Either 20 percent of available rental units must be rented to households with incomes less than 50 percent of the county median income (adjusted for family size), or 40 percent of the units must be set aside for households with incomes less than 60 percent of the county median income. (The rent can be adjusted in future years as median income changes.) The maximum gross rent, including utilities, paid by households in qualifying units may not exceed 30 percent of maximum qualifying income. The federal program mandates a 15-year period for maintaining the unit as a low-income unit. If the rent restrictions are not followed, there are provisions for recapturing the tax credits used.[34]

Despite the large role Section 42 plays in multifamily production (figure 3.4), surprisingly little welfare analysis of the tax credit program has appeared in "traditional" sources of housing program analysis. Reports

Figure 3.4. *Section 42 Units as a Share of the Multifamily Market 1987–2000*

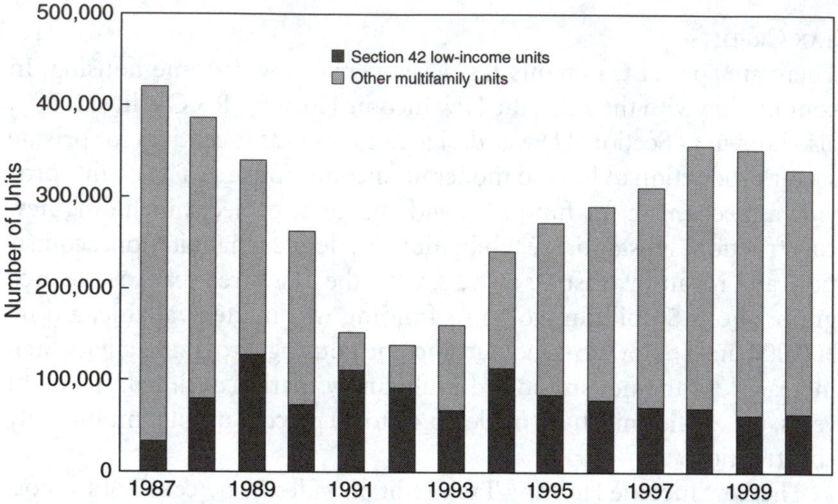

Section 42 low-income units
Other multifamily units
Number of Units
500,000
400,000
300,000
200,000
100,000
0
1987 1989 1991 1993 1995 1997 1999

Source: U.S. Census Bureau, and National Council of State Housing Agencies.

by the U.S. General Accounting Office (1990), ICF Incorporated (1991), and the U.S. Congressional Budget Office (1992) have criticized the program on the following counts:

- As noted, a certain percentage of units must be set aside for low-income households, but these households do not necessarily come from PHA waiting lists for subsidized housing.
- In most projects receiving credits, developers also receive or arrange for tenants to receive other subsidies, including vouchers or Section 8 certificates; there is little, if any, coordination between programs.
- In at least some cases, compliance monitoring by responsible state agencies may be weak. Particular concerns have been raised about enforcing the 15-year rule.
- Like other unit-based programs, economic evaluation showed that vouchers or other housing allowances would improve tenant welfare at much lower cost to the public purse. ICF Incorporated (1991) roughly estimated that a dollar in tax credit raised tenant welfare by 53 cents, while a dollar of voucher raised tenant welfare by 96 cents.

- Additional evidence is provided by Malpezzi and Vandell (1996), who are unable to find evidence that Section 42 housing activity has any positive impact on total housing activity in states.

Despite these disadvantages, tax credits are popular with developers, and few countervailing voices are heard except at the U.S. Department of the Treasury and from a few housing economists concerned with their low transfer efficiency.

Tax Treatment of Owner-Occupied Housing

The major "wedge" between taxation of owner-occupied housing and the ideal is that while we do not tax the asset's operating income, we permit the deduction of two of the major costs of producing that income: property taxes and interest. To be deductible, interest must be paid on "true" indebtedness (money paid as compensation for the use of money). Generally, "points" are deductible for mortgages and used to finance purchases of principal residences. Construction-period interest and property taxes in connection with personal residences, vacation homes, and low-income housing are immediately deductible. (For other types of property, interest and property taxes are capitalized and then deducted over the property's "useful life.")

The (somewhat simplified) current rules on homeowner mortgage interest deduction include the following:

- Owner-occupants can deduct for both their first and second homes.
- Owner-occupants can only deduct interest on up to the first $1 million of principal (total).
- Owner-occupants can deduct interest on home equity debt that is secured by a residence over and above "acquisition debt." Acquisition debt is borrowed when the property is purchased and must be incurred within 90 days of purchase.
- There is a limit on deductibility of home equity interest: It can be the lesser of the fair market value of the house less "acquisition indebtedness" (the original mortgage, see above), or $100,000 of additional debt.

Compared to the tax treatment of rental housing, the tax treatment of owner-occupied housing has been fairly stable over the past two decades.

The major changes were the aforementioned million-dollar cap in the mortgage interest deduction, and rules placing some limits on home equity lines and other second mortgages. These were put in place in 1986. Perhaps the largest change was not a change in the taxation of housing per se but in the personal exemptions and deductions taxpayers are allowed. The Tax Reform Act of 1986 raised the personal exemption over a two-year period from $1,080 to $2,000, and the amount of the standard deduction was raised to $5,000. These changes decreased the number of itemizers, mainly among middle-class households, which included a number of homeowners. Indeed, only half of all homeowners are itemizers. On the other hand, more than 80 percent of households with 1990 income in excess of $60,000 itemize.

A number of economists have attempted to measure the subsidy implied by the "wedge" between ideal taxation and actual taxation of owner-occupied housing. The estimates vary, not least because the tax treatment of housing has varied over time; marginal tax rates change; and the price of housing and the amount of indebtedness also change. The current consensus estimates this subsidy to be about $50 billion.[35] This is about three times what HUD spends.

The current tax deductions are generally more valuable to higher-income Americans than to those of middle or lower income, on three counts:

- The higher the household's income, the greater the probability that the household itemizes (and hence can take advantage of the interest and property tax deductions).
- The higher the household's income, the greater the likely value of the house (and hence the mortgage interest deduction and nontaxation of imputed rent are more valuable).
- The higher the household's tax bracket, the greater the value of the deduction of a given amount.

Ironically, as the rate structure of the overall tax code has become more progressive, the value of the mortgage interest deduction has become more valuable to the highest-income Americans. This leads to an important, if debatable, point: If we want to favor owner-occupied housing, because of some externality or extra benefit to society, we might consider replacing tax *deductions* with tax *credits.* A credit is a dollar-for-dollar reduction in taxes. A deduction is a reduction in the amount of income subject to tax. A credit is more progressive, in the sense that it returns proportionately more after-tax income to lower-income households.

Moreover, the current tax code does virtually nothing to help those at the margin of ownership. Households in this group are not likely to itemize or to be able to place large amounts of equity in their homes. They get neither the benefit of the mortgage interest deduction nor the nontaxation of imputed rent. Green and Reschovsky (1999) present a detailed analysis. Table 3.5 gives their calculation of the distribution of the benefits by income. Green and Reschovsky show that the average value of the mortgage interest deduction to a filer with an income of more than $180,000 is about $4,000; the average value of the deduction to middle-income households, whose incomes are between $20,000 and $40,000, is about $110. About 45 percent of the benefits go to filers with incomes of more than $100,000, which compose about 9 percent of all households. About 8 percent of benefits go to households with incomes below $40,000, which make up about 60 percent of all households.

One problem with shifting from deductions to credits (or to making any other very large scale tax change) is that it could have significant effects on house prices, especially in locations like California where asset prices and mortgages are high. In turn, these changes could have large follow-on effects on mortgage and financial markets. An obvious solution would be to phase in any large change gradually, over a decade. But it is difficult to impose credible gradual changes in the tax code to fully take effect a decade hence, given the American predilection for constant tinkering with the code.[36]

Housing Finance

For almost 30 years following World War II, the U.S. housing finance system was built on regulated interest rates and government deposit guarantees (on the liability side of financial institutions' balance sheets), ensuring a steady flow of cheap money into housing. Specialized real estate lenders (savings and loans and mutual savings banks, collectively known as "thrifts") were under the Federal Reserve Regulation Q. This allowed thrifts to pay depositors a small premium over the deposit rate ceiling placed on bank rates; in return, thrifts were required to hold mortgages as the bulk of their assets. The thrifts dominated mortgage lending until the late 1970s (figure 3.5). Commercial banks were permitted to make real estate loans, but they were not required to do so. Most loans for

Figure 3.5. *Mortgage Debt Outstanding, as a Percentage of GNP, 1939–99*

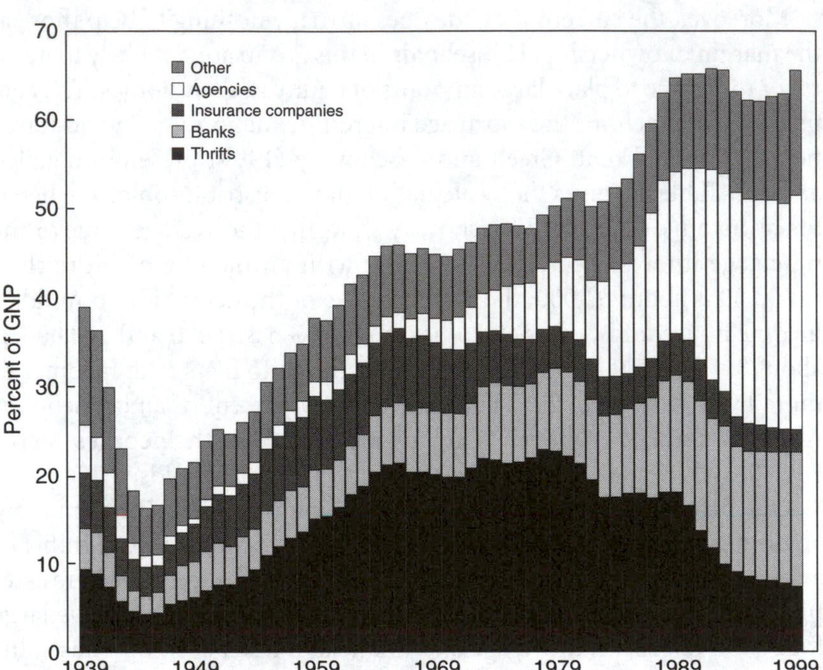

Source: Economic Report of the President.

single-family house purchases were made by thrifts, and both banks and thrifts made loans for multifamily investments, although there were other options for multifamily investment. The government guaranteed deposits for banks and thrifts. Most single-family mortgages were long-term fixed-rate instruments.

The system was somewhat different for multifamily housing. In addition to banks and thrifts, life insurance companies traditionally played a role in financing apartments, and some properties were partly financed through various syndications or partnerships. In addition to long-term financing of the finished asset, new multifamily construction requires a developed system for financing land acquisition and development and construction. Traditionally these have also been provided by thrifts and by banks, with the latter claiming a larger share of lending.

The system broke down under high and variable inflation. At the end of the 1970s it was apparent that thrifts were in serious difficulty, as they suffered "disintermediation" when savers withdrew funds as market rates elsewhere rose above the ceilings. Eventually, deposit-rate regulation was eliminated for thrifts and banks, allowing them to compete for funds on an even footing. But this did not solve the problems stemming from the fact that they had lent long at low fixed rates and were borrowing short as rates skyrocketed (figure 3.6).

Also on the liability side, individual passbook deposits became less important as a source of funds as lenders tapped the capital markets, abetted by "the agencies": the Federal Housing Administration (FHA), the Federal National Mortgage Association (Fannie Mae), the Government National Mortgage Association (Ginnie Mae), and the Federal Home Loan Mortgage Corporation (Freddie Mac). Figure 3.5, above, shows the extraordinary growth of agency securities since the late 1970s. Details of each agency's operation vary, but the essence is that each facilitates the packaging of mortgages into pools or bundles of securities. Sometimes these bundles represent whole mortgages, and sometimes they represent individual components of projected cash flow, but in either case investors are no longer required to evaluate risks involved with individual loans; instead they can rely upon the expected average behavior of a pool (Fabozzi 1988). The agencies also perform insurance

Figure 3.6. *U.S. Residential Mortgage Rates*

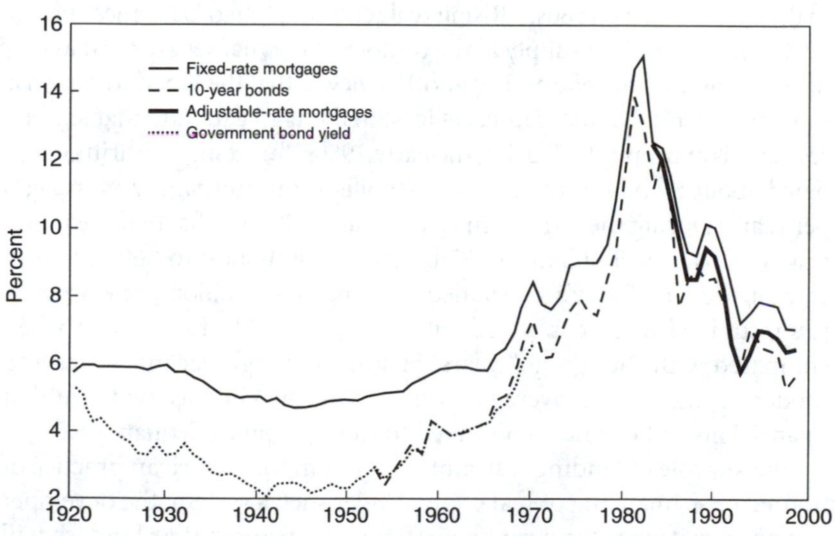

Source: Economic Report of the President, Federal Reserve.

and underwriting functions for these securities. They have multifamily programs, described below, but devote most of their attention to single-family homeownership.

Most important, on the asset side, financial institutions made more of their loans with adjustable rates, but this was not deemed sufficient by the thrifts. The Garn–St. Germain Congressional Act of 1981 effectively removed the requirement that thrifts hold most of their assets in mortgages and other housing-related investments. At first glance, deregulation on the asset side may seem to parallel the deregulation on the liability side (the removal of interest rate ceilings on deposits, as allowed by Regulation Q),[37] but policymakers did not remove deposit insurance. In fact, they increased it. These actions, coupled with regulation that ranged from lax to nonexistent[38] and an astounding lack of interest in the resulting problems from both the executive branch and Congress,[39] led to a nearly guaranteed collapse of the housing finance insurance system. Most impressive, this collapse was perfectly predictable,[40] but no real action was taken until after the 1988 election. In the end, taxpayers wound up compensating depositors for nearly $200 billion.

This regulatory failure's effects on rental housing are not easy to disentangle. Some analysts maintained that the failure resulted in a credit crunch affecting rental investment (as well as other investments), presumably because of an overreaction by lending officers and by regulators to the excesses of the 1980s.[41] Rising real rents in selected U.S. cities and the apparent reduction in supply at the bottom of the market are cited as evidence of the crunch's effects. But another view is that the U.S. currently has more than enough rental capital, at least in the aggregate, and that lending restraint is appropriate. During the early 1980s, for example, thrifts originated about $5 billion of roughly $20 billion in multifamily mortgages per year.[42] During the "go-go" mid- and late-1980s, thrifts increased their originations to $15 billion to $25 billion of $40 billion to $60 billion in constant dollars. Today's "restrained" lending of $30 billion per year looks less restrained when compared with the early 1980s, rather than when compared with the "go-go" years. Historically high vacancy rates and moderate increases in average rents can also be cited as evidence that financial institutions have continued to supply capital adequately.[43]

The key role of lending restraint stems from the American practice of nonrecourse financing of real estate. Under such a system, the developer has an incentive to undertake virtually any project that lenders will finance. If the project succeeds, the developer realizes a leveraged return on his or her equity. If the project fails, the developer can walk away. Hence, we see financial institutions toughening their underwriting standards and requiring more equity. In principle this is appropriate; in fact, the thrift crisis stemmed from bank managers acting like developers rather than bankers.[44]

Today a large majority of fixed-rate single-family mortgages are sold onto a secondary market, which finances about $400 billion per year. New multifamily mortgages originated may be sold in pools or repackaged into derivative securities, representing around $10 billion per year in recent years, or roughly one-third of total originations.

In an excellent review, DiPasquale and Cummings (1992) discuss the activities of Freddie Mac and Fannie Mae. Their key findings are that activity is moderate and highly variable; recent losses in Freddie Mac and FHA multifamily programs have led to curtailments. Drawing on analysis by Alexander (1990), DiPasquale and Cummings foresee further retrenchment in multifamily finance. The Financial Institutions Reform, Recovery, and Enforcement Act of 1989 (FIRREA) was the legislative antidote to the 1981 Garn–St. Germain Act. FIRREA increased capital requirements for thrifts and banks and introduced risk-based capital. When risk-based capital is calculated, most multifamily and "acquisition, development and control" (AD&C) loans are assigned a weight of 100, rather than the preferential 50 percent weights assigned to single-family loans. This is consistent with the international Basle agreements on banking regulation,[45] and also with the observation that thrifts did not get into much trouble with single-family mortgages per se. FIRREA also limits lending to single borrowers to 15 percent of capital. Since many U.S. thrifts are small, including some that appear to be conservatively managed but have a few large customers, this provision has been particularly controversial. FIRREA also tightens up on thrift portfolios, requiring that 70 percent of assets be in housing or related investments. FIRREA mandates increased required loan-to-value ratios and prohibit thrifts from making direct equity investments in real estate. Another FIRREA requirement is that each regional federal home loan bank develop programs to subsidize low- and moderate-income rental housing.

DiPasquale and Cummings (1992) also note that the Community Reinvestment Act of 1977 (CRA) was reinvigorated in the aftermath of the 1980s savings and loan crisis, especially post-FIRREA. Because banks and thrifts are largely local institutions, they are under political pressure to "meet the credit needs of their local communities" (DiPasquale and

Cummings 1992, 84). When this. conflicts with maximizing shareholder profits, or appears to, community groups can bring effective pressure to bear. Such community pressure has resulted in at least some participation in projects that might otherwise have remained unfinanced, or financed at higher rates, but the CRA reporting requirements are regarded as extremely onerous, particularly by small institutions.

The net effect of these changes is not completely clear. CRA and requirements that thrifts make more housing loans could, if all other factors remain equal, increase financial flows to rental housing, while tighter capital requirements and tougher underwriting would tend to decrease flows. DiPasquale and Cummings believe that the net effect will be less financial preference for rental housing. But ending on such a note begs one important question: To the extent that the United States may have invested too much capital in housing in the aggregate, and thrifts and banks have taken on inappropriate and mispriced risks, would reduced financial preference for housing be a bad thing?

Housing Regulation

Rent control, the regulation most commonly analyzed by economists, has some local importance, particularly in New York, but it covers only about 10 percent of the rental population. Far more widespread are land-use controls. The theoretical justification for such controls and for many other regulations is to control for externalities—potential costs to society that would not be borne by a property user. While such regulations may benefit society by correcting for those externalities, some observers note they can also reduce the supply of housing—particularly low- and moderately priced housing—and inhibit filtering. Land-use and growth-management controls have arguably the largest aggregate effects on housing markets.

The primary objective usually stated for zoning and other land-use controls is to correct for externalities arising from "incompatible" land uses (e.g., placing an oil refinery in the middle of a residential subdivision). But in the United States, zoning is commonly used to exclude low-income households, and many suspect it is used to exclude minority low-income households in particular. Exclusionary zoning is also referred to as "fiscal zoning."[46] From the point of view of the municipal authority (and its taxpayers), it is rational to prefer higher-income households that, it is presumed, pay more in taxes than they receive in services; low-income households are presumed to consume more in services than they pay in taxes.[47] Other hypotheses as to why "insiders" would want to exclude low-income households include the fear of crime, possible housing externalities, and concern that school achievement might suffer. For one or several of these reasons, housing that is suitable for low-income households could be "zoned out," particularly multifamily rental housing or manufactured housing. Some observers have noted that jurisdictions can be quite ambivalent (or at least confused) about their objectives. It is not unknown for a jurisdiction to impose regulations to reduce the supply of low- and middle-income units, only to also require developers of high-income properties to build a certain number of low-income units at below-market cost.[48]

Regulation's Costs and Benefits

No one would be, or should be, surprised to find that regulations raise housing prices. That is exactly what they are designed to do. What is at issue is how much they raise prices by, compared with any benefits they may confer.

Malpezzi (1996a) presents a simple model of externality-correcting regulation.[49] What potential externalities could raise social costs of housing above private costs, and hence, in principle, require regulation? Among many candidates are the following:

- *Congestion.* Building additional housing units in a community generally increases traffic locally (although it may reduce total commuting distance for many of the residents).
- *Environmental costs.* Building additional housing units may reduce the local supply of green space; affect air quality; and increase pressure on local water, sanitation, and solid waste collection systems. (The global impact is less clear.)
- *Infrastructure costs.* Building additional housing units may increase the cost of dealing with the problems listed above. Effects will vary depending on whether a particular community has exhausted economies of scale in the provision of each type of infrastructure.
- *Fiscal effects.* In addition to the obvious effects from the above, demand for local public services may increase (education, fire and police protection, or new residents believing libraries should be open on Sundays in contradiction to local custom). New residents may or may not pay sufficient additional taxes to cover the marginal costs.

- *Neighborhood composition effects.* New households may have different characteristics than existing households. If existing households prefer living among people of similar incomes or living arrangements, they will perceive costs if people different from them move in.

If such externalities are large *and* are correctly measured by the regulating authority *and* the specific policy instrument used to regulate is sufficiently precise, regulation can correct for these externalities.[50] But even if such externalities exist, departures from the rather stringent requirements for optimal regulation could leave society worse off.

Many studies have attempted to calculate the cost of regulation in one or a few markets. Only a few studies have attempted to estimate these costs across a range of markets.[51] But as Fischel (1990) has pointed out, only a few studies have attempted to measure any corresponding benefit from land-use regulation. In chapter 4, we will present results from a cross-metropolitan analysis that considers both the cost and the benefit sides.

Appendix 3.1: Measuring Consumers' Welfare—Consumption Efficiency

As discussed previously, there are three kinds of program efficiency:

- *Production efficiency,* or how much it costs the government program to produce a unit of output compared to the least-cost producer;
- *Consumption efficiency,* or how a beneficiary values a unit of the good relative to the market; and
- *Administrative efficiency,* or the shared expenditures that go to program recipients rather than administrations.

Generally, measuring production efficiency and administrative efficiency is technically straightforward (although doing it well requires careful work). This appendix focuses on the measurement of consumption efficiency.

Economists often use an important concept: *consumer surplus.* Consumer surplus is the difference between what an individual would be willing to pay for a good and what she actually has to pay. Economists refer to programs that provide assistance in the form of *things* (e.g., apartments or medical care) rather than money as "in-kind transfers" (as opposed to money transfers). It follows that consumer surplus provides a measure of "bang for the buck"—that is, how much a consumer's welfare increases (or decreases) as a result of receiving some good or service rather than money income.

The common sense behind the benefit or consumer-surplus calculation is easy to understand: The surplus is the amount of money a typical household would accept as equivalent to participating in the program (i.e., to receiving the in-kind transfer). The best way to explain this further is to use an example.

Suppose a public housing program were to offer a government-owned apartment to a low-income household at no charge. Suppose the market rental equivalent was $600 per month. But many—perhaps nearly all—low-income households would rather have $600 per month in cash and fend for themselves in the housing market than have a $600 apartment for free! On the other hand, if they are not given such a choice, but are allowed only to either take the apartment or not get assistance, many if not most would probably take the apartment. That is, the participants attach some value to the in-kind assistance; therefore, we know from common sense that the value is greater than zero but less than the market value of the unit. It turns out that, given housing demand parameters (the fraction of income households spend on housing, and how that fraction changes as incomes and prices change) and the income of the target household, economic models allow us to calculate this value.

The calculation is discussed in detail below. Suppose for the moment that we carried through such a benefit calculation and discovered that the target low-income household valued the benefits from the program at $350. That is, we estimate that the typical low-income household would have a hard time deciding between taking the free apartment or taking $350 per month in cash, so $350 is our measure of the benefit of the program.

Once we have calculated the benefit, we can also talk about the consumption efficiency (sometimes called "transfer efficiency") of a program. Consider our example again. The household receives a benefit worth $350 per month, but the program costs $600 per month, so benefits are about 58 percent of the costs. The *transfer efficiency* of the program is 58 percent.

Why do we use the market rent of the apartment as the measure of the cost? The market rent is the opportunity cost. The government could, for example, rent the apartment out to a higher-income household for the market rent of $600 and then use the money to assist low-income households. In this particular example, the government could help almost twice as many low-income households the same amount by doing this.

Thus, we see another important point: Program *efficiency* and *equity* are not always in opposition; in fact, they are usually closely related. If the government uses scarce public resources more efficiently, more people can be helped.[52]

In addition to using these methods to evaluate programs that give people things at a reduced price (such as public housing), we can use the same methods to evaluate regulations that affect individual consumption in other ways. For example, rent control could change the price and quantity of housing services consumed by certain households. We can use similar methods to evaluate both programs that deliver goods and services and policies that affect the operation of the private market. We will now examine the theory of how to measure these changes in consumer surplus.

In order to illustrate the principle of consumer surplus, we will use two housing examples. In one example, rent control will lower the price of housing, but households will consume "too little" housing.[53] In the second example, a housing program lowers the price of housing but requires the household to consume "too much" housing. We will start with the first.

Example I: Rent Control

Perhaps the simplest way to view the costs and benefits of controls on rent is to first estimate how much controlled units would rent for in the absence of controls. Then, consider the difference between that estimate and the observed controlled rent as the cost imposed on the landlord and, obversely, a benefit transferred to the tenant. But tenants under rent control are usually not free to adjust their consumption to reflect the new relative prices. Consequently, they do not generally value a reduction in rent for the unit they occupy as highly as they would value an equivalent cash transfer. The costs and benefits of rent control to existing tenants in existing rental units can be better studied by estimating changes in consumer surplus resulting from the existence of controls.[54] Figure 3.7, based on Olsen (1972), illustrates such changes for a representative consumer and his or her landlord.

Figure 3.7. *Consumer's Surplus I: Price Control with "Too Little" Housing*

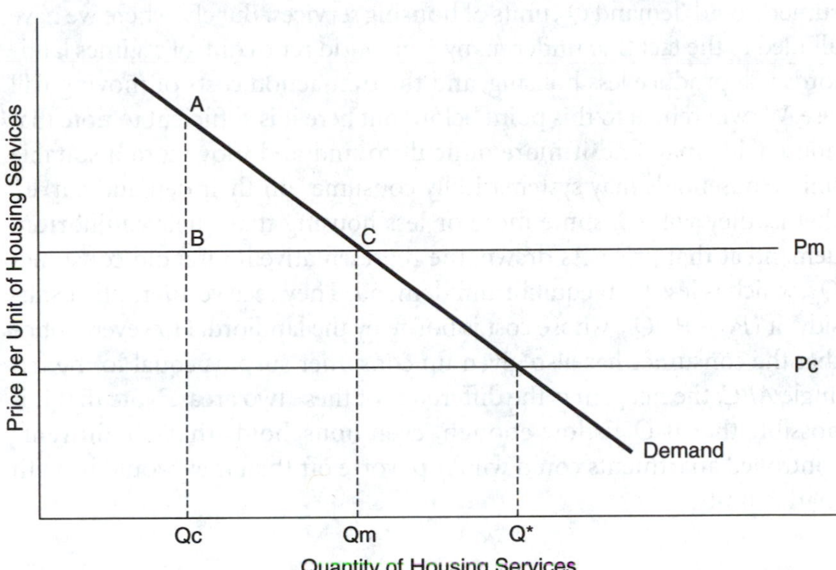

Analysis of consumer surplus rests on the fact that demand curves slope downward; that is, households *would* pay a high price for the first "bit" of housing, a little less for the next "bit," and so on down to the price actually paid for the last "bit" they consume. But in a competitive market, households pay only that last, lowest price for *all* "bits." They receive a bonus in that they are able to consume much of their housing at a lower price than the maximum amount they are willing to pay. The area under the demand curve but above the horizontal line representing the prevailing price represents this bonus. Changes in the household's welfare caused by changes in prices and in quantities consumed can be analyzed by measuring these so-called "welfare triangles" before and after the price or quantity change.

As a first approximation, the costs borne by landlords can be estimated as changes in the area of the rectangles bounded by the price line, the vertical line representing the quantity of housing services, and the axes.[55] This rectangle represents the short-run change in landlord's revenue.

Suppose that in the absence of controls the representative consumer would choose to consume Q_M units of housing services at the prevailing market price P_M, paying rent equal to $P_M Q_M$. Suppose that controls are imposed and effectively enforced, so that initially the rental price of one unit of housing services falls to P_C for all rental units. At this price the consumer would demand Q_D units of housing services. But elsewhere we have alluded to the fact that under many real-world rent-control regimes landlords will produce less housing, and the transaction costs of moving will rise. We will return to this point below, but here it is sufficient to note that households may find it more difficult to find and move into a suitable unit. Households may systematically consume "off their demand curve," that is, they will consume more or less housing than their equilibrium demand at that price. As drawn, the representative household consumes Q_C, which is less than equilibrium demand. They receive an implicit subsidy of $(P_M - P_C)Q_C$, whose cost is borne by the landlord. However, notice that the consumer has also given up consumer surplus equal to the triangle *ABC*; the net gain is the difference of these two areas. Note that it is possible that if Q_C is low enough, even households that obtain rent-controlled apartments could wind up worse off than they would be with market units.

Example II: Public Housing

Consider a housing subsidy that requires the participant to inhabit a dwelling that meets certain quality and space standards. Figure 3.8 represents such a housing subsidy for a representative participant. Given the (here linear) demand curve, in the absence of the program, at market price *Pm,* the consumer would choose a house yielding Q_M units of housing services. Suppose the government institutes a housing subsidy of (*Pm* – *Pc*) for every unit of housing consumed. If the consumer remained in the original unit, instead of paying a sum represented by the area *abjk* he or she would pay *efjk* and the government would pay *abef.* In addition to receiving the subsidy, the consumer would continue to receive consumer surplus corresponding to the area under the demand curve but above line segment *ab.*[56]

Of course, at the new lower price *Pc,* the consumer would like to consume a higher quantity, Q^*. But suppose for a moment that the housing standards are even higher, so that to participate the consumer must move to a unit yielding a larger amount of housing services, Q_C.

First, overall, note that the consumer now pays *ehmj* and the government pays *adhe* in subsidy. How much does the consumer's welfare increase relative to the cost borne by the government?

For the first Q_M units the situation is as before: The consumer receives a benefit of *abef,* representing the portion of his or her original con-

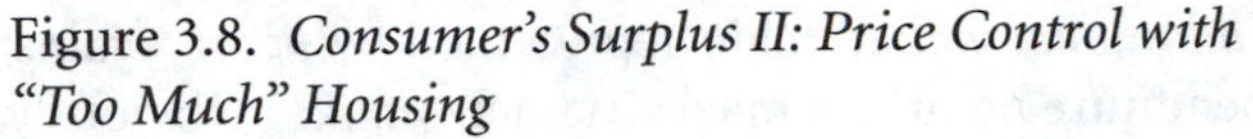
Figure 3.8. *Consumer's Surplus II: Price Control with "Too Much" Housing*

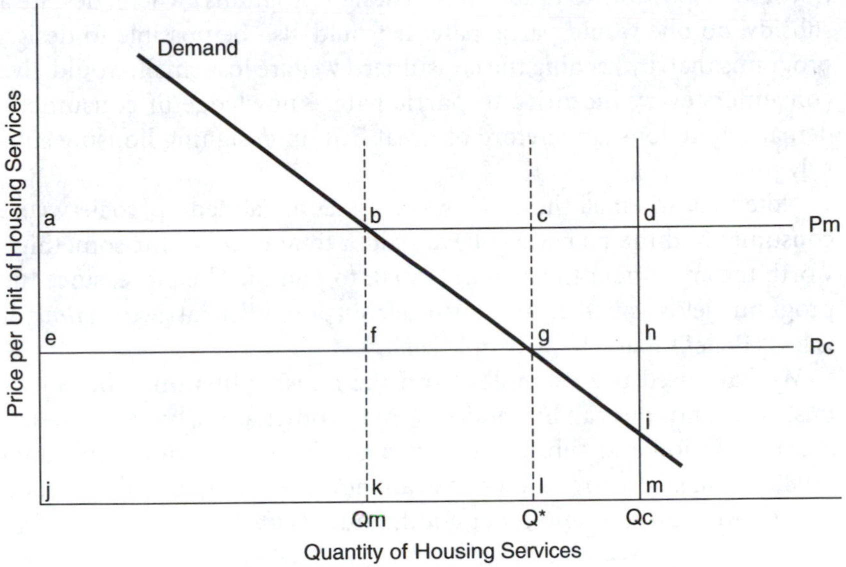

sumption now borne by the government (i.e., by taxpayers). What about the additional housing consumed? Between Q_M and Q^*, the consumer pays *fgkl* and the government pays *bcfg*. How much does the consumer actually personally value this increment? By an amount equal to area *bgkl*, which is greater than the amount the consumer spends (greater than *fglk*) but less than the sum of his or her expenditure and the government's *bcfg*. The triangle *bcg* represents the social welfare loss of this component of the program (i.e., a welfare gain to the consumer, which is less than the total cost to society *bckl*).

For the final $(Q_C - Q^*)$ units of housing services, the change is even more stark. Now even the consumer pays more than he or she gains: *ghml* is greater than his or her total benefit *giml*. Obviously, the consumer would not choose to consume this additional housing unless forced to do so by program rules. And the government (and by extension the taxpayers) ante up another *cdhg* in housing subsidy.

Adding these up, the consumer now pays *ehmj* for housing worth an amount represented by the area under the demand curve to point *i*. Suppose the consumer is free to enter the program or not, but if he or she accepts the subsidy, he or she accepts the higher standard. The consumer weighs the reduction *abef* in the amount paid for his or her original housing, and the *additional* welfare gain represented by *bikm,* against the additional expenditure he or she makes, namely *fhmk.*[57] Obviously, it would be possible to draw curves (design programs) where, despite a subsidy, no one would participate. It would also be possible to design programs that, by keeping the consumers' welfare loss small, would give consumers every incentive to participate. Knowledge of consumers' demand functions is therefore of great help in designing housing subsidy programs.

Note that, when all these gains and losses are added up, society (the consumer and the taxpayers) have paid a total of *admj* for something worth the area under the demand curve to point *i.* Therefore, since the program yields only the *new* consumer surplus, *bikm,* at a cost *bdmk,* it is less efficient than giving people cash.[58]

We have used two examples from the housing literature, but obviously these notions can be applied to many other areas, both in government provision and subsidy, and in analysis of regulation. Smeeding (1982) is one of many studies that applies these to areas such as food stamps, medical care, and other goods and services.

An Algebraic Generalization

This geometric exposition illustrates the basic method quite well, but an algebraic generalization is better suited for actually estimating the size of welfare gains and losses using a sample. Of course if demand curves happen to be straight lines, calculating numerical values involves calculating the areas of a few rectangles and triangles, and hence requires only straightforward geometry. What about other cases? It can be shown[59] that if the price elasticity of demand is constant, the benefit to consumers of a program that changes prices and quantities can be written as[60]

$$Benefit = P_M Q_M - P_C Q_C + \left\{ \left(\frac{1}{Q_M} \right)^{\frac{1}{b}} \left(\frac{b}{b+1} \right) \left(Q_C^{\frac{b+1}{b}} - Q_M^{\frac{b+1}{b}} \right) \right\}$$

where

Benefit = change in Marshallian[61] consumer surplus
Q_M = predicted housing consumption in the absence of the intervention (e.g., rent controls or government program)
Q_C = housing consumption under the intervention

$P_M Q_M$ = estimated rent in the absence of intervention, sometimes denoted R_m

$P_C Q_C$ = observed rent, in the program or under controls, also denoted R_c

b = price elasticity of demand.

In the special case where the price elasticity of demand, b, is equal to –1, the expression $b/(b + 1)$ is undefined. But it can be shown mathematically that in this special case the benefit to the consumer is

$$Benefit = P_M Q_M - P_C Q_C + P_M Q_M \left[\ln P_M Q_C - \ln P_M Q_M \right]$$

Extensions

Our focus here has been to understand the basics of consumer surplus and its application to the analysis of housing subsidies and regulations. We have abstracted from a number of important issues in such estimation, such as decomposing welfare changes into income and price effects. An excellent introduction to the different measures of welfare change, including so-called Hicksian measures as well as the simpler Marshallian measure we present here, can be found in Freeman (1979).[62] Essentially, Marshallian measures use the area under a money-income constant demand curve. But when, for example, subsidies reduce the price per unit of housing services bought by a household, the household's *real* income rises (because money income is constant but prices have fallen). Hicksian methods effectively measure the area under a demand curve, compensated for such changes in real income.

NOTES

1. For example, in the United States about 2 percent of households live in public housing. In the Netherlands, about 37 percent do so; in the United Kingdom, about 31 percent; Sweden, 23 percent; Japan, 8 percent; Canada, 4 percent; and Germany, 3 percent. Many European countries also have "social housing sectors" that are not public housing but are heavily subsidized.
2. U.S. Congressional Budget Office (1992) provides a detailed discussion.
3. See Jaffe and Louziotis's (1996) review.
4. Sources for this section include National Association of Homebuilders (1986) and various HUD reports. The section concentrates on major federal urban rental programs. The Encyclopedia of Housing (van Vliet 1998) contains many entries detailing these and a number of other programs. See also Mitchell (1985).

5. Before 1981 the main income criterion was 80 percent of the area median. The eligibility requirements are adjusted for family size, and local PHAs can impose other criteria such as family composition or (most controversially) race.

6. Some PHAs have managed their units so incompetently that HUD has taken over their management (e.g., Philadelphia).

7. Public attitudes were focused in the 1980s by the well-publicized and spectacularly filmed demolition of the Pruitt-Igoe flats in Saint Louis. Less than 20 years after their construction they were uninhabitable.

8. See Struyk (1980).

9. Since 1981, households below 50 percent of the area median, adjusted for family size.

10. In theory, rents are negotiated on a project-by-project basis, but in practice virtually all Section 8 units rent at or very near the maximum FMR for the market.

11. Or they may already live in a unit that meets the standard.

12. Again, in theory, rents are negotiated on a unit-by-unit basis but in practice virtually all units rent at or near the FMR.

13. Stegman and Holden (1987) provide details.

14. When firms are the beneficiaries they are called "industrial revenue bonds," and when the proceeds are used to subsidize owner-occupied housing they are called "mortgage revenue bonds."

15. The interest rate subsidy is shared by the enterprise/mortgagee/tenant and the bondholder.

16. See GAO's report whose title says it all: *Home Ownership: Mortgage Revenue Bonds Are Costly and Provide Little Assistance to Those in Need* (GAO 1988).

17. Allowance voucher programs can differ in several features of program design, but differences in housing standards required are particularly germane to this discussion. As it happens, the allowances studied by Mayo (1986) and by Cronin (1982) (table 3.3) were from EHAP and imposed looser standards than today's voucher program. See also Olsen (2001) for a careful and detailed review.

18. Straszheim (1981); Cronin (1981). EHAP was administered by HUD, and employed a number of consulting firms and research institutions.

19. Newman (1999) provides a recent review of these issues.

20. In 1990 the National Affordable Housing Act set forth two major sets of programs, one under the HOPE rubic, generally favored by Republicans, and one under rubric HOME, generally favored by Democrats.

21. Source for U.S. data is Casey (1992). For comparison, all renters reported a median income of $18,192 and 77 percent of all renter households reported wage or salary income. For a discussion of Britain's experiences with privatization, see Whitehead (1999).

22. We would make four conjectures about this surprising result. First, American images of public housing are bound up in abysmal, large high-rise projects such as Pruitt-Igoe (Saint Louis; demolished in 1972) and Robert Taylor Homes (Chicago), but only one-third of households live in structures with 50 or more units. Second, public housing's low rents may dominate many residents' satisfaction with their units. Third, many of the worst units are uninhabitable and are held vacant. Fourth, there may be strategic biases in tenants' answers to such questions. Without much hard evidence we would surmise the first and second are the most important.

23. Since the rationale for privatization is presumably to improve opportunities to accumulate assets, these recapture provisions.

24. To the landlord of a rental unit, the return is explicit. To the owner-occupant, the return is implicit; the owner saves money she or he would spend on rent.

25. The most common deductions are for state income taxes, property taxes, charitable contributions, and, of course, mortgage interest.

26. Compared with other capital gains, that is. Capital gains were taxed at 40 percent of ordinary income rates, which were quite high (70 percent at the margin), but nominal gains, rather than real gains, were taxed.

27. Although there was "recapture" of the accelerated part upon the property's sale, taxes deferred are taxes reduced.

28. Lengthened slightly to 18 years in 1984 and 19 years in 1985.

29. Post-1981 investors calculated depreciation on 175 percent of the declining balance in the early years of the investment, switching to straight line after about nine years. There were provisions of recapture of excess depreciation on sale, as noted above.

30. Actually, marginal rates are higher in many states because most states levy state income taxes based on federal notions of income. These marginal rates can be as high as 10 percent on top of federal tax. Some states have adjustments to income from capital, so the pass-through of changes differs.

31. Malpezzi, Ozanne, and Thibodeau (1987) present evidence that the average net depreciation of rental housing is less than 1 percent per year, and that straight line depreciation is not a bad approximation of the actual pattern.

32. The United States recognizes three types of income: active, portfolio, and passive. Active income is (more or less) income from wages and salaries. Portfolio income is (more or less) that from investments in stocks and bonds. Passive income is defined in the text.

33. When the credits are "sold" in a secondary market, however, they generally sell for between 55 and 60 percent of face value.

34. For more on the mechanics of this program, see Guggenheim (2000). Cummings and DiPasquale (1999) have undertaken a recent evaluation.

35. See U.S. Office of Management and Budget (1997).

36. See Woodward and Weicher (1989) for a defense of the mortgage interest deduction. See also Follain and Melamed (1998) and Capone (1995).

37. Regulation Q, or "Reg Q," set ceilings on the rates banks and thrifts could pay depositors. Thrifts were given a small spread above banks. During the 1970s, as inflation increased, depositors left banks and thrifts in droves for higher yielding, unregulated instruments.

38. In contrast to thrifts, banks were long diversified on the asset side, and guaranteed on the liability side, but were regulated by the Federal Reserve and the U.S. Comptroller of the Currency. Banks have problems with their real estate lending and other parts of their portfolio, but independent and relatively effective regulation somewhat limited the damage. In contrast, the main thrift regulator was the Federal Home Loan Bank Board, which was dominated by the thrifts themselves.

39. Note that the extraordinary actions (and inactions) of Congress and successive administrations were nonpartisan; both Democrats and Republicans were to blame.

40. See Kane (1983, 1985).

41. Ambrose and Benjamin (1993); Hancock and Wilcox (1992); Han (1994).

42. In 1990 dollars; derived from DiPasquale and Cummings (1992), figure 1.

43. It can be argued that without large investments in rental housing during the mid-1980s, markets would be very tight and rents very high; accepting this argument doesn't imply that the high levels of the mid- and late 1980s would be appropriate today.

44. Bank and thrift managers had incentives to increase loan volume, as lending generates substantial up-front fees. After passage of the Garn–St. Germain Act, thrifts were also allowed to take *equity* positions in real estate. In the worst cases, thrifts were used as vehicles for outright fraud. See Adams (1990) for colorful descriptions of how this was accomplished. Adams overstates the role of fraud, however. The thrift crisis would have occurred without it, albeit on a somewhat smaller scale.

45. The Basle agreements of 1988 set minimum reserve requirements for various types of financial institutions. For a review, see Wagster (1999).

46. These are not the only rationales for zoning or other urban regulations; environmental and traffic concerns also spark many growth management programs.

47. While it is often asserted that low-income households are a net fixed drain on local governments, and high-income households a fiscal bonus, it is hard to find good evidence in support of this assertion. Fiscal impacts depend on many things other than income, including density of development and demographics. See Burchell and Listokin (1978).

48. See Fischel's (1990) account of Davis, California, pp. 30 ff.

49. This simple model is from Malpezzi (1996a). Crone (1983) presents a more technically sophisticated model of externalities and land use regulation.

50. We are also abstracting from who exactly bears these costs; for the moment, assume we tax winners and compensate losers so as to share costs "fairly." And note that governments may decide that some externalities, such as a preference for racial segregation, are not "legitimate."

51. Examples of case studies of one or a few markets include Cho and Linneman (1993), Chressanthis (1986), Colwell and Kau (1982), Dowall and Landis (1982), Green (1999), Katz and Rosen (1987), Landis (1986), Pollakowski and Wachter (1990), and Schwartz, Hansen, and Green (1984). Examples of cross-market studies include Rose (1989a, b), Segal and Srinivasan (1985), and Shilling, Sirmans, and Guidry (1991).

52. Or the same people could be helped the same amount, but with lower taxes.

53. As will become clear, individual households in a housing program could consume *either* too much or too little housing. Individual households under rent control could consume *either* too much or too little, as well. We use the two different examples to highlight the fact that the same method, which is used to analyze a direct production program (public housing) can also be applied to a regulation that affects the price paid in the private market.

54. If the market for housing is not competitive—if there is an upward sloping supply curve—then there exists a corresponding producer's surplus. To date, cost-benefit studies of housing programs have assumed a competitive market.

55. Per the preceding footnote, in a competitive market the initial producer's surplus would be zero (normal profits would be part of the cost of doing business), and the post-control producer's surplus would be negative. If the supply curve were upward sloping there would be initial excess profits (positive producer's surplus) for inframarginal units.

56. Notice that since we did not draw the demand curve all the way to the origin, we have not attempted to calculate the original consumer surplus. While we can do so, in principle, usually we are interested in *changes* in consumer surplus, and you will see in a moment we can calculate such changes without calculating the original level.

57. The consumer would also have to include the transaction "costs" of entering the program (paperwork and intrusive questions), and the move to the new unit. These are easy to add, but for simplicity we have assumed them away in this example.

58. Among those arguments often put forward for in-kind housing transfers, many are some variant of the idea that markets may not in fact produce enough housing to enable a target population to purchase what they need with a straight income transfer. It can be argued that the market does not produce enough low-income housing because it is not profitable, or that discrimination denies blacks and other minorities wide choice at market prices, or that at least some homeless people have personal problems, which put them at a disadvantage in the private market. Apgar (1990) further argues that by building public housing the price of low-cost housing is reduced; this is only possible if the supply is not perfectly met. We discuss these points in more detail in chapter 4.

59. The deriviation is well known and can be found in Malpezzi et al. (1988).

60. The formula is derived from the definite integral representing the area under the demand curve, from the original market equilibrium to the new constrained consumption at the government price.

61. The Marshallian demand curve takes into account both the substitution and income effects of price changes. Hicksian demand curves take into account only substitution effects.

62. Among references that extend such welfare analysis generally see Chavas, Bishop, and Segerson (1986), Deaton and Meullbauer (1980), Hausman (1981), Silberberg (1972), and especially Willig (1976). For applications of Hicksian welfare measures to housing see Schwab (1985) and Malpezzi (1998b).

4

Six Questions for the Next Decade

Is Housing Becoming Less Affordable?

Housing advocates (Daskal 1998; Dolbeare 1999), national and local media (DeParle 1996), and some scholars, such as William Apgar of Harvard University (Joint Center 1992), maintain that the United States is experiencing a long-term decline in affordable housing. Specifically, they note that renter households, especially the young and the poor, are spending a greater portion of income on housing than they did 10 and 20 years ago.

At the same time, however, the National Association of Realtors' (NAR) housing affordability index—perhaps the most frequently cited indicator of the ability of a "typical" family to own a home—has recently declined from its highest level in 25 years.[1] This index is presented in figure 4.1. In fact, the NAR index indicates that a median-income family of four can now (by one common standard) "afford" 31 percent more than the median price of a house in the United States.

Any such affordability calculation is, by its nature, arbitrary. It is based on some normative judgment about what households "should" pay for housing. The most common rule, lent credence by its use for official calculations by the U.S. Department of Housing and Urban Development (HUD), is that spending more than 30 percent of household income on housing implies that housing is not affordable.

Figure 4.1. *NAR Housing Affordability Index Median Family Income/Qualifying Income*

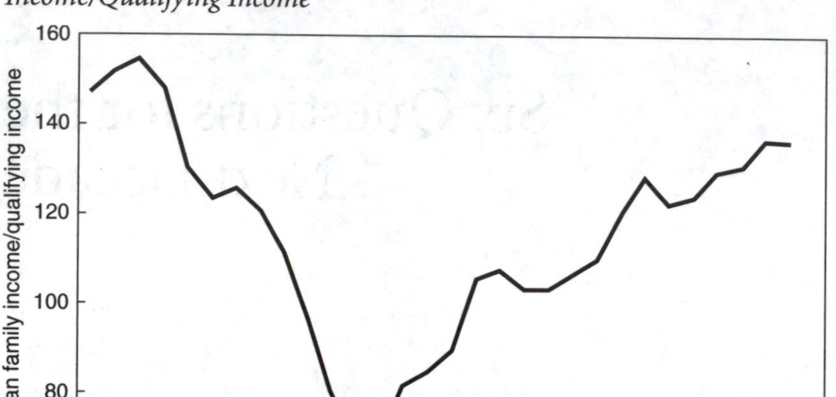

Source: National Association of Realtors.

Economists generally favor an alternative, positive definition of affordability. If households are observed to pay a given amount, then, from the economist's viewpoint, they can afford to do so. This is not a judgment about the desirability of any given payment, but simply an acknowledgment of its existence and of the household's revealed willingness to pay.

Economists point out that using a single numerical cutoff for "affordability" (whether 30 percent or any other figure) implies that an income elasticity of demand of one (a constant rent-to-income ratio) is the norm. Recall from chapter 2 that many studies suggest the income elasticity of demand within a market is less than one; see, for example, figure 2.4. That figure demonstrates that average or median within-market rent-to-income ratios fall as incomes rise, and that there is significant variation around the averages. This is true worldwide, as Malpezzi and Mayo (1987) document. This inelastic demand is consistent with housing's status as a necessity (along with food and clothing, among other goods).

Some analysts prefer to eschew the use of the term "affordability," since it can be so value-laden, but the term is in common usage, and we stick with it. Whichever definition of "affordability" one prefers, patterns and trends in housing expenditure relative to income are of intense interest.

The question before us, then, is whether we can make a broad statement about the trajectory of housing affordability in the United States. We examine affordability in the positive sense of what the trends are. We do not adopt a normative standard of affordability, but just as more is preferred to less in terms of consumption, lower is preferred to higher in these affordability figures.

It is probably no longer appropriate to focus exclusively on the family of four as the "typical" family: The percentage of households headed by married couples, both with and without children, has dropped to less than 55 percent. It is important, therefore, to also examine affordability conditions for various types of single-headed households, and in particular households with children headed by an unmarried parent.

We will also investigate contract rent-to-income ratios, a key component of consumers' ability to accumulate funds for a down payment. Specifically, we measure the amount renter families at the lowest income quartile would spend if they rented housing at the lowest rent quartile. This strategy matches up the lowest-priced housing with the lowest-income households. We examine affordability from this perspective, because we do not wish to assert the existence of an affordability crisis if households have the opportunity to spend a small fraction of their incomes on housing but are choosing to spend a larger fraction. However, if, under this "matching" scheme, low-income households are still forced to spend a substantial amount of their incomes on housing, then there is clearly a housing affordability problem.

The source of our data on the affordability of housing is tabulations we have performed using the Five-Percent Public Use Micro Sample (PUMS) of the 1990 census.[2] One yardstick of housing affordability is the rent-to-income ratio. As discussed above, HUD generally defines 30 percent of gross income as an affordable expenditure on housing. While this number or any fixed benchmark is always debatable, we will accept it as our benchmark.[3]

Our tabulations produced both not-so-bad news and bad news. The not-so-bad news is that for renter households that have the median income for renter households, housing affordability conditions appear to be reasonably good in most places. As column 1 of table 4.1 shows, in all states, households with the median renter's income need spend less than 30 percent of their incomes to rent the median-priced rental unit.[4] The highest statewide ratio of median gross rent to median renter income in the 50 states is 29 percent (Louisiana), and the minimum is 19 percent

Table 4.1. *State Indicators of Housing Affordability (Selected States), 1990*

	Median gross rent/median renter income ratio	*Calculated PITI[a] for 25th percentile value unit/median renter income ratio*	*25th percentile gross rent/ 25th percentile renter income ratio*	*Calculated PITI for 25th percentile value unit/ 25th percentile renter income ratio*	*25th percentile gross rent/ 25th percentile single mothers' income ratio*
Top States					
Alaska	19.1	14.6	26.6	20.7	45.3
Nebraska	20.2	14.3	21.0	22.3	42.6
North Dakota	20.4	12.6	25.6	20.3	51.2
Wyoming	20.6	18.9	29.1	30.6	35.8
Idaho	20.9	20.3	22.4	31.9	42.9
Bottom States					
Massachussets	27.8	45.3	36.3	85.6	43.9
Florida	27.8	23.6	37.5	38.1	53.8
Rhode Island	28.3	54.9	37.6	97.7	34.8
California	29.0	41.7	37.8	62.3	50.6
Louisiana	29.3	20.2	36.0	38.8	41.3

Source: Author's tabulations of 1990 Census PUMS data.

a. PITI = Mortgage Principal, Interest, Property Taxes, Insurance.

(Alaska); the median of all 50 state calculations is 25 percent.[5] Of course, the ratio of these two medians will mask high and low ratios experienced by specific individuals.

Let us focus on the affordability of housing to those entering the owner-occupied market. The NAR affordability index described above focuses on the relationship between median households and median house values. But consider that there are many units—specifically, half the market—that cost less than the median. For the moment, let the median renter represent the prospective first-time homebuyer.[6] Let the house with a value at the 25th percentile represent an entry-level unit. State by state, we calculate the principal, interest, and property tax required to purchase such a unit, and compare this total to the median income of renters in each state. Column 2 of table 4.1 presents this calculation.[7] The unweighted median for all 50 states is only 22 percent. In all states but California, Connecticut, Hawaii, Maryland, New Hampshire, and Rhode Island, median rental households could "afford" to make the principal, interest, and property tax payments on a home priced at the 25th percentile. This is calculated using typical industry guidelines (a 90 percent loan-to-value ratio on a 30-year fixed-rate mortgage with an interest rate of 7.5 percent). Further, because the rental burden faced by many of these households is not particularly severe, they should be able to accumulate funds for down payments. The best way to advance homeownership among this income class is to encourage savings for a down payment.[8]

When we examine lower-income households, however, a different picture emerges. We demonstrate the housing affordability problems facing households at the lowest quartile of the income distribution among renters with three exhibits. The third column of table 4.1 shows estimated rent-to-income ratios for this group. Specifically, the table presents ratios of rents at the 25th percentile to renter incomes at the 25th percentile for each state.

According to our calculations, in 23 states a renter at the 25th percentile of income would have paid more than 30 percent of income to obtain rental housing at the 25th percentile of price. This means that even if housing were perfectly matched—that is, even if the lowest income household took the least expensive rental unit, the second lowest income household took the second least expensive unit, and so on—the poorest quartile of rental households in these 23 states would typically have to spend more than 30 percent of income on housing.

Of course, household incomes and rents are never so perfectly matched, so we know that rental affordability conditions for the lowest quartile of the renter income distribution are even worse than our calculations suggest when the 30 percent standard is adopted. On the other hand, higher rent-to-income ratios for lower-income households are perfectly consistent with the housing demand literature summarized in chapter 2, which found that (in cross-section) the income elasticity of demand for housing is generally less than one. As a positive statement, households in the bottom quartile typically "afford" something more than 40 percent of their income on housing. By this standard, all 50 states appear to meet the "affordable" threshold.

We also note that rents are higher in some metropolitan areas than others. In the cross-metropolitan model we present below, we find that higher rents are clearly related to the stringency of the regulatory environment for housing. To the extent inappropriate regulations worsen affordability (especially if and when they do so without providing other corresponding benefits), we suggest the solution to the problem lies in regulatory reform, as discussed in some detail below.

Trends in Tenure Choice

It is well known that the percentage of households in the United States that owned their own homes fell from 1980 to 1990. Although the actual decline was quite small (0.24 percent), the fact that the homeowning rate fell at all was worrisome to many. After all, the United States had seen increases in its homeownership rate during every decade from the end of World War II through 1980. After the decline between 1980 and 1990, the homeownership rate moved back up to 67.9 percent during the 1990s—again, a historic high.

Should declines in homeownership, when they occur, be a source of concern? The changing demographic structure of the country might have a lot to do with why the homeownership rate declined in the 1980s. The percentage of households headed by married couples had been declining. Households headed by singles are, all else being equal, less likely than households headed by married couples to own their own homes. We may infer some reasons for this; an important one is likely that singles tend to be more mobile than married couples, and therefore are less likely to want to be tied down by homeowning, since renters face lower transaction costs.[9] If people are choosing not to become homeowners to save on such costs, the declining homeownership rate is no cause for concern.

Recent research by Myers et al. (1992) suggests the small decline in the homeownership rate from 1980 to 1990 may have understated a more pronounced long-term trend. Specifically, they demonstrate that in all but 2 of the 50 states, the homeownership rate between 1980 and 1990 fell among households headed by those in the 25- to 34-year-old age bracket. The size of these declines was often substantial, although the changes ranged from a small increase of 1.4 percent in New York to a decline of 13.4 percent in North Dakota.

Again, one could try to explain the decline as a function of changing demographic patterns. People are certainly waiting longer to marry and have children. The age of first marriage is nearly five years later than it was after World War II. Yet tabulations we have performed show that even when we control for household type, homeownership rates in the 25- to 34-year-old age bracket generally declined between 1980 and 1990. In fact, census data show that the homeownership rate for households headed by 25- to 34-year-old married couples fell in all but seven states during the 1980s.[10]

The changes in affordability conditions for young married couples mirror the overall affordability picture for median-income renters. To explain why young married couples are less likely to be owners than they were 10 and 15 years ago, we must look to two other explanations, one speculative, one certain. First, it is possible that young marrieds are far more mobile than they were in years past. Consider the increasing percentage of married couples that have dual careers, which may create incentives for each household member to move.

Second, as the tabulation from Green (1995) shows below, owning may have stagnated in the 1980s because it did not perform well financially then. Table 4.2 shows a few statewise comparisons. The ratio of median house prices to median incomes fell in 40 of the 50 states during the 1980s, after strong rises in the 1970s. But while asset prices were flat or falling in most locations, *user cost* for owner-occupied housing rose virtually everywhere between 1980 and 1990. As described in chapter 2, the components of user cost include real interest rates, property taxes, and marginal income tax rates. Real interest rates for owners were much higher in the 1980s than in the 1970s, when house price appreciation was often greater than the coupon paid on the mortgage note. Just as important, marginal tax rates were lower, meaning that the tax benefits of untaxed imputed

Table 4.2. *State Indicators of Tenure Choice (Selected States)*

	Median house price relative to median income, 1990	*Change in median house price relative to median income, 1980–90*	*Percent change in expected user cost, 1980–90*	*Percent change in actual user cost, 1980–90*	*Percent change in rent/ income of median renter, 1980–90*	*Homeownership rate, 1990*	*Percent change in homeownership rate, 1980–90*	*Homeownership rate, 1998*	*Percent change in homeownership rate, 1990–98*
Five Lowest Homeownership Rates, 1998									
Hawaii	3.6	−2.1	9.1	−6.9	−3.3	53.9	2.2	52.8	−1.1
New York	2.7	0.0	1.4	2.9	−1.5	52.2	3.6	52.8	0.6
California	4.0	−0.9	22.9	6.2	1.3	55.6	−0.3	56.0	0.4
Rhode Island	5.0	1.8	12.7	12.9	−0.1	59.5	0.7	59.8	0.3
Massachussets	4.2	1.2	9.3	13.2	2.0	59.3	1.8	61.3	2.0
Five Highest Homeownership Rates, 1998									
West Virginia	1.7	−0.8	5.1	−1.4	2.9	74.1	0.5	74.8	0.7
Kentucky	1.8	−0.2	5.6	0.4	1.1	69.6	−0.4	75.1	5.5
Mississippi	1.6	−0.6	3.0	−2.8	−0.4	71.5	0.5	75.1	3.6
Minnesota	2.0	−1.3	4.1	2.9	−1.5	71.8	0.1	75.4	3.6
South Carolina	1.8	−0.5	5.0	−1.3	−0.1	69.8	−0.4	76.6	6.8

Source: Authors' Calculations of 1990 Census PUMS data.

rent combined with the mortgage interest and property tax deduction were considerably lower than they had been before. Also, the value of personal exemptions and the standard deduction rose in 1986, and were now indexed for inflation. Thus it is certain that owner-occupied housing was not as attractive as an asset as it was in the 1970s. While this contributed to a stagnant homeownership rate during the 1980s, it by no means implied an affordability crisis.

In the 1990s, real housing prices remained stable and then rose toward the end of the decade; nominal mortgage rates fell, and so did inflation, so real rates did not change radically; and effective marginal tax rates crept up for upper-income households. Taken together, user cost fell slightly in much of the country, but not to anything like the low levels of the 1970s. Homeownership rates have increased modestly in response, and as of this writing the rate is now at a record high of 67.2 percent. We will know more about this when the 2000 Public Use Micro Sample of the U.S. Census Bureau is released.

What Will Happen to Housing Prices?

In the housing market, as in the economy generally, it has been said that "demographic is destiny." While demographics plays a profound role in housing markets, so do incomes, policy environments, and a host of other determinants. Simple extrapolations based on a single demographic correlation can be seriously misleading, a point well illustrated by the controversy surrounding Mankiw and Weil's celebrated (1989) study.

Mankiw and Weil's paper (M-W) forecast that America's aging population would cause real house prices to fall by 47 percent between 1987 and 2007. The paper is one of the most frequently cited studies in academic housing literature and has probably received more attention in the popular press than any similar paper in the past 20 years. The implications of such a precipitous decline in housing prices for housing finance are obvious: Indeed, after a summary of M-W was published in *Barrons,* the price of Fannie Mae and Freddie Mac stock both fell by more than 20 percent (they have since recovered). Other researchers (e.g., Hughes 1991) have also commented on how changing demographics might create havoc in the housing market.

Mankiw and Weil's paper was innovative because it was the first to explicitly relate the demand for housing to the age of the persons demanding housing. Mankiw and Weil simply regressed the age of a household's members on the household's home value and created an age-demand series for housing. They then constructed an age-demand time series, and regressed it along with other terms on a real house price index. From this regression they forecast the 47 percent real decline.

The reality is that real house prices rose 10 percent between 1987 and 2001 (Office of Federal Housing Enterprise Oversight). We may therefore ask why the M-W prediction is so far off the mark. In one response to M-W, Hendershott (1992) pointed out that their results were entirely the product of a time trend term estimated from 40 years of time-series data. Hendershott noted that the M-W age-demand series actually rises between 1987 and 2007, and that the in-sample forecasting performance of their time trend term is poor. From these observations he concludes that their forecast may not be reliable.

The publication and extraordinary press coverage of M-W prompted a number of other researchers to investigate the impact of changing demographics in general, and the age structure of the population in particular, on house prices. Among these are studies by Peek and Wilcox (1991b), Green and Hendershott (1996), and Myers and Pitkin (1993).

Peek and Wilcox (1991b) estimate a reduced-form macro-model that uses the cyclical component of the unemployment rate, the real after-tax cost of borrowing, household income, the size and age distribution of the population, the share of households headed by 20- to 29-year-olds, and the real price of construction materials to explain movements in house prices. House prices are measured using a series of indexes. Peek and Wilcox estimate several models, using a variety of house price indexes, and find in all their models that household incomes have a statistically significant positive influence on house prices. They also find materials' prices always have a positive influence on house prices, with a significant influence in five of the eight models. The relative size of the number of household heads aged 20 to 29 always has a negative influence, and has a significant influence in four of eight instances. Surprisingly, the influences of real after-tax interest rates and cyclical unemployment are mixed.

Green and Hendershott (1996) use a model similar to Bartik's (1987) two-step hedonic model to estimate the impact of demographic shifts on individual components (e.g., bedrooms, bathrooms) of a house in order to find how demographic shifts would affect a constant quality house price index. Specifically, they examine how age, household income, race, marital status, household size, and education levels influence the demand for the component parts of a house. They also use an age-income interactive term to act, along with education levels, as a proxy for permanent income. Finally, in creating their dependent variables, Green and Hendershott measure user cost to create a service flow of housing.

Their findings to some extent resemble those of Peek and Wilcox: Permanent household income seems to be the most important determinant of the household demand for housing services. They also find that, contrary to Mankiw and Weil's results, the demand for housing generally increases with age, even beyond the age of 45. Holding household income constant, Green and Hendershott find that the demand for housing services will move very slowly upward between now and the year 2007. This contrasts with M-W's forecast of a precipitous decline in demand.

Myers and Pitkin (1993) focus on succeeding generations' shifting demand patterns for housing. The authors simply follow cohorts across time, and, like Hendershott and Green, find that a household's demand for housing increases as the household's head ages. Myers and Pitkin argue that Mankiw and Weil erroneously compared the household demand of different generations at a single point in time. When a 50-year-old in 1970 becomes a 60-year-old in 1980, her demand does not resemble that of a 60-year-old in 1970, because the two individuals have implicit differences in characteristics outside of age. The "newer" 60-year-old's income and past level of housing consumption has been higher. By following cohorts from 1960 through 1970 to 1980, Myers and Pitkin are able to determine that the demand for housing actually rises with age. Green and Hendershott get at this same result through their permanent income proxies.

So far, the results obtained in the aftermath of Mankiw and Weil's original paper have been remarkably robust. Without exception, these papers have found that demographics will have either a small or positive effect on future house prices.

A brief consideration of economic theory should convince us that a prediction of a steep decline in real house prices over a 20-year period does not make much sense.[11] Houses do involve a great deal of sunk cost, so housing supply does not respond immediately to changes in market conditions. But over the longer term, the housing market does adjust to changing market conditions through the filtering process (see Olsen 1969), and therefore, in the long run, house prices should be equal to the marginal cost of housing production. The changing age pattern of the population is fairly predictable. Should the market expect a baby bust to cause the demand curve for housing to shift inward, the market will "filter down" the supply curve until a new equilibrium point is reached. If the long-run housing supply curve is perfectly elastic, the price of housing will return to its original point.

How Does Regulation Affect the Housing Market?

When the supply of any commodity is restricted, the commodity's price rises. To the extent that land-use, building code, housing finance, or any other type of regulation is binding, it will worsen housing affordability. However, the size of the effect is an empirical matter.[12]

Of course, the mere fact that regulation drives up the cost of housing does not suggest that regulation is bad, as we demonstrated in chapter 2. For example, the landmark laws introduced by the New York City Tenement Commission (1901), which required landlords to provide sanitary housing and called for the elimination of overcrowded housing conditions, certainly drove up the cost of housing units. Nevertheless, the regulations' public health benefits alone almost surely made them worthwhile.

This point is underscored by the publication of *Not in My Backyard,* the report of the Kean Commission (formally, the Advisory Commission on Regulatory Barriers to Affordable Housing 1991). The commission's objectives were to assess regulation of the housing industry, including rehabilitation as well as new construction, with a special emphasis on the effect regulations have on housing affordability. The title of the report is rather ideologically charged, as is the report's cover letter to then-Secretary of HUD, Jack Kemp, from Thomas Kean, former governor of New Jersey, and Thomas Ashley, the chair and vice-chair of the commission, respectively. One might infer from the report's title and the accompanying cover letter that land-use regulations have no place in a nation that wishes to provide all its people with affordable housing. The sad point is that the title and letter led to the report being needlessly stereotyped, as by Godschalk (1992), who called it "an advocacy report whose direction was set by . . . Kemp's position long before the commission was convened" (423).

Yet the report engages in far more than mere regulation-bashing. Throughout the report's recommendations are words such as "review," "flexibility," and "reform." The report generally calls for regulations to be modified so that current regulatory objectives, such as environmental protection and the efficient provision of infrastructure, are maintained while the burden these regulations place on the housing market is minimized. Regulation issues in both central cities and suburbs are addressed. The report's long list of specific recommendations includes reducing restrictions on manufactured housing, "granny flats," and single-room occupancy units; and setting impact fees based on costs rather than on what the traffic will bear. The report also calls for changes to building entitlement process, including a greater role for states in moderating some local governments' excessive regulatory tendencies. In short, the report calls on policymakers to solve a constrained optimization problem: to minimize the cost of providing housing subject to meeting certain societal requirements.

The effects of various regulations on the cost of housing have barely been considered, if not ignored completely, by those implementing regulatory policy. As Godschalk (1992) suggests, commencing discussion between regulators and the housing community might enable us to maintain certain societal objectives while reducing the cost of providing housing.[13]

Measuring Regulation

While economists endorse cost-benefit analysis of regulation in practice, Fischel's (1990) review highlights the fact that most empirical analyses of regulations by economists have, in fact, focused on their costs and ignored potential benefits. Planners and regulators tend to discuss potential benefits without much reference to costs.

Malpezzi (1996a) constructs several measures of the restrictiveness of the land-use regulatory environment across a number of metropolitan areas, and uses those measures in models explaining rents, asset prices of housing, tenure choice, and several "externality" outcomes (neighborhood satisfaction, segregation, and congestion). In multivariate models, Malpezzi finds that regulations do raise rents; this is, by itself, unsurprising. What is perhaps more interesting is that asset prices are driven up faster than rents; that homeownership rates decline substantially with more stringent regulatory environments (primarily through indirect effects on prices); and that there is little offsetting environmental benefit to more stringent regulations, at least as yet measured.

Of course, any such cross-metropolitan measure of "regulation" has its own pros and cons. An alternative and complementary approach is to study the cost-benefit of regulation in a case study of one or more markets. Examples include studies such as Dowall (1984) and Zorn, Hansen, and Schwartz (1986), among many others. Two unpublished papers by Peterson

(1974a, b) remain among the few single market studies to consider costs *and* benefits. For example, in the Fairfax County, Virginia, market, Peterson found that the benefits of regulation (from amelioration of congestion externalities) were significant, but not sufficient to outweigh the high cost of housing produced in such a restricted environment.

The weakness of such a case study, of course, is that without additional information we are uncertain whether particular results for Fairfax County have relevance for any other market. The cross-metropolitan regulatory indicators of Malpezzi (1996a) and of broadly similar efforts such as Rose's (1989a, b) land-supply indexes, and the Angel and Mayo (1996) international regulatory indicators give up some richness of detail, but yield more readily generalizable results. For example, regardless of the index used, increased levels of regulations bring about higher house prices.

Table 4.3 presents several regulatory indicators from Malpezzi's (1996a) study. The first indicator is the unweighted sum of seven variables, which are listed below and which were collected for 56 metropolitan statistical areas (MSAs) by Linneman et al. (1990):

(1) The change in approval time (zoning and subdivision) for single-family projects between 1983 and 1988 (1 = shortened considerably, 2 = shortened somewhat, 3 = showed no change, 4 = increased somewhat, 5 = increased considerably).
(2) Estimated number of months between application for rezoning and issuance of permit for a residential subdivision of less than 50 units (1 = less than 3 months, 2 = 3 to 6 months, 3 = 7 to 12 months, 4 = 13 to 24 months, 5 = more than 24 months).
(3) Similar to (2), but for a single-family subdivision with more than 50 units.
(4) How does the acreage of land zoned for single-family use compare to demand? (1 = far more than demanded, 2 = more than demanded, 3 = about right, 4 = less than demanded, 5 = far less than demanded).
(5) How does the acreage of land zoned for multifamily use compare to demand? (1 = far more than demanded, 2 = more than demanded, 3 = about right, 4 = less than demanded, 5 = far less than demanded).
(6) Percent of zoning changes approved (1 = 90 to 100 percent, 2 = 60 to 89 percent, 3 = 30 to 59 percent, 4 = 10 to 29 percent, 5 = 0 to 9 percent).

Table 4.3. *Regulatory Indicators of Housing Costs, Circa 1990, for Selected Large Metropolitan Areas*

Metropolitan area	*City-specific regulatory index*	*State regulatory index*	*Rent control dummy*	*Census median value, 1990 ($)*	*Census median gross rent, 1990 ($)*
Honolulu	29	—	0	283,600	663
San Francisco	29	6	1	332,400	709
Boston	26	6	1	186,100	656
New York	26	5	1	209,000	503
Sacramento	26	6	0	136,700	531
San Diego	26	6	0	186,700	611
Los Angeles	25	6	1	226,400	626
Newark	25	5	1	191,400	583
San Jose	25	6	1	289,400	773
Miami	24	2	0	86,500	493
Philadelphia	24	3	0	100,800	516
Albany	23	5	1	99,300	458
Allentown	23	3	0	102,400	463
Pittsburgh	23	3	0	55,600	366
Charlotte	22	4	0	72,300	425
Cincinnati	22	2	0	71,100	367
Fort Lauderdale	22	2	0	91,800	575
Toledo	22	2	0	59,700	391
Akron	21	2	0	63,600	397
Cleveland	21	2	0	74,100	406
Houston	21	4	0	64,300	406
Indianapolis	21	5	0	66,800	413
Memphis	21	2	0	64,800	391
Syracuse	21	5	0	77,300	431
Atlanta	20	2	0	89,800	529
Baltimore	20	4	0	101,200	490
Birmingham	20	1	0	59,200	358
Columbus, OH	20	2	0	72,200	421
Orlando	20	2	0	84,300	524
Providence	20	3	0	131,100	501
Rochester	20	5	0	86,600	466
Tulsa	20	1	0	58,900	359
Greensboro	19	4	0	71,300	392
Hartford	19	5	1	170,900	589

(*continued*)

Table 4.3. *Continued*

Metropolitan area	*City-specific regulatory index*	*State regulatory index*	*Rent control dummy*	*Census median value, 1990 ($)*	*Census median gross rent, 1990 ($)*
Kansas City, MO	19	2	0	66,500	425
Portland	19	4	0	72,300	437
Richmond	19	3	0	79,300	459
Salt Lake City	19	2	0	71,000	379
Youngstown	19	2	0	50,400	344
Grand Rapids	18	5	0	70,200	436
Milwaukee	18	5	0	76,900	447
Mobile	18	1	0	55,300	329
Oklahoma City	18	1	0	54,500	368
Phoenix	18	1	0	85,300	465
San Antonio	18	4	0	57,300	380
Buffalo	17	5	1	74,000	385
Denver	17	3	0	87,800	431
Detroit	17	5	0	68,300	455
New Orleans	17	4	0	70,000	397
Tampa	17	2	0	71,300	448
Minneapolis	16	6	0	88,700	479
Saint Louis	16	2	0	70,000	415
Dallas	15	4	0	83,000	456
Dayton	14	2	0	65,000	399
Gary	14	5	0	58,100	401
Chicago	13	3	0	111,200	491

(7) A scale for adequate infrastructure, such as roads and sewers (1 = much more than needed, 2 = slightly more than needed, 3 = about right, 4 = less than needed, 5 = far less than needed).

Chicago had the lowest value of the regulatory index, 13, while San Francisco and Honolulu had the highest values at 29. The lowest possible score is 7, and the highest is 35. Figure 4.2 shows the plot of census house values against the unweighted sum of these variables. Notice the strong but nonlinear relationship between house prices and this regulatory index. That is, there appears to be a range of regulation where small changes have little measured effect. Past some threshold (roughly, when the index exceeds about 20 or 22), additional regulation has a strong effect.

Figure 4.2. *Median House Values by Development Regulation Index, 1990*

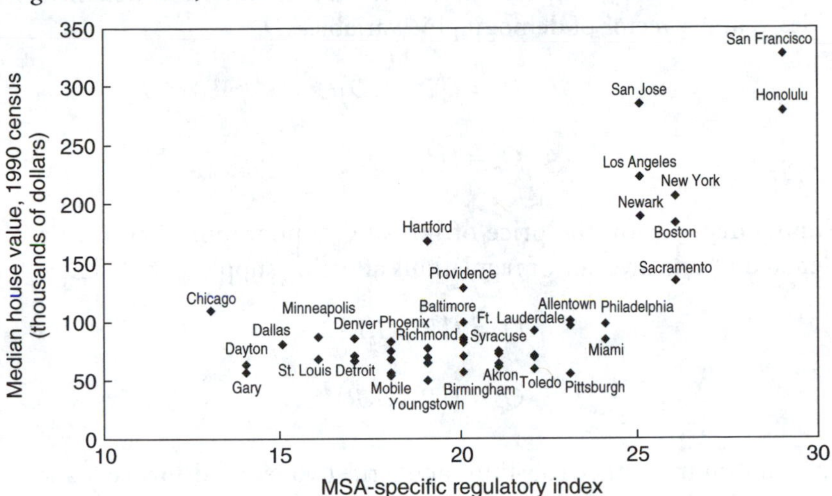

Source: Malpezzi (1996).

Table 4.3 also presents alternative regulatory indexes, based on statewide data on planning regulations and information about the presence and absence of rent control in a major part of the market. These measures are also related to prices and rents.

Of course, bivariate plots such as figure 4.2 are not by themselves conclusive. There are other variables, such as income, city growth, and physical geography, that could be correlated with regulation and could be the true cause of rising prices. To anticipate results, effects of the regulatory index in a fully specified model turn out to be remarkably similar to these two-way plots.[14]

A Model of Housing Prices, Including Regulation and Externalities

Now that we have our regulatory indexes, how do we use them? We have already noted that bivariate plots are suggestive rather than conclusive, and we have yet to consider all possible costs, or any possible benefits. We incorporate these indicators into a model of the housing market taken from Malpezzi (1996a).

We begin by considering the demand for rental and owner-occupied housing, respectively. Following a standard model of a housing market, the determinants of renter and owner demand for housing services demanded, Q_r and Q_o are the relative price of rental and owner-occupied housing (P_{hr} and P_{ho}, respectively); a vector of income and wealth variables, I, and a vector of demographic variables, D:

$$Q_r = f(P_{hr}, I, D)$$

$$Q_o = f(P_{ho}, I, D)$$

Supply depends on the price of housing; topographical constraints, denoted G; and a vector of regulations affecting supply, denoted R:[15]

$$Q_r = f(P_{hr}, G, R)$$

$$Q_o = f(P_{ho}, G, R)$$

In equilibrium, we then substitute and write two reduced-form equations of price determination:

$$P_{hr} = f_1(I, D, G, R, \varepsilon_1)$$

$$P_{ho} = f_2(I, D, G, R, \varepsilon_2)$$

The error terms ε_i are added because the relations are of course stochastic.

Next, we specify a tenure choice model driven by the relative prices of each tenure, income, and demographics, but where regulation may affect tenure. For instance, if it is nearly impossible to build apartments in a community, there will not be many renters in that community. Denoting T as the MSA specific rate of homeownership, we get

$$T = f_3(P_{ho}, P_{hr}, I, D, R, \varepsilon_3)$$

Notice that regulation R may have a direct effect on tenure, but it can also affect tenure indirectly through its partial effect on prices (see above).

Next, we specify the additional outcomes representing possible benefits of regulation. We hypothesize that, in addition to affecting P, Q, and T, regulation can potentially affect

- Average commutes (if and to the extent regulation can on balance correct congestion externalities);

- The extent of racial segregation (if and to the extent that regulation favors neighborhood "insiders" at the expense of "outsiders"); and
- Occupants' perceptions of the quality of their neighborhood (for reasons including those just listed).

Average commutes (denoted C), racial segregation (denoted S), and perceptions of neighborhood quality (denoted N), are potentially functions of income, housing prices, demographics (including racial composition of the MSA), and regulation.[16] The determinants of these outcomes can be represented as follows:

$$C = f_4\left(P_{ho}, P_{hr}, T, I, D, R, S, \varepsilon_4\right)$$

$$S = f_5\left(P_{ho}, P_{hr}, T, I, D, R, \varepsilon_5\right)$$

$$N = f_6\left(P_{ho}, P_{hr}, T, I, D, R, S, \varepsilon_6\right)$$

The hypotheses that segregation affects commutes and neighborhood opinions are conditionally entertained, but we have no prior theory suggesting that commutes or neighborhood ratings affect segregation. Again, regulation R can affect these outcomes directly, or indirectly through intervening variables such as house prices and tenure.

Thus, our initial model consists of seven equations: rental price, owner-occupied price, tenure choice, commute, segregation, and neighborhood quality, and an additional instrumental equation for the quantity of housing services. Generally, the model will be specified as linear in the logs of levels of variables (such as price, income, and population), and linear in changes, ratios (such as the percentage of owner-occupiers), and dummy variables.[17]

Population and income are significant determinants of rents, especially changes in the former and levels of the latter. Cities next to large parks and bodies of water may have higher rents, but the estimates are not statistically significant. Of the regulatory variables, the state index performs best.

For the value equation, most of the variables have the correct sign and small standard errors. The effect of metropolitan-level regulation is strongly quadratic. In order to get a measure of the joint effect of all regulatory variables, Malpezzi calculated the estimated percentage increases in rents and values given a movement from RCDUM = 0 to 1, and from first to third quartiles of the other regulatory variables.[18] Using this as one particular measure of moving from a lightly regulated environment to a heavily regulated environment, Malpezzi found, by using simulations, that rents would rise by 17 percent and house values by 51 percent. These are strong effects, but then these are fairly large changes in regulatory environments. In an auxiliary regression, Malpezzi also found that a change in regulation as suggested above reduced annual housing units constructed by an estimated 42 percent.

Regulation can affect tenure choice directly, and indirectly through intervening price variables. Regulation appears to have little direct effect; individual and joint tests do not generally reject the null. But indirect effects are also important. That is, we want to calculate the "impact multiplier":[19]

$$\frac{dT}{dR} = \frac{\partial T}{\partial R} + \frac{\partial T}{\partial P_{hr}} \cdot \frac{dP_{hr}}{dR} + \frac{\partial T}{\partial P_{ho}} \cdot \frac{dP_{ho}}{dR}$$

That is, the total effect of regulation on tenure choice,

$$\frac{\partial T}{\partial R}$$

has three components. The first effect, $\frac{\partial T}{\partial R}$, is the "direct effect" (if any) of regulations on tenure choice. The second effect, $\frac{\partial T}{\partial P_{hr}} \cdot \frac{dP_{hr}}{dR}$, comprise two parts: the effect more stringent regulation, R, has on rents (P_{hr}), time the effect a change in rent (P_{hr}) has on tenure. The third effect is the analogous effect regulation has through the asset price of owner-occupied housing; that is, $\frac{\partial T}{\partial P_{ho}} \cdot \frac{dP_{ho}}{dR}$

Regulation raises house values (which tends to reduce homeownership) and raises rents (which tends to increase homeownership). Regulation raises both rents and values, but values rise more than rents. Thus, the negative homeownership effect of regulation through an increase in value is greater than the corresponding positive homeownership effect from regulatory induced increases in rent. Taken together, the movement from a lightly regulated environment to a heavily regulated one (as defined above) decreases the homeownership rate by about 10 percentage points. For comparison, the median rate of homeownership for our sample of MSAs is 65 percent.

Regulation had little clear effect on our other measures of externalities, at least as estimated in this cross-MSA fashion. The joint effect of regulatory variables on segregation is not significant; neither is the effect of price. When we take the impact multipliers at face value, moving to a strict regulatory environment appears to reduce segregation substantially,[20] but the effect is not significant. Nothing in the equation seems to affect neighborhood ratings, except possibly the percentage of owner-occupiers, and on balance the impact multiplier is effectively zero.

The joint effect of regulatory variables on commute times (our proxy for congestion) also requires some thought. The direct regulatory variables have little effect, except for the state index, which reduces commutes. Markets with high values have more or less the same commutes as those with low values. But markets with higher rents have substantially lower commutes. The joint effects, taking the point estimates and constructing an impact multiplier, appear to reduce commutes slightly—the substantial movement in regulatory environment described above reduces commutes by about three minutes. For comparison, the average commute in our sample was 48 minutes.[21]

In summary, our results suggest that regulation raises housing rents and values and lowers homeownership rates. The former result is broadly consistent with a number of city-specific studies, some of which are discussed above, and lends credence to the idea that those individual market studies are part of a larger pattern. While this is to our knowledge the first study to focus directly on the relationship between regulation and tenure choice, it is broadly consistent with two prior literatures that suggest that tenure depends on relative prices of renting and owning, and that regulation raises rents, but somewhat less than house prices.

No statistically discernible effect was found on racial segregation or on neighborhood ratings. Effects on aggregate commutes were small. Thus, so far we have mainly documented the existence of costs without finding much in the way of benefits. That does not mean there are no benefits—there are many more possible benefit candidates, some of which we can measure and add (e.g., we can experiment with environmental and fiscal measures). And just because there is no benefit at the aggregate MSA level does not mean there is no benefit to *individual* inhabitants.

Why are these regulations so problematic? Virtually all are imposed by *local* governments. In the United States, local governments are small and fragmented, and relatively easily "captured" by insiders (current property owners), who benefit from controls and rising prices, to the detriment of outsiders (*potential* residents), who do not vote locally, run for office, or contribute funds to those who do. The Kean Commission recognized that regulations disproportionately benefit insiders, which is why most of its recommendations were not technical in nature, but political. The general thrust of the commission's report focused on the states as the potential agents for change. Local governments are directly responsible for most such regulations, but, as has just been argued, local policymakers have a systematic tendency to "overregulate," because they overweight the interests of insiders, who are their constituents. Larger, more inclusive levels of government would presumably better balance insiders' and outsiders' interests. States have some leverage over local governments, both legally and practically. In the U.S. federal system, local governments are legal creatures of the states. And as Downs (1991) points out, the federal government has greatly reduced its direct financial support—and hence its leverage—of local governments. States have relatively more fiscal clout with local governments than they did a decade ago. However, the states have shown little inclination to get involved so far. This could change, Downs points out, in response to a perceived statewide "crisis," or perhaps in response to a future federal mandate.

What's Happening to the Bottom of the Rental Market?

Two central facts about the bottom of the rental market are easy to characterize: Housing quality has improved dramatically for most low-income households, but they are paying much larger shares of their income. Figure 4.3, from data supplied by Weicher (1991) and U.S. Department of Housing and Urban Development (1996), illustrates. It is somewhat more difficult to explain the causes behind these two facts and derive clear policy implications.[22]

One widely held view is that, for reasons yet to be clearly established, the bottom has fallen out of the market, particularly the rental market. When we look at the overall rental market, vacancy rates, rents, and other indicators seem favorable: Production is up, vacancies are up, and contract rents are rising in line with other prices. Like the apocryphal statistician who puts his head in the oven and his feet in the freezer and decides, on average, he is comfortable,[23] these aggregate statistics mask gains in the top of the market and losses at the bottom. This point of view is well expressed in the Joint Center for Housing Studies' (1992) *State of the Nation's Housing:*

> Over the past 15 years, the supply of market-rate units renting for $300 or more has steadily grown while the supply of subsidized or otherwise affordable units has steadily shrunk. . . . Between 1974 and 1980, the number of privately owned

Figure 4.3. *Two Low-Income Housing Problems*

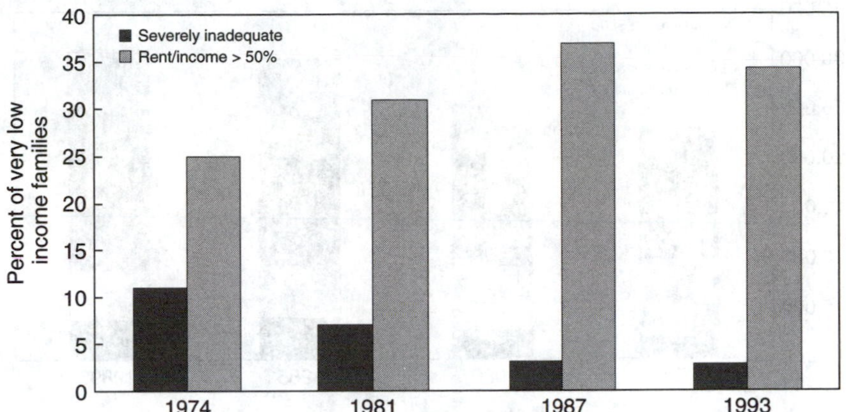

Source: Weicher (1991), U.S. Dept. of HUD (1996). Data comparability subject to verification. "Very low income" families have family size-adjusted incomes below 50 percent of area median.

> unsubsidized units renting for less than $300[24] fell by 1.4 million units . . . [and the number of such units] . . . fell from 5.3 million in 1985 to 5.0 million in 1989. . . . The supply of subsidized units, meanwhile, grew significantly. . . . This increase was not enough, however, to offset the losses of low-cost unsubsidized units. The total number of affordable rental units . . . declined from 9.9 million in 1974 to 9.3 million in 1980, and to 9.0 million in 1989 (4).

Figure 4.4 presents the Joint Center's data supporting this argument (from their Appendix A-12). The figure clearly shows a decline in number of private unassisted units with a gross rent of less than $300, and an increase in subsidized units that does not quite make up the difference.

Is there another side to the story? First, some of the same arguments made in the affordability section can be made here. Utilities rose substantially during the 1980s, while contract rents lagged behind. And utility payments do not vary much by income.[25] For yet another perspective on figure 4.4, reexamine the relationship between subsidized and low-cost units. Of the roughly 4 million federally subsidized households, just more than one million households receive vouchers or Section 8 Existing certificates. To the extent that these allowances are used in low-cost housing,[26] units that appear to disappear from the low-income stock have not disappeared; they have just been subsidized. At most, if the 1,060,000 certificates and vouchers in 1989 had been put in place since 1974, and if they all came out of the below-$300 private stock, the drop in low-cost private rental would be reduced by 38 percent. What of the 3 million supply-side

Figure 4.4. *Number of Rental Units, By Real Gross Rent, 1974–1989*

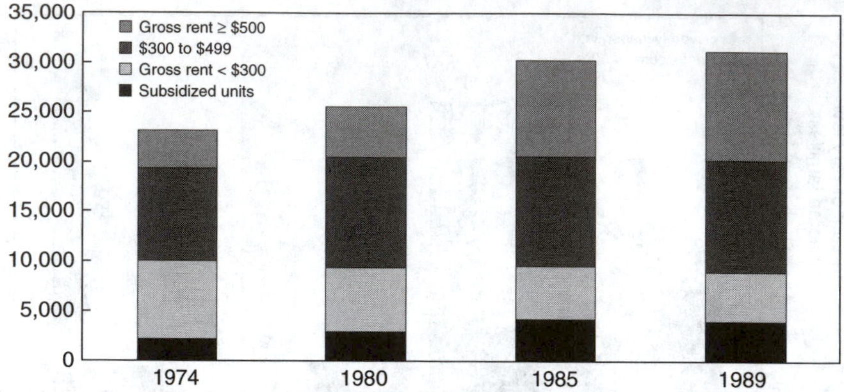

Source: Joint Center for Housing Studies (1992).
Note: Rents in 1989 dollars.

subsidized units in place in 1989? Murray (1983) and Swan (1973) have estimated the degree of substitution between subsidized and purely private housing construction. Murray's results, discussed in detail in chapter 2, suggest for every 100 subsidized units built, 85 units are ultimately removed from the stock. While Murray does not address this issue, we would expect those losses to come largely from the bottom of the stock. Only if public construction is a net addition to the stock should we be surprised at figure 4.4.

Despite our critical look at some oft-cited aggregate data, we are far from sanguine about low-cost supply. The data just presented are open to various interpretations and are not sufficient to settle the elasticity of supply for this market segment. Ideally, we would like to examine *variation* in the markets for low-cost housing. Housing markets are local and diverse, and it behooves us to analyze disaggregated data to see if the bottom is firmer in some cities than others.

A natural place for economists to begin the study of low-cost housing is to examine its relative price. Thibodeau (1992) published an extensive set of MSA-specific price indexes for units of varying quality levels. Using American Housing Survey data, he estimated tenure-specific hedonic indexes in 59 large metropolitan areas, and then used the results to price various representative bundles (vectors representing metropolitan averages of housing characteristics for various categories). We use his results for the average metropolitan "substandard" rental units and average "standard existing" rental units.[27] The ratio of these two predicted rents is our relative price of substandard housing. Thibodeau also estimated the number of substandard and total rental units in each market, permitting straightforward calculation of the percentage of each MSA's housing stock that is in each category.

Malpezzi and Green (1996) plot this relative price measure against the share of substandard rental units in the stock. At one extreme, Colorado Springs has only 5 percent substandard rental (by this particular definition), and the estimated price of a representative substandard unit is 95 percent of the estimated price of a standard quality existing unit. At the other extreme, 23 percent of New York's housing is substandard, and its relative price is about 77 percent of a standard unit. Kansas City and Birmingham also have low relative prices for substandard units, even though it is less than 15 percent of their rental markets. Low-quality housing thus exhibits typical market behavior: It is relatively inexpensive where there is a lot of it, and expensive where it is more scarce.[28] The slope of the regression line of the relative price of substandard housing on the share of market housing substandard is –0.63, with a corresponding *t*-statistic of 2.9. There is a less than 1 chance in 100 of observing a *t*-statistic that size if there were no negative relationship.

But this result is merely descriptive; what *determines* the relative price of substandard housing? One possible determinant is the regulatory environment in each market. Malpezzi and Green (1996) argue that the benefits of some restrictive urban regulations accrue to middle- and upper-income households but that costs are borne disproportionately by the poor. This occurs because land-use regulation tends to restrict the development of low-cost housing.

If the latter point were true, we would expect higher *relative* prices for low-quality units in heavily regulated markets. And we do ondeed find that the relative price of low-quality units is strongly correlated with the supply of land available for development.[29] Of course, this is still descriptive. Let us now focus on the effect of regulation, controlling for other variables, on the first- and third-quartile prices in the market. Specifically, we extend the results from the question above, which asked how regulation affects the housing market. There, we examined the relationship between regulatory measures and median house prices and rents; now we replace the median price with the first and third quartiles of each metropolitan area's distribution.

Another question raised above and in some of the literature is whether filtering works. In order for filtering to work, new units, which are mostly at or near the top of the quality level of the stock, must not simply displace low-quality units. Thibodeau's (1992) count of substandard rental units is presented for each year of the metropolitan American Housing Surveys. Most MSAs were surveyed in the mid-1970s and again in the early 1980s. Thus, we can construct the annual growth in the substandard stock during this period and compare that growth to additions from new construction. We measure the latter using a three-year average of permits per capita near the end of the period. Malpezzi and Green (1996) show that the correlation is clear: High-quality new construction is associated with growth in the low-quality stock as well. More specifically, our results imply that new units constructed each year produce a roughly 2.5 percent increase in the stock of substandard rental units. The number is quite substantial, considering that the number of permits in 1995 was equal to slightly less than 1.4 percent of the existing stock at the beginning of that year. Consequently, it is fair to say that the stock of substandard housing remains a fairly fixed share of all housing, lending support to the filtering hypothesis: Regardless of the quality of new construction, enough of the old stock is converted into lower-quality housing to keep this share of the market constant.[30]

Interestingly, the effect of this change is stronger at the bottom of the market than it is at the middle and top. Malpezzi and Green (1996) show that the corresponding simulated effects on third-quartile, median, and first-quartile rents are increases of about 17, 18, and 21 percent, respectively. That is, the percentage rent increases from more stringent regulation are largest at the bottom of the market. In the owner market, the simulated increase in value from the regulatory shift is 49 percent at the third quartile, 53 percent at the median, and 60 percent at the bottom. These differences between effects at top and bottom, though modest, are consistent with the notion that stricter regulations tend to be more binding on the bottom of the housing market.

Our final look at the bottom of the market (or at least the middle to bottom) focuses on vacancy rates. In the aggregate, current rental vacancy rates are about 8 percent, somewhat above their 25-year average of 6.6 percent. But given that we have observed a decline in the supply of affordable units, we must look to see how vacancy rates vary by rent levels. Unusually low vacancy rates for low-rent units, compared with the rest of the market, can be viewed as evidence that the bottom of the market is not functioning properly, because it is unable to meet a market need.

Recent data suggest that, in the aggregate, vacancy rates are actually higher in the low-to-moderate range and lower in both the very low cost and high-cost ranges. For example, in the final quarter of 2000, units on offer for $200 to $299 had a 10.0 percent vacancy rate, while those over $500 were at 6.3 percent. The relatively high vacancy rates for units going for between $200 to $400 may appear puzzling, given the high rent burdens among low-income households. Participants at a 1990 Urban Institute housing policy seminar advanced two possible explanations. First, there is a mismatch between the size of families and the number of rooms available among low-cost rental housing; and second, the vacant units at the bottom are so dilapidated that most will never be rented even at these low offered rents.[31] But these observations are not an indictment of how well the market "works"—that is, how well it responds appropriately to economic incentives. Available square feet or bedrooms per person are certainly measures of quality, as is the general state of a unit's repair. If lower-quality housing is available at a lower price, and low-income people are choosing not to live in it, the market is operating properly, and the problem becomes the entirely normative issue of what constitutes an appropriate minimum living standard.

But these aggregate data have serious problems. First, the census data are not stable. In the late 1980s, the vacancy rate in the highest rent category was sometimes more than double the national average, while in the lowest rent category it was as low as half the national average. Since the Census Bureau does not like to release data with substantial sampling errors, this must reflect either substantial nonsampling error or true underlying instability. Secondly, the data do not deal with spatial issues. For instance, the fact that vacancy rates for low-cost housing are high relative to higher-cost rental housing in a place like New Orleans is not particularly useful information for low-income households seeking the economic opportunity necessary to shed their low-income status.

Let us examine variation in low- and moderate-income vacancy rates among U.S. metropolitan areas. HUD publishes estimates of vacancy rates for units renting below the fair market rent (FMR) in 44 large metropolitan areas, and corresponding vacancy rates for the entire market (see U.S. Department of Housing and Urban Development, 1992, table 9). In the typical large MSA, about 60 percent of rental units are priced below FMR, ranging from 81 percent in New Orleans to 43 percent in Dallas.

In the late 1980s, 25 of 44 MSAs had higher vacancy rates for such units than for the market as a whole; 10 markets had the same rates; and in only 9 markets were rental markets tighter than average for units renting below FMR. (The vacancy rates were estimated using metropolitan AHS data for the latest years available, ranging from 1987 to 1990.) Just as important, when we performed a simple regression using per capita income to explain the difference between vacancy rates in the stock below FMR and the stock at or above FMR, the *t*-statistic on per capita income is less than one. Therefore, low-income people in areas with strong economic opportunities will not necessarily face unusually low vacancy rates in the low-cost sector.

In summary, in this section we have used three indicators—prices, production, and vacancy rates—to investigate whether the bottom of the U.S. housing market works. All these indicators suggest that the bottom of the housing market works similarly to all other markets—when it is allowed to. When overly stringent local land-use regulations are imposed, however, the relative price of low-cost housing rises, production falls, and vacancies tighten.

Does the Housing Market Work for Minorities?

Relationships between race and housing markets are complicated. We will briefly investigate six interrelated questions:

(1) Are U.S. housing markets segregated?
(2) Is there significant discrimination in the markets for housing and related markets, particularly finance?
(3) What effects are observed on prices blacks pay for housing, relative to whites?
(4) What effects are observed on tenure choice?
(5) What are the relationships between race, housing location, and employment?
(6) What is known about race and the provision of housing finance?[32]

Perhaps the first point to be made in this section is that the great majority of published research on race and housing has been on black Americans. Hispanics, Native Americans, and other racial and ethnic groups have been relatively neglected. Most of our discussion will focus on blacks, but we will try to address housing issues with respect to other minority groups as well. We also note the real difficulties that arise in any classification of households by race or ethnicity. Yinger (1995) provides a brief discussion of this important problem.[33]

It is well known that racial and ethnic minorities are not as well housed as white citizens; illustrative indicators can be found in figure 4.5.

Figure 4.5. *Incidence of Housing Problems, by Renter's Race*

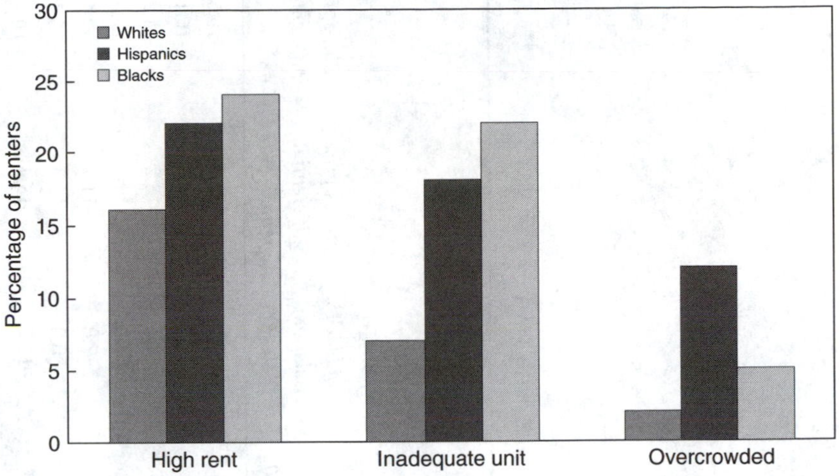

Source: 1993 American Housing Survey.

But it is also well known that minorities have lower average incomes than whites; thus many—but not all—of these housing differences can be accounted for by differences in income.

Are Housing Markets Segregated?

That *segregation* exists is not in doubt. Casual observation of most American cities confirms this, as do any number of empirical studies. One measure, for example, is the percentage of a city's blacks that live in neighborhoods with 90 percent or more blacks. Reynolds Farley recently tabulated this data for 50 metropolitan areas[34] and found that, on average, 37 percent of the black population lived in such neighborhoods in 1990. Eight large MSAs had more than half their black population living in such neighborhoods; Chicago had 71 percent, followed by Saint Louis with 70 percent. But on the other hand, this 37 percent in 1990 was down from 44 percent isolated, on average, in 1980. By this measure, segregation increased only in Detroit (57 to 61 percent), Buffalo (48 to 51 percent), and New York City (28 to 31 percent).[35] Table 4.4 presents data for 20 large metropolitan areas, sorted by the black population in 1990.[36]

U.S. cities are segregated by income as well as race. Significant segregation also exists by ethnicity, especially for Native Americans and various

Table 4.4. *Race and the Housing Market in Selected Metropolitan Statistical Areas (MSA)*

Largest city in MSA	*1990 black population (1,000s)*	*Percent of MSA population black, 1990*	*Farley's measure of black isolation, 1980*	*Farley's measure of black isolation, 1990*	*Percentage change in Farley's measure of black isolation, 1980–90*	*Black price differential, renters (%)*	*Black price differential, owners (%)*
New York	2,250	26	28	31	10.7	−0.7	−16.6
Chicago	1,333	22	80	71	−11.3	−6.6	−16.1
Washington	1,042	27	46	37	−19.6	−18.2	−24.2
Los Angeles	993	11	20	7	−65.0	−12.2	−17.5
Detroit	943	22	57	61	7.0	−11.7	−2.6
Philadelphia	930	19	53	53	0.0	−13.3	−25.3
Atlanta	736	26	49	43	−12.2	−18.4	−16.7

Baltimore	616	26	58	53	−8.6	−0.5	−17.8
Houston	611	19	50	30	−40.0	−13.4	−18.3
New Orleans	430	35	50	47	−6.0	−9.1	−9.7
Saint Louis	423	17	73	70	−4.1	−10.3	−19.1
Newark	423	23	44	41	−6.8	−2.9	−19.5
Dallas	411	16	51	29	−43.1	−15.3	−10.3
Memphis	399	41	59	58	−1.7	−16.3	−12.4
Miami	398	21	41	33	−19.5	−13.2	−20.7
Norfolk	398	29	40	24	−40.0	−15.0	−10.8
Cleveland	356	19	67	67	0.0	−12.7	−25.2
Oakland	304	15	16	5	−68.8	—	—
Charlotte	232	20	33	32	−3.0	—	—
Boston	210		25	19	−24.0	−10.8	−23.5

Source: Farley (1991); Malpezzi, Ozanne, and Thibodean (1980).
Notes: — =not available.

Hispanic ethnic groups.[37] But the most significant and persistent segregation is that of African Americans.

Several recent studies have shown that taken as a whole, racial segregation is declining from a peak circa 1970; but it is declining slowly in general and hardly at all in some metropolitan areas.[38] Segregation is generally highest in Northeastern and Midwestern cities, and lowest in the South and West.

What are some of the correlates of segregation? A simple analysis can be undertaken by regressing Farley's Black Isolation Index for 1990 against its determinants.[39] This index is the percentage of the black population that lives in neighborhoods that are 90 percent or more black. The most statistically significant effect in this simple model is that in cities with higher proportions of black citizens, blacks are more segregated. Interestingly, in cities with higher proportions of Hispanic citizens, blacks are less segregated. Faster growing cities have lower degrees of black isolation. This result is not surprising, since the creation of new housing even on the city's fringe can open up a wide range of housing possibilities for minority as well as other households. The overall size of the metro area and the poverty rate have no statistically significant effect on black isolation.

Is There Discrimination in the Housing Market?

Whether observed segregation is caused by market forces or by systematic *discrimination* in the housing market is open to discussion. Segregation may be related to overt discrimination in the housing marketplace, or it may occur in the absence of such discrimination as a result of individual decisions by consumers in the majority population, the minority population, or both.

A number of studies support the idea that whites prefer to live with other whites.[40] While black preferences have not been studied as often, it appears blacks have a higher preference than whites for integration.[41] Classic papers by Schelling (1969, 1972) demonstrate theoretically that when whites and blacks have such divergent preferences it is very difficult to obtain a stable racial equilibrium in an integrated neighborhood. Thus, segregation can occur as a market process if preferences diverge. Segregation can also occur due to overt discrimination in real estate brokerage (or finance, a point to which we return later). Of course, possible explanations for segregation are not mutually exclusive.

Race and Housing Prices

What effects do segregation and discrimination have on *housing prices* paid by minorities? The most obvious market effect of systematic white prejudice would be premiums paid by whites to live in white areas (or its obverse, discounts for black neighborhoods). Results from many (but not all) empirical studies are consistent with this hypothesis.[42] For example, using AHS hedonic indexes, Follain and Malpezzi (1981) find blacks consistently pay less for both renter and owner-occupied housing.[43] Simple statistics can be found in figure 4.6.

But these studies did not, in general, control for the location and racial composition of their neighborhoods. Further, there is a range of economic models of racial discrimination, some of which yield black premiums and some of which yield black discounts.[44] It is quite possible for discrimination to cause blacks to pay higher prices for housing outside black neighborhoods, but that in marketwide hedonics this effect is swamped by the lower housing prices faced by the majority of blacks who do not live in predominantly white areas. This may account for the studies that have found black *premiums* rather than discounts.[45]

The hypothesis that such price differentials confound different neighborhood and individual price efforts can be tested in three ways. First, and least directly, this hypothesis would lead us to expect marketwide

Figure 4.6. *Rent Burdens, by Income, for Blacks and All Renters*

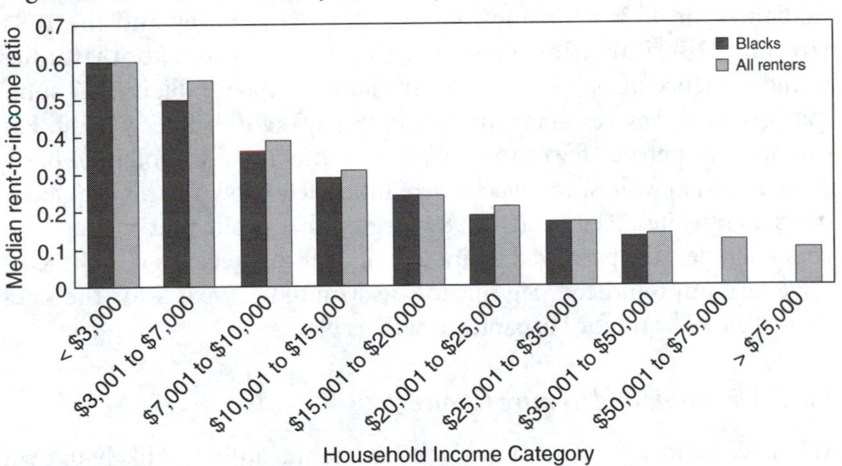

Source: 1993 American Housing Survey.

estimates of black discounts to be smaller when the market is less segregated. In fact, when we plot Malpezzi, Ozanne, and Thibodeau's (1980) estimated discounts by Farley's isolation measure, there is indeed a tendency for more segregated MSAs to have steeper discounts for blacks. However, there is great variation around the trend, suggesting that variation in segregation per se does not explain variation in the discounts fully.

The second method is to apply hedonic regression models, but to control for the racial composition of the neighborhood as well as the household. Chambers (1992) was able to use a data set for Chicago that permitted identification of racial neighborhood composition as well as race of the respondent. He constructed separate dummy variables for blacks in black areas and blacks in white areas. While Chambers found that the discount generally fell as neighborhoods became more integrated, he did not find a statistically significant actual premium for blacks in white areas. Kiel and Zabel (1996) supplemented AHS data from Denver, Philadelphia, and Chicago with neighborhood data. Without the neighborhood data, Kiel and Zabel found substantial black discounts, but they generally found that neighborhood effects, including race, dominated the race of the individual household. This is consistent with Follain and Malpezzi's interpretation of the racial discount as a neighborhood effect.

The third test involves matched-pair testing of real estate brokers' behavior to determine differences in the number of potential units recommended to and shown to similar shoppers of different races or ethnic background. Two careful and large-scale studies have been carried out focusing on the discriminatory behavior by real estate market participants: the 1977 Housing Markets Practices Survey and the 1991 Housing Discrimination Study.[46] Using paired testers, both studies found evidence of significant discriminatory behavior. Figure 4.7 summarizes some key results from Turner, Struyk, and Yinger (1991). For example, 48 percent fewer units were recommended to potential black renters than to whites, and blacks were ultimately shown 10 percent fewer units than whites. Newberger (1989) argues that profit-maximizing brokers will reflect the perceived prejudices of their market even if they themselves are unprejudiced. Significant discrimination exists for the sales market as well, and for Hispanics as well as blacks.

Race, Demand, and Tenure Choice

When we control for incomes, blacks are significantly less likely to own their homes, as shown in figure 4.8. In the 1960s and 1970s, when house

Figure 4.7. *Homeownership Rates, by Income Decile and Race/Ethnicity*

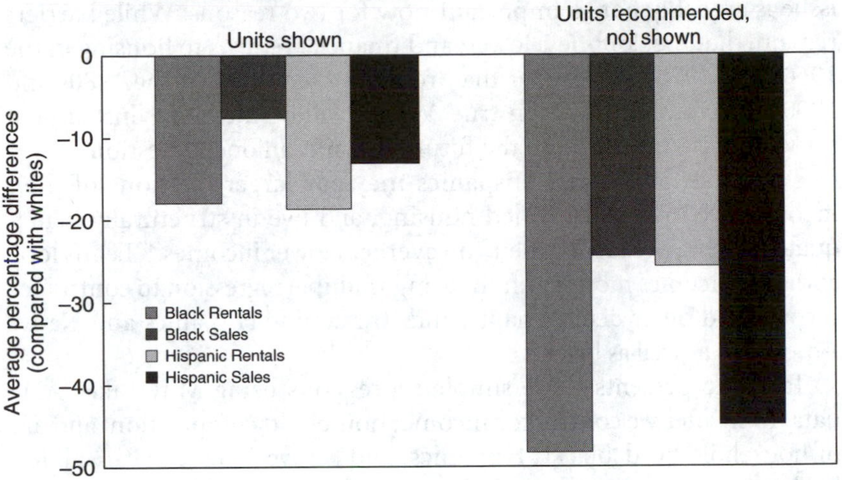

Units shown
Units recommended, not shown
Average percentage differences (compared with whites)
0
−10
−20
−30
−40
−50
Black Rentals
Black Sales
Hispanic Rentals
Hispanic Sales

Source: Turner, Struyk, and Yinger (1991).

Figure 4.8. *Discrimination in Housing Availability*

Homeownership rate (percent)
100
80
60
40
20
0
White
Black
American Indian
Asian
Hispanic
1
2
3
4
5
6
7
8
9
10
Household income decile

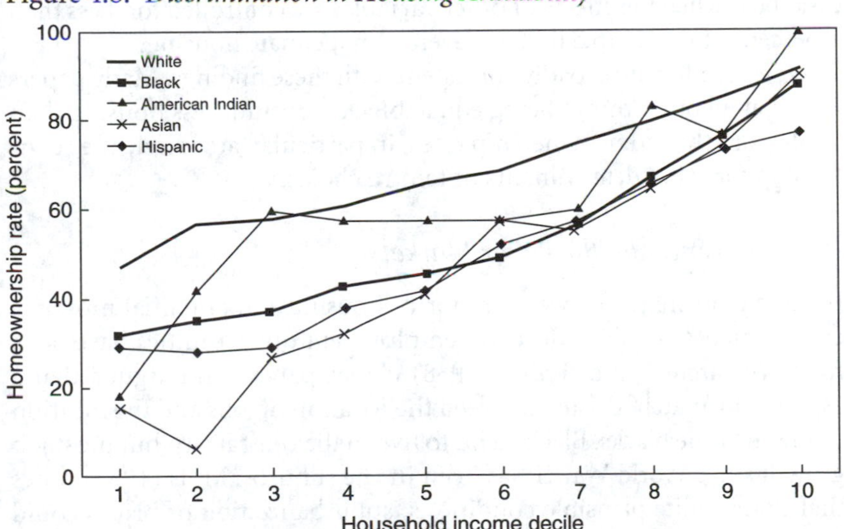

Source: 1993 American Housing Survey.

prices rose rapidly and inexpensive fixed-rate debt was readily available, the social and financial barriers to blacks entering the owner-occupied housing market prevented them from easily accumulating wealth. The issue is arguably not so important now for two reasons: While barriers remain, they are doubtless lower; and financial returns to housing in the 1960s and 1970s were better than returns to equities. In the 1980s and 1990s the converse has been true. Which will be the better instrument for wealth accumulation in the future remains an open question.

Of course, blacks and Hispanics may pay larger fractions of their income, live in more crowded housing, and live in structurally inadequate housing because of their (on average) lower incomes.[47] Let us look at these outcomes more carefully, using multiple regression to control for income and other determinants, and to examine Hispanics and Native Americans as well as blacks.

Table 4.5 presents some simple regressions using Milwaukee AHS data. Even after we control for income, household composition, and age of household head, blacks, Hispanics, and Native Americans are all less likely to own their homes than whites.[48] Hispanics and Native Americans are more likely to live in crowded housing than whites, although blacks and whites are about equal on this measure. Relationships between housing inadequacy and race and ethnicity, on the other hand, tend to disappear when the effects of other variables are controlled for. Less than 2 percent of the sample lives in severely inadequate housing.

Other studies are broadly consistent with these findings. Many papers find that all other things being equal, blacks consume less housing than whites and that homeownership rates, in particular, are lower, after controlling for other determinants of tenure choice.[49]

Race, Housing, and the Labor Market

Is there a mismatch between minority housing and potential minority employment? Possible effects on employment opportunities have been much researched since Kain's (1968) classic paper. Kain argued that a "spatial mismatch" existed between the location of jobs and the location of low-income blacks. Blacks tend to live in the central city, but most job growth since World War II has been in the suburbs. Mills (1985) notes that under quite plausible conditions, suburbanization of blacks could in fact stimulate central-city employment as well.[50]

Recently, the debate has been revived by William Julius Wilson (1987, 1996), who strongly supports the hypothesis of a link between household

Table 4.5-A. *Milwaukee Linear Tenure Choice Regression*

Dependent Variable: Homeownership Dummy
Owner = 1, cash renter = 0

Source	DF	F value	Prob > F	Adj. R-squared
Model	10	209.12	0.0001	0.3879
Error	3274			
C Total	3284			

Variable	*Parameter estimate*	*Standard error*	*T for H0: parameter = 0*	*Prob > |t|*
Intercept	–2.1692	0.1157	–18.8	0.0001
Log HH income	0.1631	0.0117	14.0	0.0001
Number of adults in HH	0.0182	0.0105	1.7	0.0829
Number of children in HH	0.0401	0.0068	5.9	0.0001
Married dummy	0.2016	0.0179	11.3	0.0001
Household head's age	0.0307	0.0025	12.2	0.0001
Household head's age, squared	–0.0002	0.0000	–8.4	0.0001
Black respondent	–0.0801	0.0235	–3.4	0.0006
Hispanic respondent	–0.0950	0.0432	–2.2	0.0279
Native American respondent	–0.2314	0.1601	–1.4	0.1485
Dummy for receive housing subsidy	–0.2987	0.0310	–9.6	0.0001

Table 4.5-B. *Milwaukee Crowding Regression*

Dependent Variable: Persons Per Room

Source	DF	F value	Prob > F	Adj. R-squared
Model	10	595.05	0.0001	
Error	3296			
C Total	3306			

Variable	*Parameter estimate*	*Standard error*	*T for H0: parameter = 0*	*Prob > |t|*
Intercept	1.0112	0.0430	23.5	0.0001
Log HH income	–0.0648	0.0043	–14.9	0.0001
Number of adults in HH	0.1355	0.0039	34.7	0.0001

(*continued*)

Table 4.5-B. *Continued*

Variable	*Parameter estimate*	*Standard error*	*T for H0: parameter = 0*	*Prob > |t|*
Number of children in HH	0.1279	0.0025	50.8	0.0001
Married dummy	0.0125	0.0066	1.9	0.0598
Household head's age	−0.0073	0.0009	−7.8	0.0001
Household head's age, squared	0.0000	0.0000	5.4	0.0001
Black respondent	0.0055	0.0087	0.6	0.5267
Hispanic respondent	0.0555	0.0160	3.5	0.0005
Native American respondent	0.1641	0.0598	2.7	0.0061
Dummy for receive housing subsidy	0.0090	0.0116	0.8	0.4353

Table 4.5-C. *Milwaukee Severe Housing Inadequacy Regression*

Dependent Variable: Severely Inadequate, HUD Definition

Source	DF	F value	Prob > F	Adj. R-squared
Model	10	12.32	0.0001	
Error	3296			
C Total	3306			

Variable	*Parameter estimate*	*Standard error*	*T for H0: parameter = 0*	*Prob > |t|*
Intercept	0.3032	0.0368	8.3	0.0001
Log HH income	−0.0284	0.0037	−7.7	0.0001
Number of adults in HH	−0.0054	0.0033	−1.6	0.1045
Number of children in HH	0.0006	0.0022	0.3	0.7780
Married dummy	−0.0012	0.0057	−0.2	0.8287
Household head's age	0.0012	0.0008	1.5	0.1420
Household head's age, squared	0.0000	0.0000	−2.2	0.0275
Black respondent	−0.0008	0.0074	−0.1	0.9134
Hispanic respondent	0.0188	0.0136	1.4	0.1689
Native American respondent	−0.0207	0.0511	−0.4	0.6855
Dummy for receive housing subsidy	−0.0431	0.0099	−4.4	0.0001

(and housing) location and employment opportunities. Several papers claim to find little or contradictory evidence to the spatial mismatch hypothesis.[51] But most careful recent studies support Kain's position.[52] Ihlandfeldt (1993) has extended the model to Hispanics and finds evidence of significant spatial mismatch for these individuals as well.

Those who focus on decentralization strategies find the evidence from the Gautreaux program heartening. Named after one of the original plaintiffs, the Gautreaux program was instituted in 1976 by the Chicago Housing Authority in response to a lawsuit brought against them for racially discriminatory practices. To simplify, under this program a nonprofit agency selects a modest number of black households each year, provides them with housing vouchers, and facilitates their move to (generally more integrated) suburbs. Participating households are carefully screened beforehand and are provided with extensive counseling and other outreach services, in addition to the vouchers.

Several evaluative studies by James Rosenbaum and his associates show that participating households do better post-move in employment and child school performance, among other improvements.[53] Of course, any attempt to generalize the Gautreaux program's evidence would be hampered by the program's small size (about 7,000 households over more than 20 years), the intensive resources available to each participant (unlikely to be replicated in a truly large-scale national program), and, not least, the fact that those households who applied to participate and who survived the screening process were not representative of the larger population.

It is important to keep the spatial mismatch hypothesis in perspective. Few advocates would argue it is the only or even the largest determinant of racial differences in incomes and other economic and social outcomes; race matters independently of space.[54]

Race and Housing Finance

Possible racial discrimination in the housing *finance* market has been a controversial issue, especially since the *Atlanta Constitution* and the *Wall Street Journal* published a series of articles based on Home Mortgage Disclosure Act (HMDA) data collected by the Federal Reserve Board (Dedman 1988). HMDA data show clearly that blacks are rejected for loans much more often than whites. By itself this means little, however, because blacks may simply have lower incomes, have poorer credit histories, or buy in riskier neighborhoods than whites. A number of studies have tried to control for these variables to see if there is a racial residual that would indicate discrimination. Many papers have been written, but the debate still rages.

As mentioned above, potential racial discrimination in mortgage markets hit the public consciousness with the publication of a series of stories in the *Atlanta Constitution,* followed by articles based on simple tabulations of HMDA data in other major newspapers. In one widely cited HMDA tabulation, blacks were found to be rejected for mortgages in 34 percent of cases; Hispanics, 22 percent of the time; and whites, 14 percent of the time.[55]

HMDA data include several other variables likely to be correlated with the expected profitability of the mortgage, such as household income and location of property within the census tract. Generally, multivariate analysis using these variables reduces but does not eliminate racial differences in rejection rates. However, the HMDA data do not include a number of other variables that would be expected to be important predictors of expected profitability, and hence acceptance/rejection, such as the applicant's credit rating. In 1990 the Federal Reserve Bank of Boston undertook to collect such additional data from cooperating Boston-area banks. Munnell et al. (1992) found that once credit histories and loan-to-value ratios were accounted for, the racial differential in Boston rejection rates fell from a ratio of 2.7 to 1.6. That is, using the Boston white average of an 11 percent rejection rate, blacks in identical circumstances would be rejected an estimated 17 percent of the time. Clearly this is still a serious difference.

The Boston Fed study has been subject to intense debate. For example, Liebowitz (1993) claims that once a small number of outlying observations are removed from the data, the racial differential disappears.[56] Zandi (1993) argues that when additional variables are added, including subjective measures of whether the applicant meets lending guidelines, the racial effect diminishes. Carr and Megbolugbe (1993) review and critique several such criticisms, and reestimate the Boston Fed model with changes suggested by the critics. In general, they find that the size of the racial effect is not terribly robust with respect to specification, although they note that a racial differential persists in most specifications. They also point out that including subjective variables on the right-hand side is not desirable when the whole point of the exercise is to test for discrimination.

Another criticism of the Boston Fed study (and of many of the follow-up studies, both pro and con) is that examining only one stage of the lending process—whether the mortgage is approved, given that an application has been submitted. Other studies, such as those that look at default rates by race, are also generally single-equation models.[57] Yezer, Phillips, and Trost (1994) criticize single-equation models of the accept-reject decision, noting that these models assume that loan terms are independent of the underwriting decision. This implies that loan officers do not tell borrowers that they can avoid rejection by increasing down payments, providing more documentation of assets, securing coborrowers, and so on. It also implies that borrowers who are initially rejected never ask for their loan to be reconsidered after enhancing their credit by increasing the down payment or by getting cosigners. Yezer, Phillips, and Trost maintain that in the Boston Fed data set, borrowers routinely ask to have their application reconsidered, and consequently, the threat of rejection is a reason for increasing the down payment and not an independent causal of how variables affect discrimination as assumed in single equation models. The fact that the loan underwriting process often involves negotiations could well produce false positive indications of discrimination where none exist.

LaCour-Little (1996) undertook a simulation study to see how serious the problem might be. LaCour-Little generated a series of synthetic data sets, then deliberately introduced varying levels of discrimination, defined as increasing the probability of rejecting a black applicant given the application's characteristics. Application characteristics can be defined to mirror observed differences in black-white income, loan-to-value ratio, and so on, or they can be adjusted (e.g., to make black and white applications have the same distribution of characteristics). The degree of lender bias can be varied from 0 percent (equal probabilities by race, given credit history, loan-to-value, etc.) to 100 percent (all blacks denied, whatever their situation). Once such a synthetic data set is constructed—where we *know* the level of discrimination because it is built into the data—different statistical models can be applied, to see whether the estimated degree of discrimination mirrors the "true" level. In fact, LaCour-Little found that the most common single-equation models consistently indicated discrimination when none was present, except in the (implausible) case where whites and blacks have the same distribution of incomes, credit histories, and so on. Of course these results do not answer the question of whether lending discrimination exists; rather, they suggest that many currently cited studies, both pro and con, based on single-equation estimation may give misleading results.

In a popular magazine article, the economist Gary Becker, one of the pioneers of economic models of discrimination, noted that loan default rates for blacks and whites are roughly equal in Boston.[58] Becker argues that if blacks were discriminated against, we would observe lower default rates for blacks. Several authors have challenged Becker's line of argument. Carr and Megbolugbe (1993) argue that racially disparate treatment remains illegitimate even if in the event such default rates are equal. Yinger (1995) points out that

> The average white applicant may be a very low credit risk while the average minority applicant is a moderate credit risk; if so, the average creditworthiness of minority loan recipients could be below that of whites even if minorities must meet a higher hurdle to get a loan (76).

Berkovec et al. (1994) is probably the best-known study to date that examines the Becker hypothesis. Using data on FHA-insured loans, matched to census tract data to construct neighborhood variables, Berkovec et al. estimate logit models of default. They find that, if anything, blacks are more likely to default than whites, all things being equal—the opposite of the Becker hypothesis prediction under discrimination. Hispanic, Asian, and Native-American borrowers are indistinguishable from whites in the Berkovec et al. model.

However, the Berkovec et al. study is also subject to criticism.[59] First, there are the general problems of specification and simultaneity discussed above. Berkovec et al. had a rich, but not unassailable, data set; FHA-insured borrowers are not representative of all borrowers; and their model is a single equation. Yinger (1995) also notes that studies that focus on the risk of default neglect the fact that, conditional on default, losses may be lower for blacks than whites.[60] Thus, if proportional losses (conditional on default) were smaller for blacks, equal default rates would imply lower-than-expected losses and higher profitability for lending to blacks.

The discussion so far has focused on possible discrimination regarding the borrower. Lenders (and others, such as appraisers or insurers) could also discriminate against the property or, more specifically, on the basis of neighborhood. Such discrimination is called redlining.[61] The Boston Fed study also tested for redlining by including the racial composition of the property's neighborhood, and found no significant effect. But other studies find that when total financial flows to a neighborhood are examined, black neighborhoods receive less financing than white ones, provided that the studies control for income and some other neighborhood characteristics.[62]

This brief review has only scratched the surface of one of the more difficult, contentious, and important housing-related research issues today. Problems of data collection and specification remain, and different analysts have different—often strong—prior beliefs. Many economists find it hard to believe that financial institutions would give up profitable lending opportunities to indulge in racial prejudice. A reasonable corollary is that the consolidation of the banking industry, and the rise of the secondary market, makes mortgage lending more of an arm's-length transaction than ever, presumably reducing such discrimination as may exist. A counterargument is that such disparate treatment may be implicit or unwitting, or at least subtle, as when a loan officer provides better assistance or coaching to an applicant of his or her own race or ethnicity.[63] Further, there is a documented institutional history to discrimination.[64] For example, prior to 1947 the FHA limited underwriting in racially mixed areas, and until the mid-1970s appraisal texts recommended lowering appraisals in nonwhite neighborhoods.[65] Thus, it is perhaps not surprising that some other economists studying the problem have strong opinions in the other direction. Careful experiments based on the paired-testing principle (as applied to the field brokerage) might go a long way toward resolving these issues for many, but in today's legal environment, submitting such synthetic mortgage applications can be problematic.

Final Comment

Most research on all these issues has focused on black Americans. To date surprisingly little research has been done on Hispanics, and even less on Native Americans, Asians, or other racial and ethnic groups.[66]

Early expectations were that fair housing legislation would (in the words of HUD's first secretary, Robert Weaver) lead to "a situation in which white and nonwhite families not only live in a spatially mixed community but also accept one another, associate without self-consciousness, and do not look forward to release from each other as neighbors."[67] Despite undeniable progress, the United States remains far from this goal.

Is Homelessness a Housing Problem?

The most severe problems in the purview of housing economists are those of the homeless. They are also the most complex. Many hypotheses have been advanced in the past decade. Among them are that homelessness is due to the loss of low-cost housing stock in general or to cutbacks in supply-side housing programs in particular; that homelessness is due to de-institutionalization of the mentally ill; that homelessness is due to chemical dependency; and that homelessness is due to falling real incomes and rising unemployment for blacks or school dropouts. Finally, one level of consensus exists: Few serious analysts still treat the homeless as a homogenous population.

Figure 4.9, from Burt and Cohen's (1989) survey of shelter and soup kitchen users, shows that the majority of the homeless are single males; of this group, the majority have some institutional history (drug treatment, mental health problems, prison, etc.). This suggests that their homelessness may be symptomatic of problems that go deeper than "mere" shelter deprivation, and that may not be successfully addressed with traditional supply-side *or* demand-side housing programs, or income transfers in general (figure 4.10).[68] However, a significant portion of the homeless, especially women and families, have no institutional history; for these people, income transfers may be more efficacious.[69] Addressing the problems of the homeless will require integrating housing assistance with other social services and improving employment prospects.

Figure 4.9. *Homeless Household Composition*

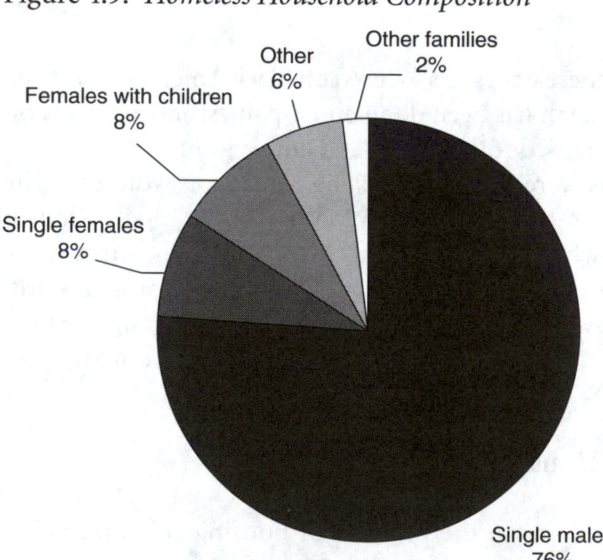

Source: Burt and Cohen (1989).

Figure 4.10. *Personal Problems of the Homeless*

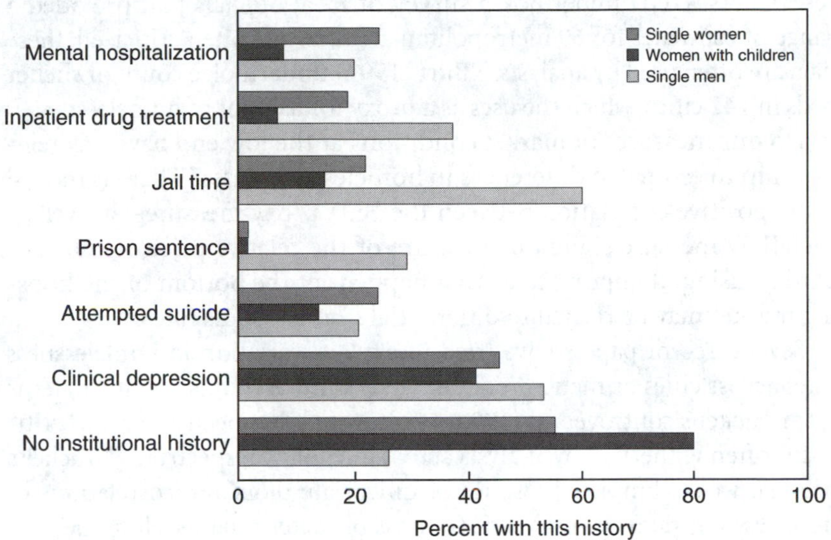

Source: Burt and Cohen (1989), p. 50.

As homelessness came into the national consciousness, housing activists often asserted that increases in homelessness were caused by the shift from supply-side to demand-side housing programs, which they often viewed as a reduction in, if not the end of, housing assistance.[70] Soon afterward, a wealth of data on nonhousing correlates of homelessness became available, such as the Burt and Cohen (1989) data just presented. As a reaction to overstatements about the housing policy–homelessness nexus, the role housing market conditions play in homelessness may have been downplayed.[71] The two views—that homelessness is best viewed as a social pathology, versus the view that homelessness is inevitably related to changes in the operation of the bottom of the housing market—are well argued in Jencks (1994) and O'Flaherty (1996).[72]

A number of recent studies have provided empirical evidence on the relative roles played by differences in macroeconomic and social conditions *and* housing market conditions in determining city-to-city differences in urban homelessness rates.[73] Of course the first difficulty in analyzing homelessness rates is measuring them. Because by definition the homeless have no fixed place of address, they are inherently difficult to count or survey. The Census Bureau undertook a preliminary study that was designed to produce a lower bound. Instead, it was misrepresented in the press as an attempt to produce an authoritative count, and the Census Bureau has since refused to make its counts available to researchers. HUD undertook a survey of local officials that provided a range of estimates for 60 metropolitan areas. While often criticized, these data are often used by analysts.[74] Burt (1992) undertook a count of shelter beds in 147 cities, which she uses as a proxy for a count of homelessness.[75]

Do our measures of market conditions at the low end have any relationship to estimated differences in homelessness rates? There is indeed some positive correlation between the Burt proxy measure—as well as the HUD measure—and our measure of the relative price of substandard housing. It appears that what happens at the bottom of the housing market may be related to differential homelessness rates.

Several recent papers have tried to explain variation in homelessness rates across cities or metro areas. In a sense, much of this literature stems from Tucker's controversial (1990) study, which has been subject to criticism (often withering) by analysts across the political spectrum.[76] Tucker's original work comprised a series of univariate plots and correlations of homelessness rates against a series of possible determinants. He argued, on the basis of this work, that housing market conditions, particularly housing shortages due to rent control, explained most of the variation in homelessness rates. There have been many criticisms of Tucker's work, most focusing on the fact that a series of univariate analyses is no replacement for a multivariate study; and many critics have pointed out that Tucker added his own estimates of homelessness (from ill-documented sources) for several cities. When those self-estimates are excluded, results are not robust.

We can get a sense of the debate with a simple multivariate model of homelessness. Table 4.6 presents regression results explaining the 1990 census estimate of the homeless in major metropolitan areas (normalized by dividing by the population of the metropolitan area). The equation succeeds in explaining one-third of the variation in homelessness, which is quite interesting given that the dependent variable is measured with such a large degree of error. Point estimates suggest that larger cities have lower rates of homelessness. We might expect cities with a high degree of poverty to have a higher degree of homelessness, but the coefficient for this variable is effectively zero, as are coefficients for population growth and climate.

We expected the age distribution of population in the metropolitan area to matter quite a lot, given that the great majority of the homeless are single individuals. In fact, according to the signs of these point estimates,

Table 4.6. *Determinants of Homelessness*

Dependent Variable: HUD 1990 Estimate, Homeless Per 1000 Pop

Source	DF	F value	Prob > F	Adj. R-squared
Model	10	7.25	0.0001	0.3316
Error	116			
C Total	126			

Variable	*Parameter estimate*	*Standard error*	*T for H0: parameter = 0*	*Prob > | t |*
Intercept	2.9870	1.1743	2.54	0.0123
Percent families below poverty level	0.0044	0.0204	0.21	0.8306
Log MSA population	−0.1380	0.0547	−2.53	0.0127
Annual growth rate of population	−1.4280	5.6994	−0.25	0.8026
Percent of population under 18	−0.0348	0.0255	−1.37	0.1747
Percent of population ≥ 65	−0.0156	0.0234	−0.65	0.5151
Rent control dummy	0.1410	0.1839	0.77	0.4447
Heating degree days	−3.93E-06	3.00E-05	−0.11	0.9093
1st quartile of census contract rent	0.0024	0.0011	2.22	0.0282
Rental vacancy rate	−0.0005	0.0179	−0.03	0.9791
New York City dummy	3.2070	0.5308	6.04	0.0001

Source: U.S. Dept. of Housing and Urban Development.

metropolitan areas with large populations under the age of 18 have fewer homeless, and those with larger elderly populations have fewer homeless. This is consistent with survey data on the personal characteristics of the homeless, as researched by Burt and Cohen (1989), but the coefficients are not significantly different from zero.[77] The rent-control dummy does not significantly affect homelessness, in contrast to assertions made by Tucker and others. However, other housing market conditions do matter. The rent variable (first quartile of census contract rent) is positive; that is, the higher the rent, the higher homelessness. On the other hand, vacancy rates had no significant effect. We expected higher vacancy rates to be associated with lower rates of homelessness. Also, in preliminary regressions New York City was found to be an extreme outlier, and a separate dummy variable was put into the equation (this is functionally equivalent to deleting New York from the sample).

Of course, a number of potential causes of homelessness are omitted for lack of data. For example, we have no MSA-specific estimates of the incidence of mental illness or drug use. Thus we cannot use these results to make useful statements about the relative contribution of housing market conditions and, for example, social pathologies. But if it is reasonable to assume that these omitted variables are not highly correlated with housing market outcomes, the evidence does suggest that housing markets matter.

We also found that the results were less than robust when reasonable changes were made in the model. This is perhaps unsurprising, given that so many of these and other potential right-hand variables are intercorrelated. For example, markets with higher rents tend to have lower vacancy rates. In some models, the rent variable "out-performed" vacancies, while in other reasonable variations of the model, vacancy rates seemed more important. This kind of problem will exist to some degree for most cross-MSA modeling efforts, but it seems particularly problematic for our homelessness regressions. Quigley (1990) also found that models explaining cross-metropolitan variation in measured homelessness were not terribly robust.

Another shortcoming is the fact that housing market conditions are probably endogenous, as are some missing variables on the right-hand side, such as the incidence of mental health problems. Early and Olsen (1996) use instrumental variables to estimate such equations; when they do so, most housing market variables are no longer significant in their model. These results cast doubt on housing conditions as *the* cause of homelessness, but an alternative explanation is that, given the errors inherent in constructing instrumental variables Early and Olsen's test, while probably the best to date, may fail to reject null hypotheses for lack of statistical power.

Perhaps the most persuasive evidence that housing market conditions ultimately affect homelessness is O'Flaherty's pathbreaking (1996) treatise. While O'Flaherty does offer some cross-city comparisons, ultimately he relies on a blend of case studies, tightly reasoned theoretical arguments, and some time-series analysis of aggregate data to argue that the bottom of the housing market functions less well today than in prior years, and that its failure is linked to a significant portion of the rise in homelessness.

Surely homelessness is much more than a housing problem, as Jencks (1994) and Lowry among others emphasize. But taken together, the studies discussed above suggest that economic, social, and housing market conditions probably matter in determining differences in homelessness rates among cities. Proving so to the satisfaction of all participants in the debate, however, has proven difficult. Recent work by Early (1998, 1999) suggests that most current housing subsidy programs, whatever their other merits, have little direct effect on homelessness. Our own simple results, consistent with prior work by Lowry, Quigley, O'Flaherty, and others, suggest that improving the bottom of the housing market, especially keeping rents low, can help ameliorate this problem.

NOTES

1. The NAR index is calculated by first computing the qualifying income required at current interest rates to purchase the median-priced home, assuming 20 percent down and a 25 percent payment-to-income ratio. The index is the ratio between median-family income and this qualifying income.

2. Some of the following tabulations have appeared in Green (1995). For California, we used a smaller sample because of the computational constraints.

3. Some PUMS data (e.g., some rent data) are presented in ranges. For such data we assign the midpoint of the range to obtain point estimates.

4. Note that this calculation is not exactly the median rent-to-income ratio, because the ratio of medians is not identically the median of individual household ratios. Both kinds of calculations are commonly used by housing analysts, and usually give qualitatively similar results.

5. The District of Columbia is not included in these calculations.

6. In fact, the typical first-time homebuyer will usually have an income above the median renter, so our calculation is conservative.

7. For brevity, table 4.1 presents the data for the five states with the lowest rent-to-income ratios (column 1) and the five highest. Data for all 50 states can be obtained from our web site at http://www.bus.wisc.edu/realestate. The discussion in this section is based on all data.

8. Downs (1985) has a particularly clear discussion of the role savings plays in down payments.

9. The transaction costs of owning include financing costs, search costs, and selling costs.

10. Incidentally, we should probably disregard the magnitude of the increase in rate in Nebraska, because our sample size for this state in 1980 was quite small.

11. In chapter 2 we noted the relative paucity of empirical studies on the long-run supply elasticity. See Muth (1960), Follain (1979b), and Malpezzi and Maclennan (2001), who find it to be close to perfectly elastic, albeit in a long run that can comprise well over a decade. Poterba (1991) and Topel and Rosen (1988) find lower elasticities.

12. In addition to our discussion, see fine reviews by Fischel (1990) and Pogodzinski and Sass (1990), and an excellent case study by Pollakowski and Wachter (1990).

13. See also the interesting commentaries on the Kean Commission report from several points of view by Anthony Downs, William Fischel, Chester Hartman, and Bernard Siegan in Fannie Mae's *Housing Policy Debate* 2 (4), 1991.

14. State-level regulatory data were collected from American Institute of Planners (1976). That body collected detailed information on state regulation of land use and related interventions. Malpezzi constructed a series of dummy variables on the presence or absence of

- State comprehensive land-use planning;
- State coastal zone management plans;
- State wetlands management regulations;
- State floodplain management;
- State designation of certain areas as "critical" for land-use regulation;
- State enabling legislation for "new towns";
- State-required environmental impact statements; and
- State regulations preempting local regulations for "developments of greater than local impact."

As with the MSA data, Malpezzi experimented with data reduction techniques, but settled on a simple additive index, SREG1. Possible values of the index range from 0 to 8.

Malpezzi's final regulatory variable is the simplest. Based on data from National Multi Housing Council (1982) and U.S. Department of Housing and Urban Development (1991), he constructed a dummy variable for the presence of rent control, RCDUM.

15. Many models also note that supply prices depend on the price of inputs. Good data on input prices, especially land, are not available. However, the prices of inputs are themselves determined by variables on the right-hand side (Q, G, and R), so we can substitute those directly for P_i. In other words, the observed effects of a change in the regulatory environment on output supply price is partly a direct effect and partly through effects on the price of inputs, or

$$\frac{dP_h}{dR} = \frac{\partial P_h}{\partial R} + \frac{\partial P_h}{\partial P_i} \cdot \frac{dP_i}{dR}$$

That is, our model and data will enable us to determine the change in price due to a change in regulation, but will not permit us to decompose this change into direct output price and indirect input price effects. The former can stem from regulation's effect on the elasticity of substitution between inputs.

16. On commuting, see for example, Domencich and McFadden (1975) and Meyer, Kain, and Wohl (1966). Representative models of segregation can be found in Schnare (1974) and Yinger (1979). The literature on neighborhood quality includes Boehm and Ihlanfeldt (1991), Brown (1980), and Diamond (1978).

17. Malpezzi (1996a) presents results from simple ordinary least squares regressions determining rents and house values, using logarithmically transformed census data as the dependent variable. Malpezzi, Chun, and Green (1998) present a similar model, but use hedonic price indexes for the dependent variables, and an instrumental variable for regulation. Qualitatively, results are similar in the two studies; we discuss selected results from the former study here. Malpezzi (1999) considers the relationship between regulation and price changes in a dynamic model.

18. Specifically, an increase in REGTEST from 18 to 22.5, in REGTESTSQ from 324 to 506, and in SREG1 from 2 to 5.

19. An impact multiplier is the sum of the direct effect plus a one-round effect through intervening variables. See Intriligator (1978).

20. The point estimate of the percentage of blacks living in neighborhoods over 90 percent black falls by 15 percent.

21. Of course all these particular numerical results are arbitrary in the sense that they are calculated on the basis of a large and arbitrary choice of change in the independent (regulatory) variables. They are also subject to change as specification and methods of estimation vary. Other benefit measures (e.g., environmental variables) remain to be tested. But we believe these first results are sufficient to demonstrate that the effects of regulation on house prices (rents and asset prices) and on tenure choice can be substantial.

22. Since housing quality has improved, even for very low income families, while rent burdens have generally increased, most economists suggest that increasing household purchasing power with vouchers or housing allowances is the direction the public sector should take. The private sector seems able to supply adequate housing when such purchasing power is available. But see Apgar (1991) for an economic defense of supply-side strategies.

23. Then, of course, he computes a confidence interval and is no longer sure.

24. In constant 1989 dollars.

25. For example, the 1989 AHS shows that median electricity payment for all renters is $41 per month; for renters below the poverty level it is $39. Median gas payment for renters with gas utilities is $27 per month; renters below the poverty level pay $29. Median monthly shelter cost, including utilities, is $424 for all renters, $281 for poor renters. Again, identifying utility payments as part of the problem does not make the problem disappear; rather, it is not particularly a housing problem. Rising utility payments for low-income households can be dealt with much more efficiently with vouchers than with supply-side programs.

26. Authoritative data are hard to develop because a number of studies suggest low-cost landlords inflate their rents to the FMR. See Drury et al. (1978).

27. The exact definition of these bundles can be found on pp. 148–49 of Thibodeau (1992). Of course not all low-cost units are substandard, nor are all substandard units low cost. But in order to study relative prices we have to base our definition on some measure of the quantity of housing services rather than rents. To our knowledge, no better definition of the bottom of the market based on characteristics of the units exists, and we believe what happens to units so defined would be correlated with other reasonably defined low-quality units.

28. Perhaps this appears unremarkable, but in this exploratory work we have not yet controlled for differences in demand for low-quality housing. This will be rectified in future work. And there are analysts who believe rental housing is produced in an uncompetitive market. See Gilderbloom and Appelbaum (1987).

29. More specifically, we regress the relative price of housing against the percentage of land unavailable for development. Segal and Srinivasan (1985) surveyed urban planning officials and obtained estimates of the percentage of otherwise developable suburban land removed from possible development during the study period. About one-third of the MSAs studied had no land removed; at the other extreme, Sacramento had 43.5 percent removed. The coefficient on percentage of land unavailable for development was significant at the 99 percent level of confidence.

30. See Weicher and Thibodeau (1988) for a microlevel study consistent with these MSA aggregates.

31. See Turner and Reed (1990), pp. 32–33.

32. Broad reviews of the literature on racial issues in housing markets can be found in Yinger (1979, 1995), Galster (1992), Kain (1992), Calomiris, Kahn, and Longhofer (1994), and LaCour-Little (1999), among others.

33. Yinger (1995), pp. 5–12.

34. Farley (1991), cited in Turner (1992), pp. 186–87.

35. There are a number of different indices of segregation extant. Massey and Denton (1993) present a good review of several measures. Broad trends as described here seem robust to choice of measure. See also Harrison and Weinberg (1992) for data on economic segregation.

36. Data for additional MSAs are available at our web site, http://www.bus.wisc.edu/realestate. Discussion is based on the full data set.

37. See Abramson and Tobin (1994) and Massey and Denton (1987).

38. McKinney and Schnare (1989), Farley (1991), Massey and Denton (1987), and Cutler, Glaeser, and Vigdor (1999).

39. Full regression results discussed here are available at our web site, http://www.bus.wisc.edu/realestate.

40. See Bobo, Schuman, and Steeh (1986) and studies cited therein.

41. According to authors including Leigh and McGhee (1986).

42. Including Yinger (1978) and Follain and Malpezzi (1981).

43. Black discounts were observed for renters in 29 of 39 metropolitan areas, and for owners in 37 of 39. The simple average of 39 premia/discounts were a 6 percent discount for renters and a 15 percent discount for owners. Malpezzi, Ozanne, and Thibodeau (1980) improved the specification and enlarged the sample; rent discounts were observed in 49 of 59 MSAs and owner discounts in all 59. Some of these data are the last two columns of table 4.5.

44. See Galster (1992), Schill (1994), and Yinger (1979, 1995) for reviews of these models.

45. Such as Reifel (1994) and Kain and Quigley (1975).

46. See Wienk et al. (1979), Turner and Mikelsons (1992), Turner, Struyk, and Yinger (1991), Galster (1990), Wienk (1992), and especially Yinger (1991, 1995).

47. The measure of housing inadequacy is constructed by HUD and takes about two pages to describe fully; it is basically an indicator for severe structural and/or heating problems in the unit.

48. The coefficient on Native Americans is negative but the standard error is large. There were only six Native Americans in the regression sample. Results were similar for logit models of tenure choice and housing inadequacy.

49. Struyk (with Marshall, 1975), Long and Caudill (1992), Gabriel and Rosenthal (1991), and Megbolugbe and Cho (1996).

50. Mills's argument is based on results from Mills and Price (1984) which finds that, all things being equal, employment suburbanizes fastest where black-white differences between central cities and suburbs are the greatest. It follows that integrating the suburbs, even modestly, could slow down (though not stop) the suburbanization of jobs.

51. See Ellwood (1986), Harrison (1974), and Jencks and Mayer (1990); but see also the critique of these studies in Kain (1992).

52. For example, Ihlanfeldt and Sjoquist (1989, 1990a, b), McMillen (1993), and O'Regan and Quigley (1991, 1998).

53. For example, Rosenbaum and Popkin (1991) and Rosenbaum (1991, 1993).

54. Holzer (1991, 1994) and Kain (1992) provide cogent reviews of this literature.

55. See Munnell et al. (1992), Dedman (1988), Quint (1991), and Thomas (1991, 1992).

56. See also Day and Liebowitz (1994) and Browne and Tootell (1995).

57. Maddala and Trost (1982), Rachlis and Yezer (1993), Yezer, Phillips, and Trost (1994), and Phillips and Yezer (1996) are among the papers that discuss this issue.

58. Becker (1993) is the recent article; his classic model can be found in Becker (1957).

59. See, for example, Galster (1993).

60. Yinger cites Quercia and Stegman (1992) in support, but notes that much research remains to be done on this point.

61. LaCour-Little and Green (1998). Schill and Wachter (1993) provide a recent review.

62. See Bradbury, Case, and Dunham (1989).

63. Hunter and Walker (1996).

64. Schill and Wachter (1995).

65. Dane (1993).

66. However, the literature on other racial and ethnic groups is growing, albeit from a small base. See, for example, Krivo (1995), Frey and Farley (1996), Nealigh and Brewer (1991), Painter, Gabriel, and Myers (2001), and Macpherson and Sirmans (2001).

67. Weaver (1956), cited in Goering (1986), p. 4.

68. Of course, such personal problems are often exacerbated by, and in some cases arise from, homelessness. But for evidence that many social problems predate homelessness see Rossi (1989).

69. Other data presented by Burt and Cohen suggest that most homeless are unemployed well before they are homeless.

70. Burt (1992, p.4) quotes former director of the Coalition for the Homeless, Robert Hayes, on the causes: "housing, housing, and housing."

71. The role of the housing market was emphasized on the other end of the political spectrum by journalist William Tucker, in a series of provocative articles and a book Tucker (1990).

72. Quigley (1996) is a nice critical review of the Jencks and O'Flaherty studies.

73. Quigley (1990), Lowry (1992), Burt (1992), and Park and Ying (2000) are among the contributions to this literature.

74. Tucker's well-known book made use of this data, but Tucker made additions and adjustments to the HUD counts with a rather casual method. His already weak statistical results are further weakened when unadjusted data are used. See Lowry (1992) for a good critique.

75. While Burt acknowledges the large errors inherent in such a proxy variable, other methods have large errors as well. She reports a surprisingly high correlation of .83 with the HUD count, and .93 with a previous survey of shelter providers undertaken for the Burt and Cohen study (Burt 1992, p. 132). Garfinkel and Piliavin (1994) provide a good critical review of the literature counting the homeless. See also the many papers in the special issue of *Housing Policy Debate* (vol. 2, no. 3, 1991) on counting the homeless.

76. Appelbaum et al. (1991), Bohanon (1991), Early and Olsen (1996), Elliott and Krivo (1991), Gilderbloom et al. (1992), Honig and Filer (1993), Lowry (1992), and Quigley (1990).

77. Since the fraction of population under 18, and the fraction over 65, are fairly highly correlated, we also examined the *F*-statistic for the joint hypothesis that the two age variables together were different from zero. We could not reject this null either.

5 Conclusions

Policies and Programs Evaluated in Light of the Facts

Several recurring questions about the most appropriate housing policies and programs emerge from our examination of U.S. housing markets. Questions include whether it is better to subsidize housing by focusing on bricks and mortar, or by focusing on people; how housing should be taxed; and what is the best approach to regulating housing and urban development.

A wide range of evidence suggests that demand-side programs are a more efficient use of scarce public resources than are supply-side programs. A few arguments in favor of supply-side subsidies, such as the pecuniary externality argument of Apgar (1990), could be more carefully evaluated. Research by Murray and others suggests that supply-side programs (with the exception of older-style public housing) generally do not provide net additions to the stock. It is clear that the effects of different program types hinge on the price elasticity of the housing supply, a key parameter that is still in dispute, despite a number of recent studies.

Tax policies affecting housing could be improved in numerous ways. For example, if the tax code is supposed to stimulate homeownership, we could convert the mortgage interest deduction into a credit.[1] However, many of these changes would be politically difficult to undertake and would require careful phasing. Credits generally meet more distributional objectives at a lower cost than deductions and can have a higher impact on homeownership. However, any major change in the tax code should be phased in over time to avoid any unnecessary shock to prices in the financial system.

In many localities, prices are raised by regulation. That may be unsurprising, but past the inflection point where the effects of regulation "takes off," it has been very hard to find much measurable benefit. Generally, any reform of these regulations is difficult because of the high degree of autonomy of local governments in the U.S. system of planning and land-use regulation. Adoption of explicit cost-benefit criteria, as has been done in the environmental areas, is one possible step forward.

Options for Future Housing Policies

While emphases on specific programs will change from time to time, with periodic interest in supply-side programs, we believe demand-side programs like vouchers will continue to dominate at the federal level.[2] Despite homeownership's place in American political culture, the U.S. private rental sector has not become a residual sector per se. Most poor people rent, but most renters are not poor. In the early days of explicit housing subsidies, public housing was the centerpiece program. Now vouchers and other housing allowance strategies focus on using the private rental supply. However, there are still some significant supply-side initiatives, including the Low-Income Housing Tax Credit and various state programs. In our view, the burden of proof is now on advocates of supply-side programs: We would support such programs' expansion and/or reintroduction only after careful research showing that they could actually complement demand-side programs successfully.

Overall, the private sector fills its assigned role fairly well. But the United States can do better. We would particularly focus on exclusionary zoning, restrictions on conversion of houses to apartments, and other impediments to low-cost rental housing.

There is a broad political consensus as well as economic evidence that traditional public housing doesn't "work." There is less consensus about what should replace it. There is also a lack of agreement about the extent to which we should subsidize housing *on budget*. Tax expenditures, as we have seen, are large and have broad support, although they can be inefficient and inequitable. But there is no apparent move to view housing as an entitlement, or other large-scale expansion of on-budget housing subsidies.

As noted above, the shift to vouchers has enabled more low-income households to benefit, at less cost to the taxpayer. But vouchers have less political support from the real estate industry than supply-side programs, even though the two options' aggregate long-run effect on the industry is about the same.

There has been increased awareness of the importance of a reasonable regulatory framework for housing, but this has not yet been translated into many concrete reforms. Restrictive zoning practices and "growth management" programs create severe problems in selected markets.

It is worth reminding ourselves of the limits of policy. In market economies like the United States, government policies have effects, but the market itself is the major determinant of how well people are housed. With a proper regulatory environment in place, ensuring elastic supply, housing conditions will improve at an equal pace with the state of the economy generally. Economic development is the most effective way of improving housing conditions in all countries. To a considerable degree, what is good for the economy is better for housing. This is probably as close as we will come to a universal truth in housing policy.

One area not touched on above that is worth mentioning is the provision of an infrastructure of an appropriate standard with appropriate pricing. Research by Aschauer (1989) and Dalenberg and Ebert (1988) suggests that the United States has been systematically under-investing in infrastructure over much of the recent past. While this conclusion can be disputed,[3] if true it has powerful implications for housing costs, quality, and location. A related issue is the existence and nature of "impact fees," which in theory are charges for the marginal cost of trunk infrastructure.[4]

Perhaps the most critical immediate need is more careful review of the costs and benefits of zoning, building codes, environmental regulations, growth management schemes, and the like. Such evidence as exists suggests that many of these regulations increase costs, often without corresponding benefits, and probably affect low- and moderate-income rental more than other types of housing, (see Malpezzi and Green 1996).

We would argue that another proximate goal would be to avoid the displacement of private investment by public activities. Murray (1983) found that each 100 new units of publicly subsidized housing caused a drop of almost 85 units in private construction; other studies indicate that U.S. public housing actually has a negative economic rate of return (i.e., it is worth less than what it cost to build).[5] Similar displacement effects and inefficiencies may well exist in other countries, although they have yet to be carefully documented.

We also saw that while tax incentives can have large supply effects, they can lead to large revenue losses. Caps on the mortgage interest deduction (such as those currently in place in the United Kingdom) may mitigate some of the worst effects. A household tax credit for mortgage interest may be preferable to a deduction on equity grounds, or, in a progressive tax system, deductions may be limited to the basic (lowest) tax rate.

In the United States, we often have a schizophrenic attitude toward low-income housing. We bemoan the state of the low-cost market, particularly the rental market, and subsidize about one-third of eligible households. We even add additional regulations in the form of "inclusionary" zoning to force developers to build a few units of low-cost housing that other regulations have made unprofitable. But we seem to be unwilling to take the fundamental steps required to remove impediments to the production of affordable housing, such as exclusionary zoning. On the other hand, these subsidies often do not come close to canceling regulatory costs. Costs and benefits of specific regulations can and should be measured; those whose benefits exceed costs should be strengthened and enforced, those that do not should be removed or modified.

There are strong economic arguments for reducing our current reliance on off-budget expenditures for housing. While rarely measured, the effects of such expenditures can be powerful. The United States provides a good example of the problems such an entitlement can cause: The roughly $50 billion tax expenditure on housing dwarfs on-budget expenditures and subsidizes mainly inframarginal investors and consumers. The expenditure is politically nearly impossible to roll back.

In our view it is not a good idea to subsidize one tenure group at the expense of another. Horizontal equity measured in the usual ways (e.g., income) will be violated. Instead, the regulatory playing field should be leveled. Regulatory reforms in land, infrastructure, finance—specifically in rent regulation—and rationalizing taxes can further tenure neutrality.

Rent controls can be a particularly inefficient means of subsidizing housing consumption by some renters at the expense of others. If such controls are strong enough and if left in place long enough, many tenants themselves will lose more from disequilibrium in consumption than they gain in lower rents. And there is a lot of overlap in the income distributions of landlords and tenants; as income redistribution, rent control simply doesn't work.

It is also a good idea to remove roadblocks to the financing of rental housing, but not at the expense of the safety and soundness of the banking system (see the lamentable history of the thrifts). There may be scope for encouraging the secondary market for multifamily rental in the United States, but this should be undertaken within a market framework.

NOTES

1. See Green and Vandell (1999) and Green and Reschovsky (1998).
2. Perhaps they will be administered by the states, but funded by the federal government.
3. See Holtz-Eakin and Rosen (1993).
4. See Nelson (1988).
5. See Mayo et al. (1980).

References

Abramson, Alan J., and Mitchell S. Tobin. 1994. "The Changing Geography of Metropolitan Opportunity: The Segregation of the Poor in U.S. Metropolitan Areas, 1970 to 1990." Washington, D.C.: The Urban Institute.

Ackerman, Bruce A. 1975. *Economic Foundations of Property Law*. Boston: Little, Brown.

Adams, James Ring. 1990. *The Big Fix*. New York: John Wiley and Sons.

Advisory Commission on Regulatory Barriers to Affordable Housing. 1991. "Not in My Backyard: Removing Barriers to Affordable Housing." Washington, D.C.: U.S. Department of Housing and Urban Development.

Alexander, Barbara. 1990. *Will 1990 Signal the End of a Demand-Driven Housing Market?* New York: Salomon Brothers.

Ambrose, Brent W., and John D. Benjamin. 1993. "A Test for the Existence, Cause, and Relative Severity of the 1990–1991 Credit Crunch." Paper prepared for the January 1993 meetings of the American Real Estate and Urban Economics Association meeting, Anaheim, California.

American Institute of Planners. 1976. *Survey of State Land Use Planning Activity*. Report to U.S. Department of Housing and Urban Development. Washington, D.C.: American Institute of Planners.

Anas, Alex, and Richard J. Arnott. 1991. "Dynamic Housing Market Equilibrium with Taste Heterogeneity, Idiosyncratic Perfect Foresight and Stock Conversions." *Journal of Housing Economics* 1 (1): 2–32.

Angel, Shlomo, and Stephen K. Mayo. 1996. "Enabling Policies and Their Effects on Housing Sector Performance: A Global Comparison." Paper presented to the Habitat II Conference, Istanbul, Turkey, June.

Apgar, William C., Jr. 1990. "Which Housing Policy Is Best?" *Housing Policy Debate* 1 (1): 1–32.

Appelbaum, Richard P., Michael Dolny, Peter Drier, and John I. Gilderbloom. 1991. "Scapegoating Rent Control: Masking the Causes of Homelessness." *Journal of the American Planning Association* 57 (2): 153–64.

Arnott, Richard J. 1987. "Economic Theory and Housing." In *Handbook of Regional and Urban Economics,* vol. 2, edited by E.S. Mills. Amsterdam: North Holland.

Aschauer, David. 1989. "Is Public Infrastructure Productive?" *Journal of Monetary Economics* 23 (2): 177–200.

Bailey, Martin J., Richard F. Muth, and Hugh O. Nourse. 1963. "A Regression Method for Real Estate Price Index Construction." *Journal of the American Statistical Association* 58: 933–42.

Bartik, Timothy J. 1987. "The Estimation of Demand Parameters in Hedonic Price Models." *Journal of Political Economy* 95: 81–88.

Barzel, Yoram. 1989. *Economic Analysis of Property Rights.* Cambridge, U.K.: Cambridge University Press.

Baumol, William J. 1982. "Contestable Markets: An Uprising in the Theory of Market Structure." *American Economic Review* (January): 1–20.

Becker, Gary S. 1957. *The Economics of Discrimination.* Chicago: University of Chicago Press.

———. 1993. "The Evidence against Banks Doesn't Prove Bias." *Business Week* 19 April. p. 18.

Belden, Joseph N., and Robert J. Wiener, eds. 1999. *Housing in Rural America: Building Affordable and Inclusive Communities.* Newbury Park, Calif: Sage Publications.

Berkovec, James, Glenn Canner, Stuart Gabriel, and Timothy Hannan. 1994. "Race, Redlining, and Residential Mortgage Loan Performance." *Journal of Real Estate Finance and Economics* 9 (3): 240–58.

Black, J. Thomas, and James Hoben. 1985. "Land Price Inflation." *Urban Geography* 6 (1): 27–49.

Blackley, Dixie M. 1999. "The Long-Run Elasticity of New Housing Supply in the United States: Empirical Evidence for 1950 to 1994." *Journal of Real Estate Finance and Economics* 18 (1): 25–42.

Blackley, Dixie M. and James R. Follain. 1996. "In Search of the Linkage between User Cost and Rent." *Regional Science and Urban Economics* 26: 409–31.

Blanck, David M. and Louis Winnick. 1953. "The Structure of the Housing Market." *Quarterly Journal of Economics* 67(2): 181–203.

Bobo, Lawrence, Howard Schuman, and Charlotte Steeh. 1986. "Changing Residential Attitudes towards Desegregation." In *Housing Desegregation and Federal Policy,* edited by John M. Goering. Chapel Hill: University of North Carolina Press.

Boehm, Thomas P. 1993. "Income, Wealth Accumulation, and First-Time Homeownership: An Intertemporal Analysis." *Journal of Housing Economics* 3: 16–30.

———. 1995. "A Comparison of the Determinants of Structural Quality between Manufactured Housing and Conventional Tenure Choices: Evidence from the American Housing Survey." *Journal of Housing Economics* 4 (4): 373–91.

Boehm, Thomas P., and Keith R. Ihlanfeldt. 1991. "The Revelation of Neighborhood Preferences: An *N*-Chotomous Multivariate Probit Approach." *Journal of Housing Economics* 1 (1): 33–59.

Bohanon, Cecil. 1991. "The Economic Correlates of Homelessness in Sixty Cities." *Social Science Quarterly* 72: 817–25.

Borsch-Supan, Axel. 1986. "Household Formation, Housing Prices and Public Policy Impacts." *Journal of Public Economics* 30: 145–64.

Box, G.E.P., and D. Cox. 1964. "An Analysis of Transformations." *Journal of the American Statistical Association*, Society Series B, 26: 211–52.

Bradbury, Katherine, and Anthony Downs. 1981. *Do Housing Allowances Work?* Washington, D.C.: Brookings Institution.

Bradbury, Katherine L., Karl E. Case, and C.R. Dunham. 1989. "Geographic Patterns of Mortgage Lending in Boston." *New England Economic Review* (September): 3–30.

Braid, Ralph. 1984. "The Effects of Government Housing Policies in a Vintage Filtering Model." *Journal of Urban Economics* 16: 272–96.

Bromley, Daniel W. 1989. "Property Relations and Economic Development: The Other Land Reform." *Land Economics* 17: 867–77.

Brown, H. James. 1980. "Micro Neighborhood Externalities and Hedonic Housing Prices." *Land Economics, 56:* 125–41.

Browne, Lynne E., and Geoffrey M.B. Tootell. 1995. "Mortgage Lending in Boston: A Response to the Critics." *New England Economic Review* (September/October): 53–78.

Brueggeman, William, and Richard Peiser. 1979. "Housing Choice and Relative Tenure Prices." *Journal of Financial and Quantitative Analysis* 14 (4): 735–41.

Brueggeman, William, and Thomas Thibodeau. 1986. "Tax Reform's Assault on Rental Housing: Measuring the Impact." *Real Estate Review* 15 (Winter): 38–45.

Burchell, Robert W., and David Listokin. 1978. *The Fiscal Impact Handbook*. Center for Urban Policy Research. New Brunswick, N.J.: Rutgers University.

———. 1995. "Influences on United States Housing Policy." *Housing Policy Debate* 6 (3): 559–617.

Burt, Martha. 1992. *Over The Edge: The Growth of Homelessness in the 1980s*. New York: Russell Sage Foundation; Washington, D.C.: Urban Institute.

Burt, Martha A., and Barbara E. Cohen. 1989. *America's Homeless: Numbers, Characteristics, and Programs that Serve Them*. Washington, D.C.: Urban Institute. Report No. 89–3.

Butler, Richard V. 1982. "The Specification of Hedonic Indexes for Urban Housing." *Land Economics* 58 (1): 96–108.

Calomiris, Charles W., Charles M. Kahn, and Stanley D. Longhofer. 1994. "Housing Finance Intervention and Private Incentives: Helping Minorities and the Poor." Part 2. *Journal of Money, Credit and Banking* 26 (3): 634–78.

Capone, Charles A., Jr. 1995. "Taxation and Housing Tenure Choice: the Case for Moderate-Income Homeownership." *Journal of Housing Economics* 4 (4): 328–49.

Capozza, Dennis R., Richard K. Green, and Patric H. Hendershott. 1996. "Taxes, Mortgage Borrowing and Residential Land Prices." In *Economic Effects of Fundamental Tax Reform*, edited by Henry Aaron and William Gale. Washington, D.C.: Brookings Institution.

———. 1999. "Tax Reform and House Prices: Large or Small Effect?" *National Tax Association Proceedings: 1998* (19–24). Washington, D.C.: National Tax Association.

Carr, James H., and Isaac F. Megbolugbe. 1993. "The Federal Reserve Bank of Boston Study on Mortgage Lending Revisited." *Journal of Housing Research* 4 (2): 277–314.

Case, Bradford, and John M. Quigley. 1991. "The Dynamics of Real Estate Prices." *Review of Economics and Statistics* 22 (1): 50–58.

Case, Bradford, Henry Pollakowski, and Susan M. Wachter. 1991. "On Choosing among Housing Price Index Methodologies." *AREUEA Journal* 19 (3): 286–307.

Case, Karl E., and Robert J. Shiller. 1987. "Prices of Single Family Homes since 1970: New Indexes for Four Cities." *New England Economic Review* (September/October): 45–56.

———. 1989. "The Efficiency of the Market for Single-Family Homes." *American Economic Review* 79 (1): 125–37.

———. 1990. "Forecasting Prices and Excess Returns in the Housing Market." *American Real Estate and Urban Economics Association Journal* 18: 253–73.

Casey, Connie H. 1992. *Characteristics of HUD-Assisted Renters and Their Units in 1989.* Washington, D.C.: U.S. Department of Housing and Urban Development.

Chambers, Daniel. 1992. "The Racial Housing Price Differential and Racially Transitional Neighborhoods." *Journal of Urban Economics* 32 (2): 214–32.

Chavas, Jean-Paul, Richard C. Bishop, and Kathleen Segerson. 1986. "Ex Ante Consumer Welfare Evaluation in Cost-Benefit Analysis." *Journal of Environmental Economics and Management* 13 (3): 255–68.

Cho, Man, and Peter Linneman. 1993. "Interjurisdictional Spillover Effects of Land Use Regulations." *Journal of Housing Research* 4 (1): 131–64.

Chressanthis, George A. 1986. "The Impact of Zoning Changes on Housing Prices: A Time Series Analysis." *Growth and Change* 17 (3): 49–71.

Christensen, L.R., D.W. Jorgenson, and L.J. Lau. 1973. "Transcendental Lograrithmic Production Frontiers." *Review of Economics and Statistics* 55: 28–45.

Clapp, John M., and Carmelo Giaccotto. 1992. "Estimating Price Indices for Residential Property: A Comparison of Repeat Sales and Assessed Value Methods." *Journal of the American Statistical Association* 87: 300–6.

———. 1994. "The Influence of Economic Variables on Local House Price Dynamics." *Journal of Urban Economics* 36 (2): 161–83.

———. 1999. "Revisions in Repeat Sales Indexes: Here Today, Gone Tomorrow?" *Real Estate Economics* 27(1): 79–104.

Colwell, Peter F., and James B. Kau. 1982. "The Economics of Building Codes and Standards." In *Resolving the Housing Crisis,* edited by M. Bruce Johnson. San Francisco: Pacific Institute for Public Policy Research.

Council of Economic Advisors. Annual. *Economic Report of the President.* Washington, D.C.: Council of Economic Advisors. Available at http: //www.whitehouse.gov or at http: //w3.access.gpo.gov.eop.

Crone, Theodore M. 1983. "Elements of an Economic Justification for Municipal Zoning." *Journal of Urban Economics* 14 (September): 168–83.

Cronin, Francis J. 1981. "Participation in the Experimental Housing Allowance Program." In (*Housing Vouchers for the Poor: Lessons from a National Experiment,* edited by R. Struyk and M. Bendick. Washington, D.C.: Urban Institute Press.

———. 1982. "The Household's Decision to Accept or Reject a Conditional Transfer Offer." *Southern Economic Journal* 49 (1): 218–34.

Cummings, Jean L., and Denise DiPasquale. 1999. "The Low-Income Housing Tax Credit: An Analysis of the First Ten Years." *Housing Policy Debate* 10 (2): 251–308.

Cutler, David M., Edward L. Glaeser, and Jacob L. Vigdor. 1999. "The Rise and Decline of the American Ghetto." *Journal of Political Economy* 107 (3): 455–506.

Dalenberg, Douglas, and Randall Ebert. 1988. "Public Infrastructure and Economic Development." Federal Reserve Bank of Cleveland Economic Commentary. January 15.

Dane, Stephen. 1993. "A History of Mortgage Lending Discrimination in the United States." *Journal of Intergroup Relations* 20 (1): 16–28.

Daskal, Jennifer. 1998. "In Search of Shelter: The Growing Shortage of Affordable Rental Housing." Washington, D.C.: Center on Budget Priorities.

Day, Ted, and S.J. Liebowitz. 1994. "Mortgages, Minorities and Discrimination." School of Management Working Paper. Dallas: University of Texas.

de Leeuw, Frank. 1971. "The Demand for Housing: A Review of the Cross-Section Evidence." *Review of Economics and Statistics* 53 (1): 1–10.

———. 1993. "A Price Index for New Multifamily Housing." *Survey of Current Business* 73 (2): 33–42.

de Leeuw, Frank, and Larry Ozanne. 1981. "Housing." In *How Taxes Affect Economic Behavior*, edited by Henry Aaron and J. Pechman. Washington, D.C.: Brookings Institution.

de Leeuw, Frank, and Raymond Struyk. 1975. *The Web of Urban Housing*. Washington, D.C.: The Urban Institute.

Deaton, Angus, and John Meullbauer. 1980. *Economics and Consumer Behavior*. Cambridge, U.K.: Cambridge University Press.

Dedman, William. 1988. "The Color of Money." *Atlanta Journal-Constitution*, 1–16 May.

Demsetz, Harold. 1964. "The Exchange and Enforcement of Property Rights." *Journal of Law and Economics* 7 (October): 11–26.

———. 1966. "Some Aspects of Property Rights." *Journal of Law and Economics* 9 (October): 61–70.

———. 1967. "Towards a Theory of Property Rights." *American Economic Review* 57 (May): 347–73.

DeParle, Jason. 1996. "Slamming the Door." *The New York Times Magazine*, 20 October, 52 ff.

Diamond, Douglas B., Jr. 1978. "A Note on Inflation and Relative Tenure Prices." *Journal of the American Real Estate and Urban Economics Association* 6: 438–50.

Diewert, W.E., ed. 1991. *Price Level Measurement*. Amsterdam: North Holland.

DiPasquale, Denise. 1999. "Why Don't We Know More about Housing Supply?" *Journal of Real Estate Finance and Economics* 18 (1): 9–24.

DiPasquale, Denise, and Jean L. Cummings. 1992. "Financing Multifamily Rental Housing: The Changing Role of Leaders and Investors." *Housing Policy Debate* 3 (1): 77–116.

DiPasquale, Denise, and Langley C. Keyes, eds. 1990. *Building Foundations: Housing and Federal Policy*. Philadelphia: University of Pennsylvania Press.

———. 1992. "The Markets for Real Estate Assets and Space: A Conceptual Framework." *AREUEA Journal* 20 (2): 181–98.

———. 1999. *Out of Reach: The Gap between Housing Costs and Income of Poor People in the United States*. Washington, D.C.: National Low-Income Housing Coalition.

Domencich, T.A., and D. McFadden. 1975. *Urban Travel Demand: A Behavioral Analysis.* Amsterdam: North Holland.

Dowall, David E. 1984. *The Suburban Squeeze: Land Conversion and Regulation in the San Francisco Bay Area.* University of California Press.

Dowall, David, and John Landis. 1982. "Land Use Controls and Housing Costs: An Examination of San Francisco Bay Area Communities." *AREUEA Journal* 10: 67–92.

Downs, Anthony. 1985. *The Revolution in Real Estate Finance.* Washington, D.C.: Brookings Institution.

———.1991. "The Advisory Council on Regulatory Barriers to Affordable Housing: Its Behavior and Accomplishments." *Housing Policy Debate* 2 (4): 1095–1137.

Drury, Margaret, Olson Lee, Michael Springer, and Lorene Yap. 1978. *Lower-Income Housing Assistance Program (Section 8): Nationwide Evaluation of the Existing Housing Program.* Washington, D.C.: U.S. Department of Housing and Urban Development, Policy Development and Research.

Early, Dirk W. 1998. "The Role of Subsidized Housing in Reducing Homelessness: An Empirical Investigation Using Micro-Data." *Journal of Policy Analysis and Management* 17 (4): 687–96.

———. 1999. "A Microeconomic Analysis of Homelessness: An Empirical Investigation Using Choice-Based Sampling." *Journal of Housing Economics* 8 (4): 312–27.

Early, Dirk W., and Edgar O. Olsen. 1996. "Causes of Homelessness in the United States: An Empirical Investigation Using Data from the 1990 Census." Working Paper, Southwestern University, Department of Economics.

Elliott, Marta, and Lauren Krivo. 1991. "Structural Determinants of Homelessness in the United States." *Social Problems* 38: 113–31.

Ellwood, David T. 1986. "The Spatial Mismatch Hypothesis: Are There Teenage Jobs Missing in the Ghetto?" In *The Black Youth Unemployment Crisis,* edited by R. Freeman and H. Holzer. Chicago: University of Chicago Press.

Fabozzi, Frank J., ed. 1988. *The Handbook of Mortgage Backed Securities.* Chicago: Probus Publishing.

Fallis, George, Arthur J. Hosios, and Gregory V. Jump. 1995. "Housing Allowances, Nonprofit Housing, and Cost-Effective Program Choices." *Journal of Housing Economics* 4 (2): 136–52.

Farley, Reynolds. 1993. "Neighborhood Preferences and Aspirations Among Blacks and Whites." In G. Thomas Kingsley and Margery Austin Turner, *Housing Markets and Residential Mobility*. Washington, D.C.: Urban Institute Press.

Fischel, William A. 1990. *Do Growth Controls Matter? A Review of Empirical Evidence on the Effectiveness and Efficiency of Local Government Land Use Regulation.* Cambridge, Mass.: Lincoln Institute of Land Policy.

———. 1991. Comment (on Downs). *Housing Policy Debate* 2 (4): 1139-60.

Follain, James R. 1979a. "A Study of the Demand for Housing by Low and High Income Households." *Journal of Financial and Quantitative Analysis* 14 (November): 769–82.

———. 1979b. "The Price Elasticity of the Long Run Supply of New Housing Construction." *Land Economics* 55: 190–99.

———. 1982. "Does Inflation Affect Real Behavior? The Case of Housing." *Southern Economic Journal* (January): 570–82.

Follain, James R., Patric Hendershott, and David C. Ling. 1992. "Real Estate Markets since 1980: What Role Have Tax Changes Played?" *National Tax Journal* 45 (3): 253–66.

Follain, James R., and Emmanuel Jimenez. 1985. "Estimating the Demand for Housing Characteristics: A Survey and Critique." *Regional Science and Urban Economics* 15: 77–107.

Follain, James R., and David C. Ling. 1988. "Another Look at Tenure Choice, Inflation and Taxes." *AREUEA Journal* 16 (3): 227–29.

Follain, James R., and Stephen Malpezzi. 1980a. *Dissecting Housing Value and Rent*. Washington, D.C.: The Urban Institute.

———. 1981. "Another Look at Racial Differences in Housing Prices." *Urban Studies* 18 (June): 195–203.

Follain, James R., and Lisa Sturman Melamed. 1998. "The False Messiah of Tax Policy: What Elimination of the Home Mortgage Interest Deduction Promises and a Careful Look at What It Delivers." *Journal of Housing Research* 9 (2): 179–99.

Federal Home Loan Mortgage Association. *Secondary Mortgage Markets*. Washington, D.C.: , Dept. of Financial Research, Federal Home Loan Mortgage Association.

Freeman, A. Myrick. 1979. *The Benefits of Environmental Improvement: Theory and Practice*. Washington, D.C.: Resources for the Future.

Frey, William H., and Reynolds Farley. 1996. Latino, Asian and Black Segregation in U.S. Metropolitan Areas. *Demography* 33: 35–50.

Friedman, Milton. 1957. *A Theory of the Consumption Function*. Princeton, N.J.: Princeton University Press.,

Gabriel, Stuart A., and Stuart S. Rosenthal. 1991. "Credit Rationing, Race, and the Mortgage Market." *Journal of Urban Economics* 29: 371–79.

———. 1990. "Racial Discrimination in Housing Markets During the 1980s: A Review of the Audit Evidence." *Journal of Planning Education and Research* 9 (3): 165–75.

———. 1992. "Research on Discrimination in Housing and Mortgage Markets: Assessment and Future Directions." *Housing Policy Debate* 3 (2) 639–84.

———. 1993. "The Facts of Lending Discrimination Cannot Be Argued Away by Examining Default Rates." *Housing Policy Debate* 4 (1): 141–46.

Gaquin, Deirdre. 2001. *County and City Extra: Annual Metro, City, and County Data Book*. Lanham, Md.: Bernan Press.

Garfinkel, Irwin, and Irving Piliavin. 1994. "Trends in the Size of the Nation's Homeless Population During the 1980s: A Surprising Result." Institute for Research on Poverty Discussion Paper No. 1034–94, Revised. Madison, University of Wisconsin, Institute for Research on Poverty.

Gatzlaff, Dean H., and Donald R. Hawrin. 1997. "Sample Selection Bias and Repeat-Sales Index Estimates." *Journal of Real Estate Finance and Economics* 14(1-2): 33–50.

———. 1998. "Revisiting Cross-Tenure Differences in Housing Maintenance." *Land Economics* 74 (3): 328–42.

Gatzlaff, Dean H., and David C. Ling. 1994. "Measuring Changes in Local Housing Prices: An Empirical Investigation of Alternative Methodologies." *Journal of Urban Economics* 35: 221–44.

Gilderbloom, John I., and Richard P. Appelbaum. 1987. "Toward A Sociology of Rent: Are Rental Housing Markets Competitive?" *Social Problems* 34 (3): 261–76.

Gilderbloom, John I., Richard Appelbaum, Michael Dolny, and Peter Dreier. 1992. "Rent Control Research: A Further Study." *Journal of the American Planning Association* 58 (2): 220–24.

Glaeser, Edward L., and Bruce Sacerdote. 2000. "The Social Consequences of Housing." *Journal of Housing Economics* 9 (1/2): 1–23.

Godschalk, David R. 1992. "In Defense of Growth Management." *Journal of the American Planning Association* 58 (4): 422–24.

Goering, John M., ed. 1986. *Housing Desegregation and Federal Policy*. Chapel Hill, N.C.: University of North Carolina Press.

Goldberger, Arthur S. 1991. *A Course in Econometrics*. Cambridge, Mass.: Harvard University Press.

Goldberger, Arthur S. 1968. The Interpretation and Estimation of Cobb-Douglas Production Functions, *Econometrica* 36 (3/4): pp. 464–72.

Goodman, John L. Jr. 1978. *Urban Residential Mobility: Places, People and Policy*. Washington, D.C.: Urban Institute Press.

Goodman, Allen C. 1995. "A Dynamic Equilibrium Model of Housing Demand and Mobility with Transaction Costs." *Journal of Housing Economics* 4 (4): 307–27.

Goodman, Allen C., and Masahiro Kawai. 1985. "Length of Residence Discounts and Rental Housing Demand: Theory and Evidence." *Land Economics* 61 (2): 93–105.

Goodman, Allen C., and Thomas G. Thibodeau. 1998. "Housing Market Segmentation." *Journal of Housing Economics* 7 (2): 121–43.

Grebler, Leo, David M. Blank, and Louis Winnick. 1956. *Capital Formation in Residential Real Estate: Trends and Prospects*. Princeton, N.J.: Princeton University Press for National Bureau of Economic Research.

Green, Richard. 1995. "Does the U.S. 'Overinvest' in Housing?" Working Paper. Madison, University of Wisconsin.

———. 1996. "Should the Stagnant Homeownership Rate Be a Source of Concern?" *Regional Science and Urban Economics* 26 (3–4): 337–68.

———. 1996a. "Age, Housing Demand, and Real House Prices." *Regional Science and Urban Economics* 26 (5): 465–80.

———. 1997. "Follow the Leader: How Changes in Residential and Nonresidential Investment Affect GDP." *Real Estate Economics* 25: 253–370.

———. 1999. "Land Use Regulation and the Price of Housing in a Suburban Wisconsin County." *Journal of Housing Economics* 8 (2): 144–59.

Green, Richard K., and Andrew Reschovsky. 1998. "The Design of a Mortgage Tax Credit." *Proceedings of the 91st Annual Conference of the National Tax Association*: 401–10.

Green, Richard K., and Kerry Vandell. 1999. "Giving Household Credit: How Changing Tax Policy Could Increase the Homeownership Rate." *Regional Science and Urban Economics* 29: 419–44.

Green, Richard K., and Michelle J. White. 1997. "Measuring the Benefits of Homeowning: Benefits to Children." *Journal of Urban Economics* 41: 441–61.

Green, Richard K., Stephen Malpezzi, and Kerry Vandell. 1994. "Urban Regulations and the Price of Land and Housing in Korea." *Journal of Housing Economics* 3: 330–56.

Greenlees, John S., and Charles C. Mason. 1996. "Overview of the 1998 Revision of the Consumer Price Index." *Monthly Labor Review* (December): 3–9.

Grigsby, William G. 1963. *Housing Markets and Public Policy*. Philadelphia: University of Pennsylvania Press.

Gyourko, Joseph, Peter Linneman, and Susan Wachter. 1999. "Analyzing the Relationships among Race, Wealth, and Home Ownership in America." *Journal of Housing Economics* 8 (2): 63–89.

Hadden, Louise, and Mireille Leger. 1990. *Codebook for the American Housing Survey Database: 1973 to 1993.* Cambridge, Mass.: Abt Associates.

Hallett, Graham, ed. 1988. *Land and Housing Policies in Europe and the USA*. London: Routledge.

Halverson, Robert, and Raymond Palmquist. 1980. "The Interpretation of Dummy Variables in Semilogrithmic Regressions." *American Economic Review* 70 (June): 474–75.

Halverson, Robert, and Henry O. Pollakowski. 1981. "Choice of Functional Form for Hedonic Price Equations." *Journal of Urban Economics* 10 (1): 37–49.

Han, Jun. 1994. "1994: The End of the Real Estate Credit Crunch." *Real Estate Finance* 11 (1): 29–39.

Hanushek, Eric, and John Quigley. 1978. "An Explicit Model of Intra-Metropolitan Mobility." *Land Economics* (November): 411–29.

Hartman, Chester. 1991. Comment (on Downs). *Housing Policy Debate* 2(4): 1161–68.

Hartzell, David J., Robert J. Pittman, and David H. Downs. 1994. "An Updated Look at the Size of the U.S. Real Estate Market Portfolio." *Journal of Real Estate Research* 9 (2): 197–212.

Haurin, Donald R., Patric Hendershott, and Dongwook Kim. 1990. "Real Rents and Household Formation: The Effect of the 1986 Tax Reform Act." Working Paper 3309. New York: National Bureau of Economic Research.

Haurin, Donald R., Toby L. Parcel, and R. Jean Haurin. 2000. "The Impact of Homeownership on Child Outcomes." Working Paper. Columbus: Ohio State Economic Department.

Hausman, Jerry A. 1981. "Exact Consumer's Surplus and Deadweight Loss." *American Economic Review* 71 (4): 662–75.

Hendershott, Patric H. 1990. "The Tax Reform Act of 1986 and Real Estate." In *Building Foundations: Housing and Federal Policy*, edited by Denise DiPasquale and Langley Keyes. Philadelphia: University of Pennsylvania Press.

———. 1992. "Are Real House Prices Likely to Decline by 47 Percent?" *Regional Science and Urban Economics* 21: 553–63.

Hendershott, Patric H., and James D. Shilling. 1982. "The Economics of Tenure Choice, 1955–1979." In *Research on Real Estate*, edited by C.F. Sirmans. New York: JAI Press.

———. 1985.

Hendershott, Patric H., and Marc Smith. 1985. "Household Formations." In *The Level and Composition of Household Savings*, edited by Patric Hendershott. Cambridge, Mass.: Ballinger.

———. 1988. "Housing Inventory Change and the Role of Existing Structures, 1961–85." *AREUEA Journal* 16 (4): 364–78.

Hill, R. Carter, John R. Knight, and C.F. Sirmans. 1997. "Estimating Capital Asset Price Indexes," *Review of Economics and Statistics,* 79 (2): 226–33.

Holtz-Eakin, Douglas, and Harvey S. Rosen. 1993. "Municipal Construction Spending: An Empirical Examination." *Economics and Politics* 5 (1): 61–84.

Holzer, Harry J. 1991. "The Spatial Mismatch Hypothesis: What Has the Evidence Shown?" *Urban Studies* 28 (1): 105–22.

———. 1994. "Black Employment Problems: New Evidence, Old Questions. *Journal of Policy Analysis and Management* 13: 699–722.

Honig, Marjorie, and Randall K. Filer. 1993. "Causes of Intercity Variation in Homelessness." *American Economic Review* 83: 248–55.

Houser, Scott. 1995. "The Effects of Tenant-Based and Project-Based Housing Assistance on Poor Households' Transitions to Self Sufficiency." Paper prepared for the 1995 annual conference of the Association of Collegiate Schools of Planning.

Hoyt, Homer. 1933. *One Hundred Years of Land Values in Chicago*. Chicago: University of Chicago Press.

Huang, S. 1973. "Short Run Instability in Single Family Housing Starts." *Journal of the American Statistical Association* 68 (344): 788–92.

Hughes, J. 1991. "Changing Demographics: Homeownership and Affordability Dilemmas." *Housing Policy Debate* 2 (4): 1215–56.

Hunter, William C., and Mary Beth Walker. 1996. "The Cultural Affinity Hypothesis and Mortgage Lending Decisions." *Journal of Real Estate Finance and Economics* 13 (1): 57–70.

ICF Incorporated. 1991. *Evaluation of the Low-Income Housing Tax Credit*. Washington, D.C.: Report for the U.S. Department of Housing and Urban Development.

Ihlanfeldt, Keith R. 1980. "An Intertemporal Empirical Analysis of the Renter's Decision to Purchase a Home." *AREUEA Journal* 8: 180–97.

———. 1981. "An Empirical Investigation of Alternative Approaches to Estimating Equilibrium Demand for Housing." *Journal of Urban Economics* 9: 97–105.

———. 1993. "Intra-Urban Job Accessibility and Hispanic Youth Employment Rates." *Journal of Urban Economics* 33: 254–71.

Ihlanfeldt, Keith R., and David L. Sjoquist. 1989. "The Impact of Job Decentralization on the Economic Welfare of Central City Blacks." *Journal of Urban Economics* 26: 110–30.

———1990a. "Job Accessibility and Racial Differences in Youth Unemployment Rates." *American Economic Review* 80: 267–76.

——— 1990b. "The Effect of Residential Location on the Probability of Black and White Teenagers Having a Job." *Review of Regional Studies* 20 (1): 10–20.

Intriligator, Michael D. 1978. *Econometric Models, Techniques and Appreciation*. New York: Prentice Hall.

Jacobs, Eva E. 2001. *Handbook of U.S. Labor Statistics*. Lanham, Md.: Bernan Press.

Jaffe, Austin J., and Demetrios Louziotis, Jr. 1996. "Property Rights and Economic Efficiency: A Survey of Institutional Factors." *Journal of Real Estate Literature* 4: 137–59.

Jencks, Christopher. 1994. *The Homeless*. Cambridge, Mass.: Harvard University Press.

Jencks, Christopher, and Susan E. Mayer. 1990. "Residential Segregation, Job Proximity and Black Job Opportunities." In *Inner City Poverty in the United States,* edited by L. Lynn and M. McGeary. Washington, D.C.: National Academy Press.

Johnson, Michael S. 1981. "A Cash Flow Model of Rational Housing Tenure Choice." *AREUEA Journal* (Spring): 1–17.

Joint Center for Housing Studies. 1992. *State of the Nation's Housing: 1992*. Cambridge, Mass.: Harvard University Press.

Joint Center for Housing Studies. 1999. *State of the Nation's Housing: 1999*. Cambridge, Mass.: Harvard University Press.

Kain, John F. 1968. "Housing Segregation, Negro Employment and Metropolitan Decentralization." *Quarterly Journal of Economics* 82: 175–97.

———. 1992. "The Spatial Mismatch Hypothesis: Three Decades Later." *Housing Policy Debate* 3 (2): 371–462.

Kain, John F., and John M. Quigley. 1975. *Housing Markets and Racial Discrimination: A Microeconomic Analysis*. New York: National Bureau of Economic Research.

Kane, Edward J. 1983. "A Six-Point Program for Deposit Insurance Reform." *Housing Finance Review* 2: 269–78.

———. 1985. *The Gathering Crisis in Federal Deposit Insurance*. Cambridge, Mass.: MIT Press.

Katz, Arnold J., and Shelby W. Herman. 1997. "Improved Estimates of Fixed Tangible Wealth, 1929–95." *Survey of Current Business*. Washington, D.C.: Bureau of Economic Analysis. Available at http://www.bea.doc.gov/bea/an/0597niw/maintext.htm.

Katz, Lawrence, and Kenneth T. Rosen. 1987. "The Interjurisdictional Effects of Growth Controls on Housing Prices." *Journal of Law and Economics* 30: 149–60.

Kearl, James R. 1979. "Inflation, Mortgages and Housing." *Journal of Political Economy* 87: 1115–38.

Kiel, Katherine, and Jeffrey E. Zabel. 1996. "House Price Differentials in U.S. Cities: Household and Neighborhood Racial Effects." *Journal of Housing Economics* 5 (2): 143–65.

Knight, John R., J. Dombrow, and C.F. Sirmans. 1992. "Estimating House Indexes with Seemingly Unrelated Regressions." University of Connecticut Working Paper. Hartford, Conn.: University of Connecticut.

Knight, John R., and C.F. Sirmans. 1999. "Depreciation, Maintenance, and Housing Prices." *Journal of Housing Economics* 5 (4): 369–89.

Koutsoyiannis, A. 1975. *Modern Microeconomics*. New York: John Wiley and Sons.

Kravis, Irving B., Alan Heston, and Robert Summers. 1982. *World Product and Income: International Comparisons of Real Gross Product*. Baltimore, Md.: Johns Hopkins University Press.

Krivo, Lauren J. 1995. "Immigrant Characteristics and Hispanic-Anglo Housing Inequality." *Demography* 32 (4): 599–615.

Kurian, George Thomas. 2001. *Datapedia of the United States, 1790–2005*. Lanham, Md.: Bernan Press.

LaCour-Little, Michael. 1996. "Identification of Discrimination in Mortgage Lending Markets." Ph.D. diss., University of Wisconsin, Madison.

———. 1999. "Discrimination in Mortgage Lending: A Critical Review of the Literature." *Journal of Real Estate Literature* 7: 15–49.

LaCour-Little, Michael, and Richard K. Green. 1998. "Are Minorities or Minority Neighborhoods More Likely to Get Low Appraisals?" *Journal of Real Estate Finance and Economics* 16 (3): 301–15.

Landis, John D. 1986. "Land Regulation and the Price of New Housing: Lessons from Three California Cities." *Journal of the American Institute of Planners* (Winter): 9–21.

Lee, Gabriel S. 1999. "Housing Investment Dynamics, Period of Production, and Adjustment Costs." *Journal of Housing Economics* 8 (1): 1–25.

Lee, Lung-Fei, and Robert Trost. 1978. "Estimation of Some Limited Dependent Variable Models with Application to Housing Demand." *Journal of Econometrics* (December): 357–82.

Leigh, Wilhelmina A., and James D. McGhee. 1986. "A Minority Perspective on Residential Racial Integration." In *Housing Desegregation and Federal Policy*, edited by John M. Goering. Chapel Hill: University of North Carolina Press.

Li, Mingche. 1977. "A Logit Model of Homeownership." *Econometrica* 45 (5): 1081–97.

Liebowitz, Stanley. 1993. "A Study That Deserves No Credit." *Wall Street Journal*, 1 September.

Ling, David T., and Marc T. Smith. 1991. "Low-Income Housing Tax Credits: Does Targeting Limit Their Use to High-Income Counties?" *Journal of Housing Economics* 1 (3): 218–34.

Linneman, Peter, Anita Summers, Nancy Brooks, and Henry Buist. 1990. "The State of Local Growth Management." Wharton Real Estate Working Paper No. 81. Philadelphia: The Wharton Business School.

Listokin, David. 1991. "Federal Housing Policy and Preservation: Historical Evolution, Patterns, and Implications." *Housing Policy Debate* 2 (2): 157–86.

Long, James E., and Steven B. Caudill. 1992. "Racial Differences in Homeownership and Housing Wealth, 1970–86." *Economic Inquiry* 30 (1): 83–100.

Lowry, Ira S. 1960. "Filtering and Housing Standards." *Land Economics* 35: 362–70.

———. 1992. "Rent Control and Homelessness: The Statistical Evidence." *Journal of the American Planning Association* (Spring): 224–28.

Maclennan, Duncan. 1982. *Housing Economics*. London: Longman.

Macpherson, David A. and G. Stacy Girmans. 2001. "Neighborhood Diversity and House Price Appreciation." *Journal of Real Estate Finance and Economics* 22 (1): 81–97.

Maddala, G.S., and Robert P. Trost. 1982. "On Measuring Discrimination in Loan Markets." *Housing Finance Review* 1: 245–66.

Malpezzi, Stephen. 1990. "Urban Housing and Financial Markets: Some International Comparisons." *Urban Studies* 27 (6): 971–1022.

———. 1993. "What Can New York and Los Angeles Learn from Kumasi and Bangalore? A Comparison of Costs and Benefits of Rent Controls." *Housing Policy Debate* 4 (4): 589–626.

———. 1996a. "Housing Prices, Externalities, and Regulation in U.S. Metropolitan Areas." *Journal of Housing Research* 7 (2): 209–41.

———. 1996b. *Notes on Consumer's Surplus*. University of Wisconsin.

———. 1996c. "The Relative Merits of Project-Based and Household-Based Housing Assistance." Working Paper. Madison, Wisc.: Center for Urban Land Economics Research.

———. 1998a. "Private Rental Housing Markets in the United States." *Netherlands Journal of Housing and the Built Environment* 13 (3): 353–86.

———. 1998b. "Welfare Analysis of Rent Control with Side Payments: A Natural Experiment in Cairo, Egypt." *Regional Science and Urban Economics* 28 (6): 773–96.

———. 1998c. "Rental Housing Markets in the U.S." *Netherlands Journal of Housing and the Built Environment* 28 (6): 773–96.

———. 1999. "A Simple Error-Correction Model of Housing Prices." *Journal of Housing Economics* 8: 27–62.

Malpezzi, Stephen, Gregory Chun, and Richard Green. 1998. "New Place to Place Housing Price Indexes for U.S. Metropolitan Areas, and Their Determinants: An Application of Housing Indicators." *Real Estate Economics* 26 (2): 235–75.

Malpezzi, Stephen, and Richard K. Green. 1996. "What's Happened to the Bottom of the Housing Market?" *Urban Studies* 33 (10): 1807–20.

Malpezzi, Stephen, and Duncan Maclennan. 2001. "The Long-Run Price Elasticity of Supply of New Construction in the United States and the United Kingdom." *Journal of Housing Economics* 10 (13): 278–306.

Malpezzi, Stephen, and Stephen K. Mayo. 1987. "The Demand for Housing in Developing Countries." *Economic Development and Cultural Change* 35 (4): 687–721.

———. 1997a. "Housing and Urban Development Indicators: A Good Idea Whose Time Has Returned." *Real Estate Economics* 25 (1): 1–11.

———. 1997b. "Getting Housing Incentives Right: A Case Study of the Effects of Regulation, Taxes, and Subsidies on Housing Supply in Malaysia." *Land Economics* 73 (3): 372–91.

Malpezzi, Stephen, Stephen K. Mayo, Ricardo Silveira, and Carmello Quintos. 1988. *Measuring the Costs and Benefits of Rent Conrol in Case Study Design*. World Bank, INU Discussion Paper No. 24.

Malpezzi, Stephen, Larry Ozanne, and Thomas Thibodeau. 1987. "Microeconomic Estimates of Housing Depreciation." *Land Economics* 63 (4): 373–85.

———. 1980. *Characteristic Prices of Housing in 59 SMSAs*. Washington, D.C.: Urban Institute Press.

Malpezzi, Stephen, James D. Shilling, and Yu-Yun Yang. 2001. "The Stock of Private Real Estate Capital in U.S. Metropolitan Areas: Measurement and Determinants." *Journal of Real Estate Research*. 22 (3): 243–70.

Malpezzi, Stephen, and Kerry Vandell. 1993. "Housing Markets and Policy in Market Economies: Lessons for Formerly Socialist Economies." Paper prepared for the American Real Estate and Urban Economics Association, Mystic, Conn. October.

———. 1996. "Evaluation of the Low-Income Housing Tax Credit: Initial Analysis of Statewide Data." Paper presented to the American Real Estate and Urban Economics Association, San Francisco, January.

Mankiw, N. Gregory, and David N. Weil. 1989. "The Baby Boom, the Baby Bust, and the Housing Market." *Regional Science and Urban Economics* 19 (May): 235–58.

Massey, Douglas S., and Nancy A. Denton. 1987. "Trends in the Residential Segregation of Blacks, Hispanics and Asians: 1979–1980." *American Sociological Review* 52: 802–25.

———. 1993. *American Apartheid: Segregation and the Making of the Underclass*. Cambridge, Mass.: Harvard University Press.

Mayer, Christopher J. and C. Tsuriel Somerville. 2000. "Residential Construction: Using the Urban Growth Model to Estimate Housing Supply." *Journal of Urban Economics* 48 (1): 85–109.

Mayo, Stephen K. 1981. "Theory and Estimation in the Economics of Housing Demand." *Journal of Urban Economics* 10 (January): 95–116.

———. 1986. "Sources of Inefficiency in Subsidized Housing Programs: A Comparison of U.S. and German Experience." *Journal of Urban Economics* 20: 229–49.

Mayo, Stephen K., and Stephen Sheppard. 1996. "Housing Supply under Rapid Economic Growth and Varying Regulatory Stringency: An International Comparison." *Journal of Housing Economics* 5: 274–89.

Mayo, Stephen K., Shlomo Angel, Michael Heller, and William Stephens. 1992. *The Housing Indicators Program: Extensive Survey Preliminary Results*. World Bank. Washington, D.C.: World Bank, Urban Development Division.

Mayo, Stephen K., Shirley Mansfield, D. Warner, and Richard Zwetchkenbaum. 1980a. *Housing Allowances and Other Rental Housing Programs: A Comparison Based on the Housing Allowance Demand Experiment, Part 1: Participation, Housing Consumption, Location and Satisfaction*. Cambridge, Mass.: Abt Associates.

———. 1980b. *Housing Allowances and Other Rental Housing Programs: A Comparison Based on the Housing Allowance Demand Experiment, Part 2: Costs and Efficiency*. Cambridge, Mass.: Abt Associates.

McDonald, John R., and Daniel P. McMillen. 2000. "Residential Building Permits in Urban Counties: 1990–1997." *Journal of Housing Economics* 9: 175–86.

McKinney, Scott, and Ann B. Schnare. 1989. "Trends in Residential Segregation by Race: 1960–1980." *Journal of Urban Economics* 26: 269–80.

McMillen, Daniel P. 1993. "Can Blacks Earn More in the Suburbs? Racial Differences in Intra-Metropolitan Earnings Variation." *Journal of Urban Economics* 33: 135–50.

Megbolugbe, Isaac F., and Man Cho. 1996. "Racial and Ethnic Differences in Housing Demand: An Econometric Investigation." *Journal of Real Estate Finance and Economics* 12: 295–318.

Meier, Gerald M., ed. 1983. *Pricing Policy for Development Management*. Baltimore, Md.: Johns Hopkins University Press.

Meyer, John R., John Kain, and M. Wohl. 1966. *The Urban Transportation Problem*. Cambridge, Mass.: Harvard University Press.

Milgram, Grace. 1983. "The Rationale for Assisted Housing." In *Housing—A Reader*. Washington, D.C.: Congressional Research Service.

Mills, Edwin S. 1985. "Open Housing Laws as Stimulus to Central City Employment." *Journal of Urban Economics* 17: 184–88.

Mills, Edwin S., and Richard Price. 1984. "Metropolitan Suburbanization and Central City Problems." *Journal of Urban Economics* 15: 1–17.

Mitchell, J. Paul. 1985. "Federal Housing Policy and Programs: Past and Present." Center for Urban Policy Research. New Brunswick, N.J.: Rutgers University.

Munnell, Alicia H., Lynn E. Browne, James McEneaney, and Geoffrey M.B. Tootell. 1992. *Mortgage Lending in Boston: Interpreting HMDA Data*. Federal Reserve Bank of Boston Working Paper No. 92–7. Boston: Federal Reserve Bank.

Murray, Michael P. 1978. "Hedonic Prices and Composite Commodities." *Journal of Urban Economics* (April): 161–92.

———. 1983. "Subsidized and Unsubsidized Housing Starts: 1961–77." *Review of Economics and Statistics* 65 (3): 590–97.

———. 1999. "Subsidized and Unsubsidized Housing Stocks 1935–1987: Crowding Out and Cointegration." *Journal of Real Estate Finance and Economics* 18 (1): 107–24.

Muth, Richard F. 1960. "The Demand for Non-Farm Housing." In *The Demand for Durable Goods*, edited by Arnold Harberger. Chicago: University of Chicago Press.

———. 1973. *Public Housing: An Economic Evaluation*. Washington, D.C: American Enterprise Institute.

Muth, Richard F., and Allen C. Goodman. 1988. *The Economics of the Housing Market*. New York: Harwood Academic Publishers.

Myers, Dowell. 1992. *Analysis with Local Census Data: Portraits of Change*. New York: Academic Press.

Myers, Dowell, and John Pitkin. 1993. "The Effects of Demographics on Future House Prices." Mimeograph. University of Southern California.

Myers, D., R. Peiser, G. Schwann, and J. Pitkin. 1992. "Retreat from Ownership: A Comparison of the Generations and States." *Housing Policy Debate* 3 (4): 945–76.

National Association of Homebuilders. 1986. *Low and Moderate Income Housing: Progress, Problems, and Prospects*. Washington, D.C.: National Association of Homebuilders.

Neaeigh, Norma R., and Gwendolyn J. Brewer. 1991. "Oklahoma Native Americans: Federal Policies and Housing Programs." *Housing and Society* 18 (3): 31–37.

Nelson, Arthur C, ed. 1988. *Development Impact Fees: Policy Rationale, Practice, Theory and Issues*. Chicago: Planners Press.

Newberger, Harriet B. 1989. "Discrimination by a Profit-Maximizing Real Estate Broker in Response to White Prejudice." *Journal of Urban Economics* 26: 1–19.

Newman, Sandra J. 1999. *The Home Front: Implications of Welfare Reform for Housing Policy*. Washington, D.C.: Urban Institute Press.

Newman, Sandra J., and Joseph Harkness. 2000. "Assisted Housing and the Educational Attainment of Children." *Journal of Housing Economics* 9 (1/2): 40–63.

Newman, Sandra J., and Ann B. Schnare. 1990. "Integrating Housing and Welfare Assistance." In *Building Foundations: Housing and Federal Policy*, edited by Denise DiPasquale and Langley C. Keyes. Philadelphia: University of Pennsylvania Press.

O'Flaherty, Brendan. 1996. *Making Room: The Economics of Homelessness*. Cambridge, Mass.: Harvard University Press.

O'Regan, Katherine M., and John M. Quigley. 1991. "Labor Market Access and Labor Market Outcomes for Urban Youth." *Regional Science and Urban Economics* 21 (2): 277–93.

———. 1998. "Where Youth Live: Economic Effects of Urban Space on Employment Prospects." *Urban Studies* 35 (7): 1187–1205.

Office of Federal Housing Enterprise Oversight. "House Price Index." http://www.ofheo.gov/house/

Olsen, Edgar O. 1969. "A Competitive Theory of the Housing Market." *American Economic Review* 59: 612–22.

———. 1972. "An Econometric Analysis of Rent Control." *Journal of Political Economy*. 80: pp. 1081–1100.

———. 1987. "The Demand and Supply of Housing Services: A Critical Review of the Empirical Literature." In *Handbook of Regional and Urban Economics*, volume 2, edited by E.S. Mills. Amsterdam: North-Holland.

———. 2001. *Housing Programs for Low-Income Households.* NBER Working paper No. 8208.

Olsen, Edgar O., and D.M. Barton. 1983."The Benefits and Costs of Public Housing in New York City." *Journal of Public Economics* 20: 299–332.

Ozanne, Larry, and Stephen Malpezzi. 1985. "The Efficacy of Hedonic Estimation with the Annual Housing Survey: Evidence from the Demand Experiment." *Journal of Economic and Social Measurement* 13 (July): 153–72.

Painter, Gary, Stuart A. Gabriel and Dowell Myers. 2001. "Race, Immigrant Status, and Housing Tenure Choice." *Journal of Urban Economics* 49(1): pp. 150–67.

Park, June, and Shann-Hwa Ying. 2000. "Increased Homelessness and Low-Rent Housing Vacancy Rates." *Journal of Housing Economics* 9 (1/2): 76–103.

Peek, Joe, and James A. Wilcox. 1991a. "The Measurement and Determinants of Single Family House Prices." *AREUEA Journal* 19 (3): 353–82.

———. 1991b. "The Baby Boom, 'Pent-Up' Demand, and Future House Prices." *Journal of Housing Economics* 1 (4): 347–67.

Pejovich, Svetozar. 1990. *The Economics of Property Rights: Towards a Theory of Comparative Systems.* Boston: Kluwer.

Peterson, George E. 1974. "The Influence of Zoning Regulations on Land and Housing Prices." Urban Institute Working Paper No. 1207–1224. Washington, D.C.: Urban Institute.

———. 1974. "Land Prices and Factor Substitution in the Metropolitan Housing Market." Urban Institute Working Paper. Washington, D.C.: Urban Institute.

Phillips, Robert F., and Anthony M.J. Yezer. 1996. "Self-Selection and Tests for Bias and Risk in Mortgage Lending: Can You Price the Mortgage If You Don't Know the Process?" *Journal of Real Estate Research* 11 (1): 87–102.

Pogodzinski, J.M., and Tim R. Sass. 1990. "The Economic Theory of Zoning." *Land Economics* 66 (3): 294–314.

Polinsky, A.M. 1977. "The Demand for Housing: A Study in Specification and Grouping." *Econometrica* 42 (March): 1533–51.

Pollakowski, Henry O. 1982. *Urban Housing Markets and Residential Location.* New York: Lexington Books.

Pollakowski, Henry O., and Susan M. Wachter. 1990. "The Effects of Land Use Constraints on Housing Prices." *Land Economics* 66 (3): 315–24.

Poterba, James M. 1991. "House Price Dynamics: The Role of Tax Policy and Demography." *Brookings Papers on Economic Activity 2.* Washington, D.C.: Brookings Institution.

Pozdena, Randall J. 1988. *Modern Economics of Housing.* Westport, Conn.: Quorum Books.

Ptacek, Frank, and Robert M. Baskin. 1996. "Revision of the CPI Housing Sample and Estimators." *Monthly Labor Review* (December): 31–39.

Quercia, Roberto, and Michael A. Stegman. 1992. "Residential Mortgage Default: A Review of the Literature." *Journal of Housing Research* 3 (2): 341–80.

Quigley, John M. 1990. "Does Rent Control Cause Homelessness? Taking the Claim Seriously." *Journal of Policy Analysis and Management* 9 (1): 89–93.

———. 1995. "A Simple Hybrid Model for Estimating Real Estate Price Indexes." *Journal of Housing Economics* 4 (1): 1–12.

———. 1996b. "The Homeless." *Journal of Economic Literature* 34 (December): 1935–41.

Quint, Michael. 1991. "Racial Gap Found on Mortgages." *New York Times*, 22 October.

Rachlis, Mitchell B., and Anthony M.J. Yezer. 1993. "Serious Flaws in Statistical Tests for Discrimination in Mortgage Markets." *Journal of Housing Research* 4 (2): 315–36.

Ratcliff, Richard U. 1949. *Urban Land Economics*. New York: McGraw Hill.

Reeder, William J., Donald Lerman, John Hession, and Patrick Sullivan. 1987. *National and Rural Housing Policy: Historical Development and Emerging Issues*. Washington, D.C.: U.S. Department of Agriculture.

Reid, Margaret. 1962. *Housing and Income*. Chicago: University of Chicago Press.

Reifel, John W. 1994. "Black-White Housing Price Differentials: Recent Trends and Implications." *Review of Black Political Economy* 23 (1): 67–94.

Renaud, Bertrand. 1989. "Affordable Housing, Housing Sector Performance and Behavior of the Price-to-Income Ratio: International Evidence and Theoretical Analysis." Paper Presented to the Center of Urban Studies and Urban Planning, University of Hong Kong, October.

Renaud, Bertrand, Frederik Pretorius, and Bernabe Pasadilla. 1997. *Markets at Work: Dynamics of the Residential Real Estate Market in Hong Kong*. Hong Kong: Hong Kong University Press.

Rogers, R. Mark, Steven W. Henderson, and Daniel H. Ginsburg. 1993. "Consumer Prices: Examining Housing Rental Components." *Federal Reserve Bank of Atlanta Economic Review* (May/June): 32–46.

Rohe, William M., and Michael A. Stegman. 1992. "Public Housing Homeownership: Will It Work and for Whom?" *Journal of the American Planning Association* 58 (2): 144–57.

Rose, Louis A. 1989a. "Topographical Constraints and Urban Land Supply Indexes." *Journal of Urban Economics* 26 (3): 335–47.

———. 1989b. "Urban Land Supply: Natural and Contrived Restrictions." *Journal of Urban Economics* 25: 325–45.

Rosen, Sherwin. 1974. "Hedonic Prices and Implicit Markets: Product Differentiation in Pure Competition." *Journal of Political Economy* 82 (1): 34–55.

Rosenbaum, James E. 1991. "Black Pioneers—Do Their Moves to the Suburbs Increase Economic Opportunity for Mothers and Children?" *Housing Policy Debate* 2 (4): 1179–1214.

———. 1993. "Closing the Gap: Does Residential Integration Improve the Employment and Education of Low-Income Blacks?" In *Affordable Housing and Public Policy: Strategies for Metropolitan Chicago*, edited by L.B. Joseph. Chicago: Center for Urban Research and Policy Studies.

Rosenbaum, James E., and Susan J. Popkin. 1991. "Employment and Earnings of Low Income Blacks Who Move to Middle Class Suburbs." In *The Urban Underclass*, edited by C. Jencks and P.E. Peterson. Washington, D.C.: Brookings Institution.

Rossi, Peter H. 1989. *Down and Out in America: The Origins of Homelessness*. Chicago: University of Chicago Press.

Rothenberg, Jerome, George Galster, Richard V. Butler, and John K. Pitkin. 1991. *The Maze of Urban Housing Markets: Theory, Evidence and Policy*. Chicago: University of Chicago Press.

Rydell, C. Peter. 1976. "Measuring the Supply Response to Housing Allowances." *Papers of the Regional Science Association* 37: 31–57.

Rydell, C. Peter, C. Lance Barnett, C.E. Hillstead, Michal P. Murray, Kevin Neels, and R.H. Sims. 1981. *The Impact of Rent Control on the Los Angeles Housing Market.* Santa Monica, Calif.: Rand Corporation

Sa-Aadu, Jarjisu. 1984a. "Alternative Estimates of Direct Tenant Benefit and Consumption Inefficiencies from the Section 8 New Construction Program." *Land Economics* 60 (May): 189–201.

———. 1984b. "Another Look at the Economics of Demand Side Versus Supply Side Strategies in Low Income Housing." *AREUEA Journal* 12 (4): 427–60.

Schelling, Thomas C. 1969. "Models of Segregation." *American Economic Review* 59: 488–93.

———. 1972. "Dynamic Models of Segregation." *Journal of Mathematical Sociology* 59: 148–86.

Schill, Michael H. 1994. "The Role of the Nonprofit Sector in Low-Income Housing Production: A Comparative Perspective." *Urban Affairs Quarterly* 30 (1): 74–101.

Schill, Michael H., and Susan M. Wachter. 1993. "A Tale of Two Cities: Racial and Ethnic Geographic Disparities in Home Mortgage Lending in Boston and Philadelphia." *Journal of Housing Research* 4 (2): 245–75.

———. 1995. "The Spatial Bias of Federal Housing Law and Policy: Concentrated Poverty in Urban America." *University of Pennsylvania Law Review* 143 (5): 1285–1342.

Schnare, Ann B. 1974. *Externalities, Segregation, and House Prices.* Washington, D.C.: Urban Institute.

Schnare, Ann B., and Raymond J. Struyk. 1976. "Segmentation in Urban Housing Markets." *Journal of Urban Economics* 3: 146–66.

Schwab, Robert. 1985. "The Estimation of the Benefits of In-Kind Government Programs." *Journal of Public Economics* 27 (2): 195–210.

Schwartz, Seymour I., David E. Hansen, and Richard Green. 1984. "The Effect of Growth Control on the Production of Moderate-Price Housing." *Land Economics* 60: 110–14.

Segal, David, and Philip Srinivasan. 1985. "The Impact of Suburban Growth Restrictions on U.S. Housing Price Inflation, 1975–78." *Urban Geography* 6 (1): 14–26.

Sheppard, Stephen. 1999. "Hedonic Analysis of Housing Markets." In *Handbook of Regional and Urban Economics*, volume 3, edited by Paul C. Cheshire and Edwin S. Mills. Amsterdam: North-Holland.

Shiller, Robert J. 1991. "Arithmetic Repeat Sales Price Estimators." *Journal of Housing Economics* 1 (1): 110–26.

Shilling, James D., C.F. Sirmans, and Jonothan F. Dombrow. 1991. "Measuring Depreciation in Single-Family Rental and Owner-Occupied Housing." *Journal of Housing Economics* 1 (4): 368–83.

Shilling, James D., C.F. Sirmans, and Krisandra A. Guidry. 1991. "The Impact of State Land-Use Controls on Residential Land Values." *Journal of Regional Science* 31 (1): 83–92.

Siegan, Bernard H. 1991. Comment (On Downs). *Housing Policy Debate* 2(4): pp. 1169–78.

Silberberg, Eugene. 1972. "Duality and the Many Consumer's Surpluses." *American Economic Review* 62 (5): 942–52.

Simmons, Patrick A. 2001. *Housing Statistics of the United States.* Lanham, Md.: Bernan Press.

Simonson, John. 1980. "Everything You Always Wanted to Know about Defining Inadequate Housing, But Didn't Bother to Ask." Washington, D.C.: Office of Policy Development and Research, U.S. Department of Housing and Urban Development.

Smeeding, Timothy. 1982. "Alternative Methods for Valuing Selected In-Kind Transfer Benefits and Measuring their Effect on Poverty." Census Technical Paper No. 50. Washington, D.C.: U.S. Census Bureau.

Smith, Lawrence B., Kenneth Rosen, and George Fallis. 1988. "Recent Developments in Economic Models of Housing Markets." *Journal of Economic Literature* 26 (March): 29–64.

Somerville, C. Tsuriel. 1999. "Residential Construction Costs and the Supply of New Housing: Endogeneity and Bias in Construction Cost Indexes." *Journal of Real Estate Finance and Economics* 18 (1): 943–62.

Stegman, Michael A., and J. David Holden. 1987. *Nonfederal Housing Programs: How States and Localities are Responding to Federal Cutbacks in Low-Income Housing.* Washington, D.C.: Urban Land Institute.

Stephens, William, Ying Li, Vassilis Lekkas, Jesse Abraham, Charles Calhoun, and Thomas Kimner. 1995. "Conventional Mortgage Home Price Index." *Journal of Housing Research* 6 (3): 389–418.

Straszheim, Mahlon. 1981. "Participation." In *Do Housing Allowances Work?* edited by Katherine L. Bradbury and Anthony Downs. Washington, D.C.: Brookings Institution.

Struyk, Raymond J. 1975. "Determinants of the Rate of Homeownership of Black Relative to White Households." *Journal of Urban Economics* 2: 291–306.

———. 1977. *Should Government Encourage Homeownership?* Washington, D.C.: Urban Institute.

———. 1980. *A New System for Public Housing: Salvaging a National Resource.* Washington, D.C.: Urban Institute.

Struyk, Raymond J., with Sue Marshall. 1975. "Income and Urban Homeownership." *Review of Economics and Statistics* 57: 26–37.

Struyk, Raymond J., and Marc Bendick. 1981. *Housing Vouchers for the Poor: Lessons from a National Experiment.* Washington, D.C.: Urban Institute.

Swan, Craig. 1973. "Housing Subsidies and Housing Starts." *AREUEA Journal* 1 (2): 119–40.

Sweeney, James L. 1974. "Quality, Commodity Hierarchies, and Housing Markets." *Econometrica* 42: 147–67.

Teitz, Michael. 1991. "Housing: The Intractable Market." Paper presented to the LaFollette Institute, Madison, Wisc. May.

Thibodeau, Thomas G. 1992. *Residential Real Estate Prices: 1974–1983.* Mt. Pleasant, Mich.: Blackstone.

———. 1995. "House Price Indices from the 1984–1992 MSA American Housing Surveys." *Journal of Housing Research* 6 (3): 439–79.

Thomas, Paulette. 1991. "Morgage Rejection Rate for Minorities is Quadruple That of Whites, Study Finds." *Wall Street Journal*, 21 October.

———. 1992. "Federal Data Detail Pervasive Racial Gap in Mortgage Lending." *Wall Street Journal*, 21 March.

Thorson, James A. 1997. "The Effect of Zoning on Housing Construction." *Journal of Housing Economics* 6 (1): 81–91.

Tin, Jan S. 1993. *Housing Characteristics of Rural Households, 1991*. Washington, D.C.: U.S. Department of Housing and Urban Development.

Topel, Robert, and Sherwin Rosen. 1988. "Housing Investment in the United States." *Journal of Political Economy* 96 (4): 718–40.

Tucker, William. 1990. *The Excluded Americans: Homelessness and Housing Policies*. Washington, D.C.: Regnery Gateway.

Turner, Margery Austin. 1992. "Discrimination in Urban Housing Markets: Lessons from Fair Housing Audits." *Housing Policy Debate* 3 (2): 185–216.

Turner, Margery Austin, and Maris Mikelsons. 1992. "Patterns of Racial Steering in Four Metropolitan Areas." *Journal of Housing Economics* 2: 199–234.

Turner, Margery Austin, and Veronica M. Reed. 1990. *Housing America: Learning from the Past, Planning for the Future*. Washington, D.C.: Urban Institute.

Turner, Margery Austin, Raymond J. Struyk, and John Yinger. 1991. *Housing Discrimination Study: Synthesis*. Washington, D.C.: Urban Institute; Syracuse, New York: Syracuse University.

U.S. Congressional Budget Office. 1992. *The Cost-Effectiveness of the Low-Income Housing Tax Credit Compared with Housing Vouchers*, prepared by Leonard Burman. Washington, D.C.: U.S. Government Printing Office.

U.S. Department of Commerce, Bureau of the Census. 1976. *Historical Statistics of the United States, Colonial Times to 1970*. Washington, D.C.: U.S. Government Printing Office.

———. Periodical. *Current Construction Reports: C-20, Housing Starts*. Washington, D.C.: U.S. Government Printing Office. Available online at http: //www.census.gov.

———. Periodical. *Current Construction Reports: C-22, Housing Completions*. Washington, D.C.: U.S. Government Printing Office. Available online at http://www.census.gov.

———. Periodical. *Current Construction Reports: C-25, New One-Family Homes Sold*. Washington, D.C.: U.S. Government Printing Office. Available online at http://www.census.gov.

———. Periodical. *Current Construction Reports: C-30, Value of Construction Put in Place* Washington, D.C.: U.S. Government Printing Office. Available online at http://www.census.gov.

———. Periodical. *Current Construction Reports: Building Permits*. Washington, D.C.: U.S. Government Printing Office. Available online at http://www.census.gov.

———. 1991. *Report to Congress on Rent Control*. Washington, D.C.: Office of Policy Development and Research.

———. 1992. *The Location of Worst Case Needs in the Late 1980s: A Report to Congress*. HUD-1387-PDR. Washington, D.C.: U.S. Government Printing Office.

———. 1996. *Rental Assistance at a Crossroads: A Report to Congress on Worse Case Needs*. Washington, D.C.: Office of Policy Development and Research.

———. Periodical. *U.S. Housing Market Conditions*. Washington, D.C.: U.S. Government Printing Office. Available online at http://www.huduser.org.

———. Periodical. *State of the Cities Data Systems.* Washington, D.C.: U.S. Government Printing Office. Available online at http://socds.huduser.org/index.html.

U.S. General Accounting Office. 1988. *Home Ownership: Mortgage Bonds are Costly and Provide Little Assistance to Those in Need.* Washington, D.C.: U.S. Government Printing Office.

———. 1990. *Rental Housing: Observations on the Low Income Housing Tax Credit Program.* Washington, D.C.: Government Printing Office.

U.S. Office of Management and Budget. 1997. *Budget of the United States, Analytical Perspectives.* Washington, D.C.: Government Printing Office.

van Vliet, Willem, ed. 1998. *The Encyclopedia of Housing.* Newbury Park, Calif.: Sage Publications.

Vandell, Kerry D. 1981. "The Effects of Racial Composition on Neighborhood Succession." *Urban Studies* 18 (3): 315–33.

———. 1997. *Improving Secondary Markets in Rural America.* Federal Reserve Bank of Kansas City.

Wagster, John D. 1999. "The Basle Accord of 1988 and the International Credit Crunch of 1989–92." *Journal of Financial Services Research* 15 (2): 123–43.

Wallis, Allan D. 1991. *Wheel Estate: The Rise and Decline of Mobile Homes.* New York: Oxford University Press.

Wang, Ferdinand T., and Peter M. Zorn. 1997. "Estimating House Price Growth with Repeat Sales Data: What's the Aim of the Game?" *Journal of Housing Economics* 6: 93–118.

Weaver, Robert. 1956. "Integration in Public and Private Housing." *The Annals* 304 (March): 86–97.

Weicher, John C. 1991. "Housing Policy and Programs: A New Strategy to Alleviate Poverty." Paper presented to the LaFollette conference on U.S. Housing Policy, Madison, Wisc.

Weicher, John C., and Thomas Thibodeau. 1988. "Filtering and Housing Markets: An Empirical Analysis." *Journal of Urban Economics* 23 (January): 21–40.

Weinberg, Daniel H., Joseph Friedman, and Stephen K. Mayo. 1981. "Intraurban Residential Mobility: The Role of Transaction Costs, Market Imperfections, and Household Disequilibrium." *Journal of Urban Economics* 9: 332–48.

Whitehead, Christine M.E. 1999. "Urban Housing Markets: Theory and Policy." In *Handbook of Regional and Urban Economics*, volume 3, edited by Paul Cheshire and Edwin S. Mills. Amsterdam: North-Holland.

Wienk, Ronald E. 1992. "Discrimination in Urban Credit Markets: What We Don't Know and Why We Don't Know It." *Housing Policy Debate* 3 (2): 217–40.

Wienk, Ronald E., Clifford Reid, John Simonson, and Frederick Eggers. 1979. *Measuring Discrimination in American Housing Markets: The Housing Market Practices Survey.* Washington, D.C.: U.S. Department of Housing and Urban Development.

Willig, R.D. 1976. "Consumer's Surplus without Apology." *American Economic Review* 66 (4): 589–97.

Wilson, William Julius. 1987. *The Truly Disadvantaged: The Inner City, the Underclass, and Public Policy.* Chicago: University of Chicago Press.

Wilson, William Julius. 1996. *When Work Disappears: The World of the New Urban Poor.* New York: Alfred Knopf.

Woodward, Susan E., and John C. Weicher. 1989. "Goring the Wrong Ox: A Defense of the Mortgage Interest Deduction." *National Tax Journal* 42 (3): 301–13.

Yezer, Anthony M.J., Robert F. Phillips, and Robert Trost. 1994. "Bias in Estimates of Discrimination and Default in Mortgage Lending: The Effects of Simultaneity and Self-Selection." *Journal of Real Estate Finance and Economics* 9: 197–215.

Yinger, John. 1978. "The Black-White Price Differential in Housing: Some Further Evidence." *Land Economics* 54: 187–206.

———. 1979. "Prejudice and Discrimination in the Urban Housing Market." In *Current Issues in Urban Economics*, edited by Peter Mieszkowski and Mahlon Straszheim. Baltimore, Md.: Johns Hopkins University Press.

———. 1991. "Acts of Discrimination: Evidence from the 1989 Housing Discrimination Study." *Journal of Housing Economics* 1 (4): 318–46.

———. 1995. *Closed Doors, Lost Opportunities: The Continuing Costs of Housing Discrimination*. New York: Russell Sage.

Zais, James P., and Thomas G. Thibodeau. 1983. *The Elderly and Urban Housing*. Washington, D.C.: Urban Institute.

Zandi, Mark. 1993. "Boston Fed's Bias Study Was Deeply Flawed." *American Banker*, 19 August.

Zorn, Peter, David Hansen, and Seymour Schwartz. 1986. "Mitigating the Price Effects of Growth Control: A Case Study of Davis, California." *Land Economics* 62: 46–63.

About the Authors

Stephen Malpezzi is Professor, Wangard Faculty Scholar, and Chair of the University of Wisconsin-Madison's Department of Real Estate and Urban Land Economics (http://www.bus.wisc.edu/ realestate). Dr. Malpezzi's research includes work on economic development, the measurement and determinants of real estate prices, housing demand, and the effects of economic policies on real estate markets. Prior to joining UW, Malpezzi was an economist specializing in urban development at the World Bank from 1981 to 1990. He was affiliated with the Urban Institute from 1977 to 1981. He holds a Ph.D. in economics from the George Washington University, an M.A. in international affairs from the same university, and a B.A. in political science from LaSalle College.

At the time of this writing, **Richard Green** was Professor of Business and Wangard Faculty Scholar at the University of Wisconsin-Madison School of Business. He chaired the Department of Urban Economics and Real Estate. He has published papers on housing, commercial real estate and tax policy in academic journals and chapters in conference volumes by Brookings Institution and the National Bureau of Economic Research. Green was an advisor to the Federal Reserve Bank of Chicago. He has consulted for the World Bank, the Eastern European Real Property Foundation, National Association of REALTORS, Ernst and Young, Deloitte and Touche and CCIM. He is also a Faculty Associate of the Lincoln Institute of Land Policy in Cambridge, Massachusetts, and a Post-Doctoral Fellow of the Homer Hoyt Institute. In 1995 he won the GBA Teacher of the Year Award.

About the Authors

About the Series

The American Real Estate and Urban Economics Association (AREUEA) was organized in 1964 based on the need to improve information and analysis in the fields of real estate development, planning, finance, and urban economics. The AREUEA Monograph Series is designed to further the purposes of AREUEA by providing teachers, students, and practitioners with a comprehensive and timely presentation of recent research materials translated into a summary form that is more quickly and easily comprehended than journal articles and specialized studies. Monographs provide such a translation by reviewing old views, identifying new techniques, and describing recent findings. Accordingly, the monographs should be particularly useful as supplements to classroom instruction or the continuing professional education of practitioners.

The AREUEA Monographs are edited for style but not for content and are supervised by a committee appointed by the AREUEA Board of Directors headed by the editor. For past monographs outside commentators have been invited to add brief comments supplementing the coverage in the body of the monograph. Given the length of this monograph, remarks by outside commentators have not been included but the draft manuscript was subject to external review with comments provided to the authors. The AREUEA Monographs are distributed to association members. Naturally the opinions expressed in this monograph are those of the authors alone and do not necessarily reflect the views of AREUEA.

Anthony M. Yezer, AREUEA Monograph Series Editor
Department of Economics
The George Washington University

Index